DON'T
RETIRE...
Graduate!

For Brooke
Forever my princess

It's time to retire our definition of retirement.

- Arianna Huffington

(*Huffington Post*, September 5, 2014)

BROTMAN
Media Group
A division of Brotman Financial Group, Inc.

www.brotmanmedia.com

Eric@DontRetireGraduate.com

www.facebook.com/DontRetireGraduate/

ISBN: 978-1-7349701-0-4 (print)

ISBN: 978-1-7349701-1-1 (ebook)

ISBN: 978-1-7349701-2-8 (audiobook)

Ordering Information:

Special discounts are available on quantity purchases by corporations, associations, and others. For details, contact Brotman Media at 410-252-4555.

Course Catalog

Junior year: Gaining Influence & Acumen

Senior year: Making Your Mark & Presenting Your Thesis

Graduation Day

DON'T RETIRE...
Graduate!

ERIC D. BROTMAN, CFP ®

AUTHOR'S PURPOSE

This book has been in the works for several years and marks the completion of my 25th year as a financial advisor. My personal plan to graduate into retirement has been incorporated into my family's financial plan, and the strategies detailed in this book are the ones I'm using to reach financial independence.

My "retirement" plan is to work as an advisor, consultant, speaker, advocate, and mentor for as long as my health allows and for as long as it remains rewarding and fun. And long before I qualify for social security, I plan to be financially independent and living at the beach in a state with low income taxes.

Over the past quarter century, I have helped hundreds of families make life's big financial decisions, navigate through career and life stages, and prepare for, enter, and live in retirement. It seems to me that the script of retirement planning and living as a retiree is in many cases suboptimal and perhaps even hazardous to a life well-lived. This book aims:

1. To reframe the concept of retirement from one of retreat to one of advancement, psychologically and socially.

2. To provide insight into gaining and maintaining financial independence.

3. To equate the process of wealth building during states of career development to the advancement through a college experience— from matriculation to commencement.

A word of caution: This book is deliberately written in the first-person tense. References to "I" or "me" are specific to the author. References to "we," "us," "our firm," etc. are specific to the author's firm, BFG Financial Advisors, a division of Brotman Financial Group, Inc. All of these references are being used interchangeably in this volume for readability and convenience.

To the extent possible, I have omitted phrases like "In my opinion" and "In my mind" in the hopes of making the book readable and enjoyable. Note that unless otherwise attributable to someone else in specific cases, *everything* in this book represents my opinion and should not be used for implementation without proper professional analysis.

This book is not designed to render specific investment or planning advice. Please do not implement any of the suggestions in this book without obtaining appropriate legal, tax, and financial advice from qualified professionals who know enough about *you* and *your personal finances* to render appropriate advice for you.1

There are several instances in the book when I advocate getting professional advice because financial advisors have the training to see many vantage points that are sometimes hard to see when doing planning on your own. Even the most financially savvy individuals can benefit from some dispassionate advice, in the same way that world-class athletes still have coaches.

By the time you complete the coursework in the chapters that follow, I hope you'll be armed with the tools you need to reach financial indepen-

---

1   The opinions expressed in this commentary are those of the author and may not necessarily reflect those held by Kestra Investment Services, LLC, or Kestra Advisory Services, LLC. This is for general information only and is not intended to provide specific investment advice or recommendations for any individual. It is suggested that you consult you financial professional, attorney, or tax advisor with regard to your individual situation. Comments concerning the past performance are not intended to be forward looking and should not be viewed as an indication of future results. This material was created to provide accurate and reliable information on the subjects covered but should not be regarded as a complete analysis of these subjects. It is not intended to provide specific legal, tax, or other professional advice. The services of an appropriate professional should be sought regarding your individual situation.

dence and to graduate into retirement with dignity, optimism, and a sense of enthusiasm for the next chapter of your life.

After you complete your studies, I would love to hear about how this book helped you formulate your own plans to graduate into retirement. Please send me an e-mail at ebrotman@bfgfa.com to share your story about how you used this book, or even how you completed one or more extra-credit assignments to work your way to graduation day and financial independence.

Here's to a bright, engaging, and ever-evolving financial future!

Sincerely,

Eric D. Brotman, CFP®
CEO, BFG Financial Advisors, a Division of Brotman Financial Group, Inc.

Applying to 'Retire University'

GRADUATING INTO RETIREMENT

Bobby Bowden, the legendary Florida State University football coach, was once asked when he was going to retire, and he said, "I guess I'll retire someday if I live that long."

He also once said that retirement was the next-to-last milestone in his life and that he wasn't ready to have his last milestone next up on his list! Bowden ended up coaching until he was 80 years old.

Right now, retirement doesn't specifically celebrate the completion of anything. You haven't mastered your career such that you are ready to quit. In an ideal world, it marks the date when you are financially independent and no longer need a paycheck to thrive.

However, for many Americans it marks a different milestone—one when you are no longer healthy enough to continue to work every day or one when your skills are no longer relevant enough to keep pace with the changes in your field and you just lack the motivation (or money) to refresh those skills by returning to school.

Contrast that with graduation day, which is ideal for a celebration–not only to mark the completion of an educational program to further your knowledge, skills, and career path but also to look ahead to the next challenge in your life. When you graduate, you're moving up, moving on, and starting a new chapter in your life. You're ready to take on the world, and you're thinking, "Look out world… here I come!"

Why can't we take the energy and the benefits of your lifetime of experiences and be just as fired up about retirement as graduation? You're smarter, more capable, and more valuable than you've ever been before, so why not leverage that to your advantage?

At Retirement University (or Retire U for short), we want to redefine retirement for you and show you that there are many ways for you to get there—just like there are many college majors available to matriculating students. Maybe your course of study will lead to, "I want to do consulting or to keep working part time because I enjoy it." Maybe your course of study will lead to, "I want to play golf or travel the world." Or maybe your course of study will lead to, "I'm physically unable to work but want to live my life joyfully and to make a difference in other ways."

Some of you will be reading this book facing many years (or decades) of work before even contemplating retirement. Others of you can already see the light at the end of the nine-to-five tunnel and want to refine your planning to reach your desired destination effectively.

RETIREMENT IN TODAY'S WORLD... UGH!

The two concepts of graduating and retiring are mistakenly viewed as bookends of an adult's working life, and I believe we need to reframe retirement completely—for our own good.

Let's start with the simple meanings of these two words as defined by Merriam-Webster. To graduate is "to pass from one stage of experience, proficiency, or prestige to a usually higher one."[2] To retire is "to withdraw from one's position or occupation" or "to conclude one's working or professional career."[3]

---

2 "Graduate," Merriam-Webster Dictionary, Merriam-Webster, Incorporated, Accessed April 16, 2020, https://www.merriam-webster.com/dictionary/graduate.

3 "Retire," Merriam-Webster Dictionary, Merriam-Webster, Incorporated, Accessed April 16, 2020, https://www.merriam-webster.com/dictionary/retire.

ARE YOU KIDDING ME?

See the profound and loaded difference between these two concepts? To graduate marks success, achievement, advancement, and accomplishment. To retire marks withdrawal, termination, and ceasing to succeed, achieve, advance, or accomplish anything. Based on definition alone, I'd like to graduate repeatedly and can't imagine signing up to retire in the traditional sense.

THEY DON'T WANT ME TO RETIRE, THEY WANT ME TO DIE

The concept of retirement has been around for centuries. In the early 1700s, a New England Puritan minister, Cotton Mather, said that old people should "be pleased with the retirement you are dismissed into."[4] Note that this gem of advice comes from the same source that gave our country the Salem witch trials.

In the 1800s, the Minister President of Prussia, Otto von Bismarck, mandated that older members of society (at age 65) would be *forced* to leave the workforce and instead receive government-run financial support.[5]

In 1905, William Osler, one of the four founding physicians of Johns Hopkins Hospital in Baltimore, Maryland (and for whom the still-standing Osler Building is named), presented a landscape for adult "usefulness" as follows:

- From ages 25–40, people are in the "golden years of plenty."

- From ages 40–60, people are "tolerable."

- By age 60, people are useless and should be "put out to pasture because they are no longer constructive."[6]

Today in the United States, "retirement age" is the term to mark the arbitrary figure imposed by an employer or the government, like the age at which one becomes eligible for a pension or social security income. However, when

---

4   Mary-Lou Weisman, "The History of Retirement, From Early Man to A.A.R.P.," *New York Times*, March 21, 1999, https://www.nytimes.com/1999/03/21/jobs/the-history-of-retirement-from-early-man-to-aarp.html.

5   Mary-Lou Weisman, "The History of Retirement."

6   *US National Library of Medicine* Profiles in Science, "William Osler," NIH, Accessed April 16, 2020, https://profiles.nlm.nih.gov/spotlight/gf/feature/biographical.

social security was created in 1935, most people joined the workforce by 18 years of age, worked until they were 65, and died by age 72.

The full legal name for social security is marked by the acronym OASDI, or the Old-Age, Survivors, and Disability Insurance program. The program was designed for extremely elderly former workers and their widows and for those too impaired to work.

The idea was that people would work for their entire adult lives, until one day they either couldn't do the job anymore physically or some other reason forced them to leave their employment. Within a short period of time, they would be deceased, reasoned the designers of the OASDI program.

In 1935, 65 may have been "elderly," but in modern times, it certainly is not. Today, many people don't join the workforce until after they graduate school or college (say at 22 to 25), they may want to retire at 55, and they could live to be 107. The old model won't work in most cases, which is partly why social security has so many problems with future adequacy and availability.

While graduation invokes images of caps and gowns and wild celebration, retirement conjures up different images for everyone. Some people think of retirement today as working one job instead of two, while others think of it as time on their yacht in the Mediterranean. Clearly, they can't use the same definition or measurement to determine what retirement is or is not.

OUR DEFINITION OF RETIREMENT

For our purposes, let's use the following to define retirement: the age or moment in life when work becomes *optional.* That way, those who want to start businesses after leaving the employ of another and those who want to get the gold watch and ride off into the sunset are all covered by the same standard.

When you have achieved enough financial wherewithal to eschew income-producing activities other than those you *want* to pursue, in my mind you are "retired."

In other words, it is the absence of needing to work, not the absence of working that defines retirement.

While we're at it, I would propose that we all think of retirement as another graduation. It is a new door being opened and a new chapter of your life, full of opportunity and a myriad of life choices.

Many cultures around the world celebrate and revere their elders—those believed to be the wisest members of their society. It's hard to conceive of revering anyone who has been "dismissed into retirement" or who is "no longer constructive." In other words, after centuries of looking to our elders for advice and counsel, we are now in a world that views our seniors as useless. That's not only wrong, it's sad.

Let's find a way to create the retirement you want on your terms and open your mind to new ideas of retirement that will work for you so you can take a cue from Frank Sinatra and say, "I'm doing retirement *my way*."

HOW TO USE THIS BOOK

Much like you cannot be a junior in college until you have finished your freshman and sophomore years, this book has been written to be linear, following a chronology of choices leading up to graduating into retirement successfully. That said, if you are already in your junior year when you arrive on campus, like a transfer student, you do not have to repeat your freshman and sophomore years; feel free either to skip those chapters or to view them as refresher courses before you take on new material.

This book has been designed like a college syllabus. Each chapter is structured as a course that will end with a short, fun, post-course exercise so that you can make sure you've picked up the key elements of each class. This will help you determine your readiness to advance and on which courses you feel you need to devote additional energy in order to graduate successfully. You will have a chance to grade yourself on your own progress along the way.

Each chapter will also include an extra-credit assignment (because no one likes tests or homework, but everyone likes extra credit!). The extra-credit assignment at the end of each chapter will be the *one* step you can take to make sure you ace each course.

As each year of college builds on prior years, so too will this book. This book also espouses the merits of "work-life integration," as opposed to the ever-sought but never-caught "work-life balance."

Throughout this book, you'll be preparing for the shifting of priorities and attitudes and striving for self-actualization along your educational journey. And hopefully, after reading this book, completing these courses, and attempting the extra-credit assignments, you'll be ready for your big day in a cap and gown and to graduate into retirement.

CHOOSING THE BEST RETIREMENT UNIVERSITY FOR YOU

If you are a college graduate, no doubt you remember the daunting process of getting into college in the first place. Getting into Retire U can be challenging as well, especially when you consider the course of study you want to pursue.

Fully Funded Retirement has some of the toughest entry standards but may also be the most rewarding course of study. If that's critical to your happiness and your personal definition of success, let's take steps to get you accepted into that program.

Work Until I Die is an alternate course of study but one that might be less than optimal. If this is currently your best option, let's find ways to get your grades up, including taking advantage of as many extra-credit assignments as possible.

Coming out of high school, in addition to simply making the grades, you also had to build a résumé of activities, especially those in which you played a leadership role.

You may have taken a prep course to get ready for your standardized tests. You took the SAT or ACT at least once and possibly a few times.

You met with college counselors or other advisors, and you read the annual *U.S. News & World Report* college rankings issue. Perhaps you even completed some aptitude testing to determine the priorities you envisioned in your future school of choice.

All of that happened *before* you ever set foot on a college campus. Similarly, retirement requires years of preparation and planning. If you wait for the last semester of your senior year to try to catch up on all your classes, you may not make it.

YOUR FIRST JOB AND RETIREMENT

While spending more than a decade planning for college sounds ridiculous, retirement planning should ideally be started the moment young people start their first job.

Within a week or so of starting employment, they are encouraged to participate in their company's retirement plan and are asked to make important elections for their future. Those same young people need to make decisions (often for the first time) about budgeting and cash flow, paying down student loans, housing options, transportation solutions, and a laundry list of other "adulting" concepts.

When you are 22 years old, the idea of retirement couldn't be more remote—you can't begin to imagine being as old as 30, much less what it will mean to be 65–70.

For most young people, the idea of retirement is not one they are equipped to understand. Who begins their first job and is already thinking about not working anymore? Instead, they are focusing on the more immediate and urgent tasks of managing their daily affairs (financially and otherwise), learning the ropes in their new occupations, and thinking about making weekend plans. If they are long-term planners, they may be thinking about graduate school or potential career advancement, not about the end of their careers.

Just like choosing an educational path, planning for retirement is a process. For most people, it takes years of discipline to become financially independent; it doesn't happen overnight.

In preparing for college, you generally want to visit a dozen or more campuses to get a feel for the culture and environment. Do you want an urban or rural campus? Would you prefer a large public university or a small liberal arts college? How close to home would you like to be—close enough to spend weekends or to take laundry home or far enough that you'll be home only for extended breaks throughout the year? How does the campus *feel*— the classrooms, the dormitories, the student union? And of course, you need to consider the cost of attendance and determine affordability.

In preparing for retirement, you need to answer similar questions. What type of housing options feel right for you? Do you want an active 55-plus community, a continuing-care retirement community, or a condominium for independent living? Do you want to be in the mountains, in the city, or at the beach? How close do you want to be to your children and grandchildren? Is it important to be near high-quality hospitals? What about the impact of taxes and the cost of living? Can you afford to potentially spend decades of retirement without running out of money? Preparing for financial independence requires almost as many steps as graduating from college requires individual classes.

BECOMING AND STAYING WEALTHY

It is generally much easier to *stay* wealthy than it is to *become* wealthy, much like it is easier to *stay* educated than to *become* educated. While wealthy families can take the review course to stay that way, non-wealthy families need to enroll in the full program to get there.

Our objective here is to help families who want to begin building wealth to do so and to plant the seeds for various action steps that can be taken at appropriate thresholds of wealth. Remember that the goal is financial independence—the absence of *needing* to work, not the absence of actual work itself.

There are only three sources of income possible in the financial world:

1) People at work

2) Money at work

3) Charity

While you are working at a job or career, your labor is creating income for you and your family. Eventually, you need to have enough assets working for you to create income so that you can end your working years. If you lack the working assets to create enough income when your paychecks stop coming, the only other possibility is to rely on some form of benefactor, like a family member, charitable organization, or government agency.

HANG WITH THE RIGHT CROWD

While you spend time and energy picking friends in school who share your interests, it is also advisable to choose companions with positive habits and who can be good influences on you during your years together.

In building wealth, there are a number of good habits that will help you accomplish your financial independence goals, and choosing the right spouse, friends, and others who will be supportive of those efforts may make a difference for you. In other words, if your best friend or spouse has a habit of very expensive dinners or vacations and you follow along, it could impact your wealth building adversely. Remember being asked, "If your friends jumped off a bridge, would you jump, too?" That concept applies here just as much; if your spouse, partner, or friend jumps off the financial planning "bridge," you don't have to follow.

You can compare the primary wealth-building steps to the best practices that helped you graduate from high school. Those were to go to class, turn in homework, and study diligently for exams. You won't have to copy off a friend's paper to steal the answers at Retire U because the answers can be summed up as follows:

1. Pay yourself first.

2. Stay free from adverse debt.

3. Spend less than you make.

4. Build a risk management plan, including an emergency fund.

5. Diversify among types of accounts.

6. Diversify among traditional asset classes.

7. As appropriate, expand into alternative asset classes.

8. Consider income investments as you approach retirement.

9. Maintain a current estate plan.

10. Hire an independent Certified Financial Planner™ practitioner and assemble your own personal dream team of advisors.

These steps will be covered in detail as we work toward our degree from Retire U.

Pay yourself first

The most important bill you need to pay each month is the one to yourself. Once you have eliminated adverse debt and created positive cash flow and a risk management plan, it is time to set up an automatic bill payment to your own savings and investment accounts. It may also be helpful to "hide" these funds outside of your ATM or checkbook access so that the process can be predictable, sustainable, and self-completing. This will help ensure that you are building wealth and not merely growing an account to spend eventually on consumerism.

A word about automatic bill paying: When you decide on an amount to save or invest, I urge you to make it an automatic deduction or transfer of some kind. Whether it is from your paycheck or your checking account, if the savings and investment deposits are automated, you can spare yourself from the psychological torture of deciding if now is a good time to invest or if you want to make a contribution in a given month. The only way this step works in your favor is to avoid the self-talk and rationalization that can be hazardous to your wealth-building efforts. In this case, autopilot is often the best way to get where you want to go.

Stay free from adverse debt

Until and unless adverse debt can be eliminated, no level of financial independence can be achieved. This debt must be wiped off your family's balance sheet before other steps can be undertaken. This includes all credit card debt and consumer debt, all 401(k) loans, any unfavorable or variable student loans, all margin loans, and most loans against life insurance policies. It does not include debt that is leverage for real property (a mortgage or home equity line of credit, for example), as long as there is positive equity in the event of an immediately necessitated sale of the collateralized property.

Running up adverse consumer debt is often related to "keeping up with the Joneses," and we already understand the importance of hanging out with the right crowd to avoid the temptation to do this in the first place. Finding the right crowd sometimes begins with avoiding the wrong one.

Spend less than you make

Positive cash flow is critical to making sure that you are accruing assets and avoiding debt. However large or small your income, if you earn more than you spend, you will have the ability to begin growing wealth. If you spend more than you earn, you will need to increase your income or decrease your expenses (or both) to have any chance at building sustainable wealth.

Build a risk management plan, including an emergency fund

Later in your course, you will learn the critically important concepts of maintaining a risk management plan and an emergency fund for you and your family. In the absence of a comprehensive risk management plan and a suitable emergency fund, any wealth building can quickly be derailed by any number of adverse events or circumstances.

An *ideal* financial plan is only ideal if it works *no matter what* happens to you. If you have loose ends in your risk management plan, get them closed before attempting to build wealth or you risk losing your progress due to unforeseen events against which you have not immunized your financial plan.

Diversify among types of accounts

It is important to have both retirement (qualified) and non-retirement (non-qualified) assets in your portfolio. This is due to the various and ever-changing tax laws and to the restrictions present on retirement accounts. When you begin to diversify your portfolio, start with different *types* of accounts, which allow you to have multiple layers of working assets.

When it comes time to stop contributing and start withdrawing from the various accounts, you will find that you have a great deal of flexibility when you have different buckets of money from which to withdraw. This is true especially if they allow for tax diversification—that is, the ability to decide from which accounts to withdraw in a given year based upon your income (and income tax) situation for the year.

Diversify among traditional asset classes[7, 8]

Most investors have three primary asset classes in which to invest: Equities (stocks and stock mutual funds), fixed income (bonds), and cash (and cash equivalents). The allocation to equities appropriate for you will depend on factors including your age, years to retirement, risk tolerance, and experience and comfort as an investor. You have hundreds (if not thousands) of options for selecting equities, fixed income instruments, and cash for a portfolio, and we will dive in-depth into this topic later in this book.

The most powerful factor in determining your success in building a portfolio is in the asset allocation and diversification of the account, not in the timing or security selection. It is okay to utilize several different styles of investment management, but it is more important to get the allocation right, to contribute regularly and automatically, and to manage the *behavioral* risks (often with the help of your financial advisor). Behavioral risks can hurt the portfolio as much as any other type of risk, if not more.

As appropriate, expand into alternative asset classes[9]

While the primary asset classes discussed previously are a good starting point, as your portfolio grows, it may make sense to add alternative investments to create additional diversification. Note that these alternative investments, in and of themselves, tend to have greater risk associated with them, including liquidity risk. Thus, they are not for everyone. However,

---

7 Mutual funds are sold only by prospectus. Please consider the charges, risks, expenses, and investment objectives carefully before investing. A prospectus containing this and other information about the investment company can be obtained from your financial professional. Read it carefully before you invest or send money. All hypothetical case study results are for illustrative purposes only and should not be deemed a representation of past or future results. These examples do not represent any specific product, nor do they reflect sales charges or other expenses that may be required for some investments. No representation is made as to the accurateness of the analysis. All hypothetical portfolios are intended only as illustrations of the math involved rather than the results of any specific investments.

8 Using diversification as a part of your investment strategy neither assures nor guarantees better performance and cannot protect against the loss of principal due to changing market conditions.

9 Alternative investments are often speculative, lack liquidity, lack diversification, and are not subject to the same regulatory requirements as mutual funds, may involve complex tax structures and delays in distributing important tax information, and may involve substantial fees. These products often execute trades on non-US exchanges. Investing in foreign markets may entail risks that differ from those associated with investments in US markets. These investments may not be appropriate for all investors.

if you have built some working assets (say $100,000), it may make sense to begin introducing one or more alternative investments as a small piece of your portfolio.

In general terms, alternative investments include real estate, managed futures, commodities, precious metals, hedge funds, hard assets and equipment, natural resources, private equity, private debt, and venture capital. Some of these are appropriate for a small piece of your portfolio when it reaches $100,000, while others are not appropriate for families unless they have amassed millions of dollars.

There are lots of variables and thresholds, and you will want to work with an independent financial advisor for assistance in determining which asset classes may be right for you.

Consider income investments as you approach retirement

With the exception of FDIC-insured savings accounts, the word "guarantee" is one that is difficult to find in any investment vehicle. Even when it is used, it is most likely backed only by a promise from an insurance company, bank, or other financial institution. That being said, there are different types of accounts that become appropriate in some cases as individuals and couples near retirement age. These are classified as income investments.

Many kinds of investments can fit that description, and they are beyond the scope of this book. However, while I firmly believe that there is rarely such a thing as a "good" or "bad" investment vehicle, there are absolutely vehicles that can be used appropriately or inappropriately for a given family situation. When used properly, they can provide additional financial security when it is needed most. You may want to explore the pros and cons of holding some of your assets in investment vehicles with fixed or stated income payments as you near and enter retirement, as they often have lifetime income benefits worth considering.

Maintain a current estate plan

We will include a discussion on estate planning documents during your coursework. Having your documents executed properly and updated as necessary to keep them in line with your family's needs and wishes and federal and state tax laws is a critical part of the process. Building wealth that you can rely upon for your lifetime is important. Having a plan for beyond your lifetime is also a strategy worth discussing with a qualified estate planning attorney.

Our firm suggests reviewing your estate planning documents with your attorney at least every five years or as major life changes occur. These changes could include a birth or death in the family, a marriage or divorce personally impacting you or your extended family (especially if it involves one or more people you have named as responsible parties), or a geographic move.

Generally, you'll want to have these documents prepared in your current state of residence, as the rules surrounding property titles and inheritance and estate tax laws vary so widely from state to state.

Hire an independent Certified Financial Planner™ practitioner and assemble your own personal dream team of advisors

It may seem self-serving but even objectively, I cannot imagine being a busy professional and a part of a busy family and trying to stay on top of all of the planning rules, laws, and concepts on my own. I encourage you to consider the services of a financial advisor to assist you on your wealth-building quest.

I am asked on a regular basis how to find a planner. My first suggestion is that you ask a friend, coworker, or family member for an introduction to their planner. You can also ask your accountant, attorney, or other advisor (insurance, real estate, etc.) for a referral. If you are unable to be introduced to advisors to interview, try LinkedIn or other online resources to find one or more advisors to consider.

When selecting an advisor, you will want to review his or her credentials and make sure that they reveal a background in financial planning. There are many industry-specific credentials and designations, some of which take years of study to earn while others are mere certificates of participation.

In general, look for the Certified Financial Planner™ (or CFP®) designation, as it is considered the gold standard for the financial-planning industry. To earn a CFP® designation, a candidate must pass six courses, prepare a financial plan for review, and pass a rigorous board exam. Additionally, the candidate must have at least three years of experience in the field and, most importantly, must maintain objectivity and act as a fiduciary while keeping the client's best interests in mind.

Note that some advisors work for various financial institutions as captive agents or employees, which can limit the range of products or services available to their clients. Other advisors are independent and have an open range of products and services manufactured by multiple financial institutions available to their clients.

At the end of the day, you wouldn't see a doctor without an MD credential so it is important to know if an advisor is a CFP® practitioner or not and also to whom the advisor is primarily responsible—their employer or their clients.

Before choosing to work with an advisor or firm, you may want to conduct a professional background check on them. You may also want to see if they have a history of complaints against them or if they have been involved in a personal bankruptcy or have had legal actions taken against them.

To research a potential advisor, you can verify that your advisor is a CFP® practitioner by going to the CFP® Board's website at cfp.net. You can also check disciplinary history by using the Financial Industry Regulatory Authority's BrokerCheck®, which is available online at finra.org.

Generally, you will want to fall within the scope of a typical client for a firm. Unless you have been referred to a specific financial advisor by a trusted friend or advisor, I encourage you to interview several planners before deciding which firm to hire. We will discuss some of the questions you might want to ask a prospective financial advisor later in this book.

You will learn about some of the risks inherent in investing and about the risk tolerance questionnaire often completed by investors during the initial financial-planning process. Some firms will stop with the risk tolerance questionnaire and will implement investment portfolios based on the questionnaire responses alone. This is called meeting the suitability standard. The suitability standard is one to which most stockbrokers, bank employees, and insurance agents are held. It says that all investment recommendations must be *suitable* for a particular client *at the time they are recommended.*

This standard is not nearly high enough in my mind, but the battles in Congress on the issue are facing stiff lobbying efforts by brokerage firms, insurance companies, and banks who want their employees to be able to sell their proprietary products when they are suitable, even when they may not be the *best* solutions for a client. While I understand the business rationale for this stance, if I were a client of these firms, I would always wonder if my best interests were being served or if I was simply getting a suitable product off the shelf.

The higher standard in the financial advisory profession is the fiduciary standard. This is the standard to which Certified Financial Planner™ practitioners are held. The fiduciary standard forces planners to put themselves in a client's shoes and to render advice that is in the *best interests* of the client *at all times.*

Taken one step further, the fiduciary standard ensures that your financial advisor renders planning advice to a client the same way he or she would to his or her own family. It doesn't mean that your advisor's family owns everything that a client does in his or her portfolio. It does mean, however, that if a client situation were to mirror the advisor's personal situation, the portfolios would look very similar.

Selecting a financial advisor is only the first step in assembling your dream team. You will also need the services of one or more of the following professionals (if your CFP® practitioner does not perform their function in-house):

- An attorney (estate planning, business planning, family planning) licensed in your home state
- An accountant or tax preparer (ideally a CPA)
- A real estate agent who knows your area
- A mortgage banker or broker
- A personal banker or credit union representative
- A property and casualty insurance agent
- A life and health insurance agent
- Your human resources liaison at work

Just as in your process for choosing a CFP® practitioner, ask for referrals from other professionals or people you trust and consider interviewing a few before making your ultimate selection. Ideally, you want these professionals to know what the others are doing and to work together for your benefit. Coordination of your planning helps avoid mistakes and may make your desired outcome more attainable.

Congratulations! You are ready to head off to start your freshman year at Retirement University. Each course you take will end with an exercise and an extra-credit assignment. So study hard, take lots of notes, don your Retire U sweatshirt, and prepare to graduate in four years with a dual degree in financial independence and retirement readiness!

Freshman Year:
Starting Out, or Refresher Courses

FIRST SEMESTER

I spent much of the first few weeks of my college career walking around the University of Pennsylvania campus sensing that I was surrounded by people smarter than I was. It was so daunting an experience that at times I even felt like I didn't belong there.

As a young adult in the financial world, feeling stressed and overwhelmed can be common, and those feelings can usually be traced to cash flow and personal debt.

In your first semester, we're going to tackle some core requirements related to cash and debt management. These include the causes of getting into debt, the struggles of dealing with debt, and some solutions and strategies for eliminating debt and getting back on the path to financial independence.

Debt is often the elephant in the room and the reason people fail to build wealth. Sometimes debt is caused by unfortunate events like medical expenses or acceptance of large student loans, but quite frequently it is caused by routine overspending.

We'll deal with extreme debt and chronic overspending like an addiction. The first steps in breaking a habit are to get past our denial and change our behavior. Like many freshmen, as we get more confident in the study skills we've learned, we'll take a heavier course load in the second semester.

Course Schedule for Freshman Year—First Semester:

- Cash Management 101: Pay Yourself First
- Debt Management 101: Regain Control Over Debt
- Debt Management 102: The Path to Freedom from Debt
- Debt Management 103: Creative Strategies to Reduce Debt Fast

Cash Management 101:

PAY YOURSELF FIRST

Most liberal arts programs have a core curriculum that students must complete in order to graduate. When I attended Penn, I had to elect 10 courses across several disciplines to start the foundation for a liberal arts bachelor's degree. This meant courses in natural science, physical science, math, English, history, and foreign languages.

Times and curriculums have changed over the years, but the basis of a well-rounded education still includes a broad range of coursework. It also helps to choose a major once you've completed a few courses in various disciplines so that you find what you like to study the most. For me, it was English and psychology. And, yes, I am a financial advisor and business owner with an English degree concentrating on late 18th-century Romantic poetry, although our firm's quarterly statements are not written in iambic pentameter.

For our purposes in graduating into retirement, the core curriculum is the series of steps that must be taken to create an effective financial plan. As with any great recipe, adding ingredients or taking directions out of order can adversely impact the outcome of a meal so in this case the sequence of steps is also important.

IT'S ALL ABOUT YOU, REALLY

Managing the educational rigors of undergraduate life means developing good study habits. For me, it meant scheduling time to complete papers and assignments and to study for exams. Thriving in college is more than just matriculating and attending classes; you also need to reinforce what you've learned in the classroom to be ready to apply that knowledge. During freshman year, some of the most valuable lessons aren't learned in class at all. Those include forming good study habits and developing solid time management.

In planning to graduate into retirement, you must develop a strategy to save, invest, and ideally grow your net worth until you reach financial independence.

On the surface, saving money sounds like a straightforward proposition. If you spend less than you make, you are saving money. But if it were really that easy, wouldn't we all be better at it naturally?

What many households do from month to month is bring in the income, pay the bills, and hope that something is remaining on the last day of the month. If you are in one of the households employing this strategy and you have money left at the end of the month (at least *most* of the time), that is an excellent start—you are living within your means. However, allow me to suggest that someone is not necessarily a great saver simply because there is money left over at the end of the month in a checking account.

The strategy I would like to suggest is one that I call "pay yourself first." The concept is simple. Each month, you put away your allocation for savings or investment first (before you pay any bills). Then you adjust your lifestyle (or budget) as if the money you saved was never earned in the first place.

Of all the checks you write every month, the one that is most important might be the one that you write to yourself. Once you are free of adverse debt and have built your emergency fund to three to six months of expenses or more, your next step toward wealth building and financial independence is to build your asset base.

Initially, set an objective to save a specific percentage of your gross income each month. At our firm, we set an initial target of 15 percent for our clients, but you can start with any percentage just to get the process underway. If your household's gross income is $10,000 per month, the initial objective will be to save $1,500 per month. If, due to cash flow considerations, you feel the need to set an intermediate goal of less than 15 percent (say $750) to get started, it is still a valuable step in the process because it helps you to create good habits.

In the example above, saving 15 percent of gross income means setting a spending limit at $8,500 a month, even though you are earning $10,000. If you can live on the $8,500 per month, you'll be able to comfortably save the $1,500 each month and won't miss it. We'll discuss in future courses where to put the $1,500 each month, but for now, let's at least agree that it won't be used for personal spending or household bills.

After you have reached the 15 percent objective, are living within 85 percent of your means, have maintained your emergency fund, and have remained free of adverse debt, it is time to set a long-term goal and to create metrics to measure your progress along the way.

If your goal is to retire in 20 years, for example, it is possible to estimate how much money you'll need to save or invest every month from now until retirement to help you reach your goal. Through the power of compounding interest and dollar-cost averaging, you can build quite a large potential nest egg by paying yourself first every month and checking your progress regularly. If you check your progress every six to 12 months, you can adjust the amount you're saving or investing each month as needed to stay on track.

Here's an example of the power of compounding interest and dollar-cost averaging:

If you were to put away $2,000 per month for 20 years (240 months), the total nominal amount of money that you would have saved or invested would be $480,000 ($2,000 x 240 months). However, if the funds were in an account that experienced a hypothetical 7 percent annualized rate of return, your account would have grown to $1,052,764. Note that the impact of taxes is not being considered in this example.

Imagine the power of setting aside 15 percent or more of your income and earning a reasonable rate of return for many years. The really important factor is to have time on your side. If you are in your 20s, 30s, or 40s and want to start saving for retirement, you have several decades to watch your accounts grow and to reach for a lofty retirement goal. For people closer to retirement, it is much harder to reach the target in fewer years. That is not to discourage anyone from getting started with saving and investing at any age but rather to encourage young people to save regularly from as early an age as possible.

Saving early and routinely, staying free of adverse debt, and paying yourself first are major determinants of financial independence and will help guide your way to reaching your goals.

If you need assistance with the calculation, you can find tools online to calculate retirement needs or you can enlist the assistance of a financial advisor. You or your advisor can create various hypothetical illustrations to build a plan and monitor it regularly. Assumptions on rates of return and inflation, along with your ability to save and invest money regularly, will help you determine how soon you may be able to reach your goal.

Once you have eliminated adverse debt and paid yourself first with 15 percent of your income each month, it will be time to get serious about creating a savings and investment plan, which we will discuss later during your studies.

Congratulations on completing your first course at Retire University! It may be too soon to decide what size cap and gown to order but you are on your way.

Let's check your progress with our post-course exercise.

POST-COURSE EXERCISE QUESTIONS

1. **TRUE** or **FALSE**: Compound interest accumulates faster than simple interest.

2. **TRUE** or **FALSE**: Assuming a 5 percent compound return, investing $1,000 per year for 40 years will grow to a larger amount of money than investing $5,000 per year for 10 years.

3. **TRUE** or **FALSE**: $100,000 in cash today has more value than $100,000 in cash 10 years from now.

4. **TRUE** or **FALSE**: Saving the money left over after paying bills every month is the best way to accumulate wealth.

5. **TRUE** or **FALSE**: If you set a goal to save 15 percent of your income, you may need to adjust your contributions if you get a pay raise.

POST-COURSE EXERCISE ANSWERS

1. **TRUE.** While simple interest only accrues on the initial principal invested, compound interest accrues on the initial principal and prior interest payments. If you invest $10,000 for five years at a 7 percent hypothetical interest rate, with simple interest the funds would grow to $13,500, and with compound interest the funds would grow to $14,026. Note that while this is good news when saving or investing, it is bad news when borrowing money, which is why credit cards and other consumer debt can be so damaging to net worth.

2. **TRUE.** In the case of investing $1,000 per year for 40 years, your total contributions are $40,000 and the future value, assuming the 5 percent hypothetical return, is $120,800. On the other hand, in the case of investing $5,000 per year for 10 years, your total contributions are $50,000 and the future value, assuming the 5 percent hypothetical return, is only $62,889. This is a simple example of the power of the time value of money and the magic of compound interest.

3. **TRUE.** Due to the impact of inflation, a dollar today is generally worth more than a dollar in the future. In this example, assuming an inflation rate of 2.6 percent, the value of $100,000 10 years from today would be worth only $77,361 in today's dollars. Conversely, to accumulate an amount 10 years from today equal to $100,000 in today's dollars, you would need to have $129,263 in your account in 10 years.

4. **FALSE.** Saving only the funds leftover after paying bills each month is not an effective way to accumulate wealth over time. The most effective way is to pay yourself first and to save or invest a target percentage (or dollar amount) at the beginning of each month, and to live on the difference all month long. This will help with budgeting and discipline, as well as creating a more predictable forecast for accumulation.

5. **TRUE.** While some savings plans such as payroll-deducted retirement accounts might adjust your contribution levels automatically upon earning a pay raise, other accounts will not. If your plan is to

save 15 percent of what you earn and you get a $5,000 annual raise, you'll need to adjust your plans to increase your annualized savings and investment by $750 (15 percent of the $5,000 raise).

EXTRA-CREDIT ASSIGNMENT

Choose a percentage of your annualized income as a savings and investment target and begin to pay yourself first with automatic deposits, contributions, or transfers to one or more accounts available to you. If you're ready for a stretch goal, challenge yourself to save at least 10 percent, and preferably 15 or 20 percent, of your gross income as a starting point every month.

Note that before undertaking this extra-credit assignment, you'll want to make sure you are free of adverse debt and that you're aware of any matching or other employer contributions for which you are eligible, as this will impact the outcome of the assignment. If you have adverse debt, instead of setting a goal to save a percentage of your income, set a similar goal to pay excess principal to your debt as a percentage of your income. This will allow you to create wealth in the long term and will also help you reduce adverse interest payments and debt service in the short run.

Debt Management 101:

REGAIN CONTROL OVER DEBT

In this course, we'll begin with awareness and detection and look at each of the warning signs of unmanageable debt in detail, and then we'll deal with solutions and strategies to solve them.

In my experience, a number of signs can indicate when a family is losing the tug-of-war with debt. Some are more obvious than others, but as with a medical issue, even the subtlest symptoms can lead to major problems if not detected and addressed early.

Below are some of the debt-related "symptoms" that should raise red flags for you:

- Inability to make the minimum payment due, or making only the minimum payment regularly
- Paying interest-only for an extended time
- Using a same-as-cash offer and not paying in full by the end of the stated period
- Transferring balances back and forth between credit cards
- Being assessed late fees on credit cards and other loans
- Exceeding your credit line and accruing fees and penalties
- Being tempted to use check-cashing services, paycheck loans, or tax-refund advances

- Using credit cards for cash advances
- Bouncing checks
- Utilizing overdraft protection on your checking account regularly
- Receiving letters and calls from collection agencies
- Having a steady stream of credit card offers that arrive in the mail, particularly those promising debt consolidation
- Being turned down for consumer credit
- Eviction, foreclosure, or repossession notices

Some of these signs can begin as the result of a job loss, illness, divorce, or other major adverse financial event. However, some of them can also begin benignly through poor record keeping, bill-paying habits, or spending decisions.

Inability to make the minimum payment due, or making only the minimum payment regularly

Over the past few years, many credit card companies have increased the minimum payment due as a percentage of total outstanding balance. This has created a hardship for some families who are able to make only minimum payments. Failure to make at least the minimum payment and to make it on time will lead to late charges and penalties, including the imposition of a default interest rate, which can sometimes be as high as 29.99 percent! That alone can cause a spiraling debt crisis and is reason enough to never miss a payment or be late with one.

Even if you do make the minimum payment on time every month, you're not entirely out of the woods. If you make only the minimum payment on a credit card, your purchases will take many years to complete and the interest adds up, often to more than the amount of your initial purchase.

As a general rule, if you can make only a minimum payment toward a purchase, don't make the purchase, regardless of how tempting the sale price or special deal might seem at the time. You will wind up paying much more for the purchase than the price tag indicates.

Paying interest-only for an extended time

During the mortgage industry meltdown in the early 2000s, there was a lot of negative press about interest-only loans and lines of credit. I am a firm believer that there is no such thing as a bad mortgage but that homeowners can select (or be encouraged to select) a mortgage that is wrong *for them*.

For homebuyers with unpredictable incomes, like business owners or salespeople earning commissions, an interest-only note can be very helpful. It permits a smaller required monthly payment during a lean month and allows for large principal payments to be made during months when income is higher, which also lowers the next month's minimum interest payment.

On the other hand, for homebuyers with predictable and steady incomes, interest-only notes are not a good idea, especially if the income coming into the household is only enough to cover the interest-only payment.

As a rule, interest-only notes aren't a bad financial tool. However, they aren't right for everyone and need to be used very thoughtfully when the optimal circumstances exist.

Using a same-as-cash offer and not paying in full by the end of the stated period

Many of us have been tempted while in department or electronics stores by the signs touting deals such as "six months same as cash" or "no interest for 18 months." While these "deals" can seem very appealing, they must be used properly to avoid adverse financial consequences.

Read the fine print in these offers. Generally, if you don't pay the full amount by the end of the stated period, interest is applied *from the date of purchase*. If you buy a $600 item with six months to pay for it interest-free and you still owe $50 after six months, the interest will be applied for all six months on the entire balance remaining as of each month. This can add several hundred dollars to your purchase price, especially since the interest rate on these programs tends to be very high.

As a rule of thumb, if you make a "six months same as cash" purchase, pay one-fifth of the purchase amount for five months. It makes your payment a bit higher each month but it helps prevent a very expensive mistake.

Transferring balances back and forth between credit cards

Sometimes described as "robbing Peter to pay Paul," this strategy can lead to a dangerous debt spiral. By making payments with one credit card to pay down another, you are paying interest on the first card each month and accruing a balance (subject to more interest) on the second card. It is better to explore refinancing options than to move payments between cards or other lines of credit in this manner.

While it is sometimes appropriate to transfer balances from a high-rate card to a lower-rate card, you do not want to create a habit of sending debt back and forth between lenders. As with the same-as-cash deals, the credit card offers to transfer balances come with significant fine print. Often, a credit card company will offer a low teaser rate for a period of six months or a year but there will be a fee on the transfer of 4 to 5 percent paid up front to the card company. Sometimes you wind up actually spending more on interest by doing the transfer than if you had just left the balance alone and made payments against it.

This is not to suggest that all balance transfer offers are a bad deal; however, make sure you understand the details and compare the total cost of doing the transfer, as opposed to only looking at the interest rate being offered. And as a rule, if you cannot afford payments on a purchase without transferring a portion of the balance to another loan vehicle, it is best to avoid making a purchase in the first place.

Being assessed late fees on credit cards and other loans

If you are paying your bills late and accruing penalties and interest, this means one of two things: 1) Your bills are exceeding your income and they are being paid late due to insufficient funds available, or 2) you need a better system of organization and bill paying to make sure bills are paid on time.

If you are unable to pay your bills due to insufficient income, there are strategies to combat insolvency. On the other hand, if you are late simply due to the lack of a good reminder system, there are systems you can use to improve your cash management skills and avoid costly mistakes. We'll discuss each of these scenarios later in this semester.

Exceeding your credit line and accruing fees and penalties

As with the fees for paying bills late, exceeding your credit line can occur for two primary reasons: 1) You have maxed out all of your available credit because your spending is exceeding your income, or 2) you need to consider a better tracking mechanism to make sure you're not accidentally overspending in a given month.

Sometimes these accidental instances of overspending in a given month can be attributed to a couple using the same credit card account and not communicating with one another about what is being spent. If that is the case, each spouse might be better off carrying a separate card and being aware of his or her own credit limits.

Being tempted to use check-cashing services, paycheck loans, or tax-refund advances

Check-cashing services, paycheck loans, and tax-refund advances are very often a terrible deal created to prey on desperate people in need. They should be considered last resort solutions. We will address emergency funds and other strategies designed to prevent the need to utilize services like these later in the semester.

Unlike most of the offers we've discussed thus far that can be used properly for consumer benefit, these options are rarely, if ever, beneficial and should be avoided if at all possible.

Using credit cards for cash advances

Credit card companies want their cardholders to accrue as many interest and fee charges as possible—that is how they make money. And since cash advances are usually the most expensive way to utilize a credit card, card companies are constantly trying to entice their customers to make them. Companies often charge fees up front to take the advance and a higher interest rate for advances than for purchases. In addition, if you carry a balance on your purchases at a lower rate, when you make your payments each month, you are paying the lower-rate purchase balance first, which means that the higher-interest cash-advance balance stays on your card for a long time.

Cash advances seem like a convenient and easy way to get cash. However, the cost to you for using that convenience is very high and should be avoided, if possible.

Bouncing checks

If there is a common theme among the warning signs, it is that some of them can be attributable either to poor systems of cash management and family communication or to expenses exceeding income. If you are bouncing checks on a joint account, it may be because you and your spouse do not know how much one another spends from day to day. We will talk about strategies to avoid this costly mistake later in this semester. If you are bouncing checks because of insufficient funds, you may want to consider paying cash more often and implementing a tracking system to keep on top of your household expenses.

Most banks clear the largest check first on any given day because it generates the most fee revenue for them. For example, let's say you have $2,000 in your bank account and you write six checks in one day in the following amounts:

- $1,975
- $500
- $200
- $100
- $50
- $50

In this case, instead of clearing the five smaller checks and bouncing one, the bank will clear the $1,975 check and the other five checks will bounce. This creates much larger fees for the bank at your expense, so you'll want to stay aware of this common banking practice. Of course, it's also better not to write checks in the first place if you have an insufficient balance to cover them!

Utilizing overdraft protection on your checking account regularly

While having a small overdraft protection feature on your checking account can be helpful in the rare occasion when you overdraw your account, it can also create a very expensive habit if you use it frequently.

Banks will charge high fees and interest for this service and will often make several small transfers to cover each overdrafted check instead of a single transfer of the available balance. Again, this creates much higher fee collections for the bank, at the consumer's expense, since there is a fee associated with each transfer.

As a rule, when using your checking account, pretend that you do not have an overdraft feature on it. If you use it once in a rare while, it won't be the end of the world, but if you rely on it as an ongoing cash management tool, it will be very expensive over time.

Receiving letters and calls from collection agencies

If you are receiving letters or phone calls from collection agencies, you know how frustrating it can be to navigate the process of cleaning up your credit. Sometimes these collection notices are for items that truly do not belong to you and you must go through a process to clean up the mistake. Other times, they are legitimate debts being collected by a third party on behalf of one of your creditors.

Having a steady stream of credit card offers that arrive in the mail, particularly those promising debt consolidation

Getting lots of credit card offers in the mail may seem like more of a nuisance than a warning sign. However, credit card companies generally send offers to two types of consumers: 1) The 1 percent of the population with the best credit who are getting exclusive offers for perk-laden cards, and 2) people with outstanding debt that they want to move to their card under a balance transfer offer.

Generally, it is not necessary to have more than two or three credit cards as a family. As a result, most of these credit card offers should go directly into the garbage—and I encourage you to shred them to try to combat identity theft. We'll discuss identity theft in detail when we cover risk management in your sophomore year.

Being turned down for consumer credit

Consumer credit is based on a formula that only an actuary could fully understand. Generally, it is easier to get credit for purchases that have collateral than for any other type of purchase. Thus, it's more likely you'd be turned down for a $2,000 purchase at an electronics store than for a $150,000 mortgage.

If you have been turned down for credit, you must receive written notification in the mail as to why you were turned down. You then are entitled to a free credit report so you can analyze the information that credit bureaus have in their records and take steps to clean up your credit, if necessary. We'll discuss this topic in depth during your sophomore year.

Eviction, foreclosure, or repossession notices

Lastly, if you are on the receiving end of an eviction, foreclosure, or repossession notice, it is safe to assume that you are already in debt well over your head. These types of actions can destroy credit for many years and often lead to personal bankruptcy.

HOUSTON, WE HAVE A PROBLEM

You've already taken a big first step toward identifying and understanding the warning signs. Some of them are based on record-keeping mishaps; some are based on spending habits or budgeting. Others are related to tricks of the trade used by banks and financial institutions to generate extra interest and fee income.

If some of these warning signs apply to you, it's time to solve the problem.

If you are in debt that is creating a financial emergency for you and your family, you will need to perform triage on your finances. If late notices are piling up, if you are in danger of losing your home to eviction or foreclosure, or if you are simply unable to pay the bills coming due and have been forced to choose which ones to pay each month, there are several steps that you can take to get back on track.

Sometimes personal bankruptcy is an option. However, before taking steps to go down that road, you can explore other planning opportunities and resources.

1. Attend debt management and financial education workshops in person, on the telephone, or online.
2. Consider using a credit counseling service.
3. Consider using a debt management service.
4. Get bankruptcy education and counseling.
5. Consult a bankruptcy attorney.

Let's address each of these steps in a bit more detail.

Attend debt management and financial education workshops in person, on the telephone, or online

Many of us resist getting help, especially when it comes to debt relief.

Many so-called credit counseling or debt management programs and workshops are scams looking to prey on unsuspecting consumers. It is critically important when you look for financial education in the area of debt relief or bankruptcy that you find a reputable provider of those services.

The United States Department of Justice maintains a website to assist consumers in need of credit counseling and debtor education information. You can find this information under the office of the United States Trustee at usdoj.gov/ust. Once you are on this site, click on Credit Counseling & Debtor Education and you will find objective information about consumer credit counseling agencies and debtor education providers, including those that are approved by the US Trustee's office and those that are inactive. You'll want to explore those approved providers in your home state.

Consider using a credit counseling service

You will find that some credit counseling services are for-profit businesses, while others are legitimate nonprofit organizations. In general, a nonprofit may be a better first call since their interests are better aligned with yours and they don't have a profit motive, which can cost you money. One such nonprofit organization is Money Management International, which includes the Consumer Credit Counseling Services (CCCS) program. This organization can be reached toll-free at 800-308-2227 or online at moneymanagement.org.

On this website, you'll find numerous resources, including educational videos dealing with all aspects of consumer credit and debt. They will provide credit counseling services, including helping consumers with budgeting, money management, and credit issues. They offer educational courses on credit card consolidation, interest rate negotiation, credit reports, and alternatives to bankruptcy.

Some of these topics, including negotiating rates with creditors, can save you substantial interest over time and may help you avoid bankruptcy and collection letters. A creditor is more likely to negotiate with you if you have a solid payment history, even if you are struggling to make minimum payments. In the end, they want to be paid and you want your debt cleaned up so a successful negotiation can be a win-win.

Whether in person or by telephone, a credit counseling service can help you come away with a personal action plan to get your financial house in order. The goal is not only to get you back on track but to try to do so without personal bankruptcy.

Consider using a debt management service

When education and credit counseling are not enough to relieve you and your family in a time of financial crisis, you can turn to a debt management service. You can find a list of approved providers on the same website for the United States Trustee listed previously. Money Management International and other similar programs can help you build a debt management plan. They become an impartial intermediary and negotiate with your creditors on your behalf to come up with a manageable and mutually acceptable debt repayment plan. The debt-planning intermediaries get involved every step of the way, even disbursing your monthly payments to various creditors on your behalf.

Additional programs specific to housing can be found on the website of the US Department of Housing and Urban Development (commonly referred to as HUD) at hud.gov. HUD can assist you with avoiding foreclosure, finding a lender, or obtaining public housing assistance. If online research doesn't yield the solutions you need, you can also find HUD offices in your home state where you can speak with someone personally.

Get bankruptcy education and counseling

Bankruptcy is a last resort in the process of debt management. Before you contact an attorney and start the process of filing personal bankruptcy, recognize that it can be a tricky process and do your homework first. Educational resources are available through the United States Trustee website under Bankruptcy Information Sheet. Here you will find the different types of bankruptcies that can be filed, generally Chapter 7 and Chapter 13.

When most people think of bankruptcy, they are picturing a Chapter 7 filing, which is a true liquidation. This means that you are looking to eliminate all of your debts and are relinquishing most of the underlying property to a trustee who will sell it to pay some of your creditors to the extent possible. Another alternative is a Chapter 13 filing, which is more of a personal reorganization. This type of plan generally allows you to keep your property with an alternative payment schedule negotiated with your creditors.

On the United States Trustee website, you can learn about how to receive a bankruptcy discharge so that you can clean up your debts. Before you file, it will be important to figure out which debts might be able to be discharged, because some—like taxes, child support, alimony, student loans, court fines and criminal restitution, and personal injury caused by driving drunk or under the influence of drugs—cannot be discharged through personal bankruptcy.

In addition to information about types of bankruptcy filings and the discharge process, you can find information about a reaffirmation agreement, which you can use to keep property and arrange to pay the debt for it, even though you have filed for bankruptcy. For example, if you have a debt discharged for your car payment, you generally cannot also keep the car. However, if you agree to pay for the car under a reaffirmation agreement, you can negotiate an alternate payment schedule to keep the car.

Before you can file for bankruptcy, you have to participate in a bankruptcy counseling session by an approved provider that can allow you to obtain the participation certificate you need to move forward with the bankruptcy filing. Money Management International is one such approved provider.

Consult a bankruptcy attorney

This book is not intended to provide legal advice nor are the websites for the government offices and nonprofit organizations listed. If you need legal advice during this process, you will need to contact an attorney. I strongly encourage legal representation throughout the bankruptcy proceedings, as the bankruptcy laws are constantly changing and vary from state to state.

An attorney can help you determine whether to file for Chapter 7 or Chapter 13, as well as review the laws specific to your home state with you. A Chapter 7 bankruptcy can generally be removed from your record or discharged within 90 days, although your creditors do have the right to file a complaint to dispute the discharge. A Chapter 13 bankruptcy generally takes five or more years to discharge because it isn't complete until you have repaid your creditors under the alternative payment plan.

Perhaps the biggest upside to bankruptcy is that once it is discharged, all of the eligible debts are wiped off your balance sheet. Another benefit is that once you have filed for bankruptcy, a foreclosure of your home is postponed and you become eligible for loan modification. If your home is worth more than $100,000 less than you owe on it (called a loan deficiency), filing for bankruptcy may be your only relief option.

Note that some assets are generally exempt from bankruptcy proceedings so that you may be able to keep them under the laws of some states. Examples include property owned by married couples titled as "tenants by the entireties" and some qualified retirement plans like 401(k) plans (subject to limits imposed by federal law). While life insurance cash values are creditor proof, they are not bankruptcy exempt, so they become available to your creditors when you file for personal bankruptcy. Since bankruptcy falls under federal law while foreclosure falls under state law, it is important to work with an attorney in your state with a specialty in this area.

Bankruptcy has some major downsides, the biggest one being that filing for personal bankruptcy damages your credit report for up to eight years. This will make it very difficult to establish or utilize credit of any kind for a long period of time. If your loan deficiencies are more modest and there is a way to avoid bankruptcy, all avenues should be explored to protect your credit.

In our next course, we'll turn to some of the strategies you can use to resolve your debt issues, regain control of your finances, and get you on the path to graduating into retirement.

POST-COURSE EXERCISE QUESTIONS

1. **TRUE** or **FALSE**: It is best to avoid having overdraft protection on your checking account.

2. **TRUE** or **FALSE**: Making credit card payments late can subject you to higher interest rates moving forward.

3. **TRUE** or **FALSE**: Credit cards can be an efficient way to get access to cash if they allow for cash advances.

4. **TRUE** or **FALSE**: Same-as-cash offers can be effective as long as the full purchase balance is paid in full before the end of the 0 percent interest period.

5. **TRUE** or **FALSE**: Declaring bankruptcy is a simple way to reduce or eliminate your debt payments.

POST-COURSE EXERCISE ANSWERS

1. **FALSE**. There is nothing wrong with having an overdraft feature on your checking account so long as it is used solely for the occasional hiccup. Using overdraft protection regularly will be very expensive and isn't a good idea. However, having overdraft protection on your checking account to prevent a rare bounced check is perfectly reasonable.

2. **TRUE**. It is critically important to make credit card payments on time. In a perfect world, they will all be made both on time and in full to avoid interest entirely. However, even if you cannot pay the bill in full, making at least the minimum payment on time will allow you to maintain the standard interest rate. Making late payments can subject your entire remaining balance to outrageously high default rates, which can be very damaging to your cash flow and financial health.

3. **FALSE**. Cash advances on credit cards are one of the most expensive ways to obtain cash. Not only are they subject to transaction fees and higher interest rates than purchases, they also ensure that payments made to the card for purchases get applied first. This means the high rate on the cash advance amount will be applied monthly until the entire card balance is paid in full. Try to avoid cash advances on credit cards at all costs.

4. **TRUE**. If you are making a major purchase and the vendor is allowing you six or 12 months to pay the principal amount without interest, using that payment plan can be an affordable and helpful strategy. However, it is critically important that every cent of the purchase amount is paid before the end of the interest-free period to avoid an outrageously high interest rate being applied to the full original debt amount retroactively. Having any balance, however small, when the interest-free period ends can be a catastrophically expensive mistake and should always be avoided.

5. **FALSE**. Bankruptcy is a time-consuming solution to debt reduction and one that can have negative consequences to your personal credit and access to capital for nearly a decade. While bankruptcy is a potential solution to a debt crisis, it should be seen as a solution of last resort in most cases.

EXTRA-CREDIT ASSIGNMENT

Take a full inventory of your debts (and if you are married, your spouse's debts). Make sure you know the full balances, the interest rates, the time to maturity, and any special considerations (like short-term interest-free terms) for each debt.

You will use this extra-credit assignment to make major progress starting in the next course, and this one step will give you an excellent foundation for creating a strategy and plan for debt reduction.

Debt Management 102:

THE PATH TO FREEDOM FROM DEBT

Like any journey, the first step to take is to figure out exactly where you are so that you can chart a path toward your destination. Becoming debt free is no exception. The material in this course is designed to assist you in regaining control of your financial future when your debt is manageable enough that you are able to help yourself.

There's no reason to be embarrassed about debt troubles; some of the greatest minds and most successful people have found themselves underwater, including Walt Disney, Abraham Lincoln, and Henry Ford.[10] The steps to take to regain control of your financial future are as follows:

1. Create a basic balance sheet to determine your assets, liabilities, and net worth.
2. Create a basic income statement to determine how much money you can afford to put toward your debt service each month.
3. Analyze your assets to determine which, if any, can be liquidated to create debt relief.
4. Review your existing debts to see if they can be refinanced or restructured to reduce interest or payments or to improve tax efficiency.
5. Put your existing (or newly refinanced) debts in order by interest

---

10 "10 Great People Who Survived Bankruptcy," Weston Legal, PLLC, Accessed April 16, 2020, https://www.westonlegal.com/bankruptcy/10-great-people-who-survived-bankruptcy/.

rate from highest to lowest to determine where extra principal should be going first.

6. Create a schedule and stick to it.

It's time to break out your calculator or spreadsheet and roll up your sleeves.

Create a basic balance sheet to determine your assets, liabilities, and net worth

The first step to determining where you stand financially is to list all of your assets and all of your liabilities, and to calculate the difference to determine your net worth.

A very simple balance sheet might look like this:

Assets

$330,000 – Primary residence
$130,000 – 401(k)
+$40,000 – Savings account
_____

$500,000

Liabilities

$180,000 – 1st mortgage
$40,000 – Student loans
$20,000 – Home equity line of credit (HELOC)
$20,000 – 401(k) loan
$20,000 – Auto loan
+$50,000 – Credit cards
_____

$330,000

Net Worth

$500,000 – Total assets
–$330,000 – Total liabilities
_____

$170,000 – Net worth

In this particular case, the net worth is a positive number, which is a good sign. A negative number would indicate that you owe more than you own, which could be a sign of serious debt issues ahead.

Even with a positive net worth, this scenario is not without challenges. First, most of the assets are illiquid. In other words, they cannot be readily sold or converted to cash without adverse consequences. Although the 401(k) account may hold liquid assets, it generally cannot be converted to cash, except in the form of a loan against the plan, unless specific criteria are met (age, plan language, hardship, etc.). In this example, only the savings account is a liquid asset.

Create a basic income statement to determine how much money you can afford to put toward your debt service each month

Unlike a balance sheet, which lists assets and liabilities and calculates net worth, an income statement will list income and expenses and will calculate cash flow. A simple income statement might look like this:

Monthly Income

$5,000 – Salary

Monthly Expenses

$1,200 – Income taxes

$1,050 – Mortgage (principal & interest @ 5.5%)

$150 – Mortgage escrow (taxes & insurance)

$100 – HELOC (interest only @ 6%)

$400 – 401(k) loan (principal & interest @ 6%)

$400 – Auto loan (principal & interest @ 4%)

$250 – Student loan (principal & interest @ 4.5%)

$1,400 – Credit cards (minimum & 10% interest)

+$1,500 – Other expenses (food, telephone, utilities)

$6,450

Monthly Cash Flow

$5,000 – Income

– $6,450 – Expenses

($1,450) – Monthly shortfall

In this scenario, the problem is clear very quickly. The monthly expenses exceed the monthly income, leading to a spiral of debt and, ultimately, bankruptcy if corrective action isn't taken quickly.

There are only two ways to improve an income statement: increase income or reduce expenses. To increase income, you would have to get a higher paying job or start working a second job to make up the difference.

Analyze your assets to determine which, if any, can be liquidated to create debt relief

In our example, only the savings account is favorably liquid enough to use toward debt principal. However, having too small a bank balance means that the next spending surprise along the way might necessitate further use of credit cards or other debt instruments. As a result, you'll want to make sure to keep an emergency fund on hand.

The concept of an emergency (or rainy day) fund is a simple one, and yet few households I encounter have such a fund. Moreover, those that do have an emergency fund have no idea how to quantify the fund beyond an amount that helps them sleep at night.

While a good night's sleep is an excellent goal, the purpose of an emergency fund is to have liquid capital available when needs arise without the need to make decisions that are expensive to execute. When I talk to clients about the moat around their financial castle, I explain that the very first (outermost) layer of defense is the emergency fund.

An emergency fund can take many forms. In its simplest incarnation, it would simply be a savings or money market account holding immediately available liquid capital. During times when money market accounts are paying 5 percent interest, that may be all the line of defense you need. However, as of this writing, most money market accounts are paying less than 1 percent interest and some savings accounts are paying basically no interest at all.

While it is important to have some cash in a readily available account like a savings or money market account, it is also appropriate to hold some of your emergency fund in assets that have a potentially better rate of return, like a certificate of deposit, or CD. As long as the CD has no penalty for early termination, you only need to hold one CD at your local bank or at a national or even online institution. On the other hand, if you would face a stiff penalty for early withdrawal, you might need to hold a series of CDs, potentially with staggered maturity (or liquidity) dates to avoid an expensive problem if you needed to access a lot of capital relatively quickly.

It may also be appropriate, if you have enough equity in your home, to maintain a home equity line of credit (or HELOC) against your house. If you have a HELOC with a zero-dollar balance, there should be no cost to maintain it. However, it is nice to have a checkbook that can access capital immediately in an emergency. The HELOC allows you to draw against the line and then to repay it, either at once or over time, with funds from your remaining assets or your income.

A HELOC can provide a lower rate of interest than revolving consumer debt like a credit card, and the interest may be tax deductible if it is used for the sole purpose of making home improvements, subject to federal limits. You'll want to check with your CPA or tax preparer to be sure you can deduct this interest, as only those taxpayers taking advantage of itemized deductions (as opposed to the standard deduction) can qualify. Some other limits regarding the use and amount of the borrowed funds also apply.

Another place to turn for quick liquidity is the cash value in permanent life insurance policies. We'll discuss this vehicle later in the book in greater detail, but if you have cash available and need it in a crunch, it can often be accessed as a loan.

If your savings and money market accounts are your first line of defense and your HELOC or life insurance cash value is your second line of defense, your third line of defense will be your non-qualified investment accounts. These include your accounts that are not qualified retirement plans or various types of IRAs.

The reason that these accounts can assist in an emergency is that the return of principal in these accounts is not taxable to you, so you would only pay a capital gains tax (at a favorable tax rate as of this writing) and only on the amount of your gain, if any, when you make a withdrawal. On the other hand, with only a few exceptions, a withdrawal from a qualified retirement plan or IRA prior to age 59½ will result in significant taxes and penalties, which you'll want to avoid paying.

One final thought about types of emergency funds: While credit cards are a convenient way to spend and to earn points toward various benefits, you will want to avoid using credit cards to handle larger financial emergencies, because they often have high, nondeductible interest rates and can get you into trouble quickly. Moreover, avoid at all costs taking a loan against a 401(k) or other retirement plan. There is no more expensive place to get funds than that for various tax reasons, and a plan loan should be only a very last resort.

Now that we have discussed where to hold an emergency fund, let's talk about *how much* to hold in one. As your household expenses increase, the size of your ideal emergency fund typically increases as well. That is because in a period of income reduction due to job loss or an injury or illness, your bills will not stop coming just because your paychecks do.

Using our simple example, if your household bills are roughly $5,000 per month, you will need to have enough of an emergency fund to cover your expenses for some time. The length of that period depends on whether your household relies on a single income or dual income and how secure you feel about your income sources.

If you are self-employed and therefore cannot be fired, you may feel a sense of job security that you wouldn't feel if you could be subject to a pink slip at any time. Of course, the flipside of that equation is that if you are self-employed, your income can vary widely based on the revenues and expenses of your enterprise.

If you determine that six months of expenses is an appropriate emergency fund, in the example above with $5,000 in monthly expenses, you will want to maintain a $30,000 emergency fund. Reasonably, you would want to hold $15,000 (or three months' worth) in a savings or money market account and the other $15,000 in a CD or similar vehicle to try to get a better return on the funds.

It would also help to have another $30,000 in available credit on a HELOC, bringing the total available capital up to $60,000 without the need to sell securities (potentially at an adverse time), to use a credit card for financing, or to take premature distributions from a qualified plan to cover the emergency.

In general, having a HELOC provides an additional layer of protection to increase the size of the cash emergency fund. The reason I like to see the cash emergency fund larger is that after an emergency that depletes the cash, available credit can be very helpful during the time needed to rebuild the cash fund in the event there is a subsequent emergency.

A few more comments about emergency funds before we move on:

- They can also be opportunity funds and should be considered as available capital for certain types of opportunities that life presents at times.
- They can also be used for major events or purchases like a new car or a family vacation, provided you have defined plans to repay the fund. Instead of paying interest to a car dealership and making payments to them, you would be making the same payments back to your own emergency or opportunity fund.
- Lastly, since the fund is designed to pay bills over time during a period of reduced income, the amount of capital that you can access in a *single day* rarely needs to be the full amount of the emergency fund. The only exception I can even contemplate when all the funds would be needed at once is to make bail, and here's hoping that is never a consideration in your household!

Back to our example, since only the savings account is liquid, we'll need to determine how much, if any, of that account should be used toward current debt principal. In this case, a $30,000 emergency fund (6 months of expenses) is adequate. The current balance is $40,000, so we'll apply $10,000 immediately to debt reduction, applying it to the highest-rate debt first (in this case the credit card balances).

Now your balance sheet would look like this:

Assets

$330,000 – Primary residence
$130,000 – 401(k)
+$30,000 – Savings account
_____

$490,000

Liabilities

$180,000 – 1st mortgage
$40,000 – Student loans
$20,000 – Home equity line of credit (HELOC)
$20,000 – 401(k) loan
$20,000 – Auto loan
+$40,000 – Credit cards
_____

$320,000

Net Worth

$490,000 – Total assets
–$320,000 – Total liabilities
_____

$170,000 – Net worth

Note that there has been no change to your net worth. You simply used $10,000 that was paying you less than 1 percent in interest to pay down debt that was costing you 10 percent in interest. After this reduction in the credit card balances, your cash flow would be adjusted as follows:

Monthly Income

   $5,000 – Salary

Monthly Expenses

   $1,200 – Income taxes

   $1,050 – Mortgage (principal & interest @ 5.5%)

   $150 – Mortgage escrow (taxes & insurance)

   $100 – HELOC (interest only @ 6%)

   $400 – 401(k) loan (principal & interest @ 6%)

   $400 – Auto loan (principal & interest @ 4%)

   $250 – Student loan (principal & interest @ 4.5%)

   $1,150 – Credit cards (minimum & 10% interest)

   +$1,500 – Other expenses (food, telephone, utilities)
   _____

   $6,200

Monthly Cash Flow

   $5,000 – Income

   – $6,450 – Expenses
   _____

   ($1,200) – Monthly shortfall

With this one modest adjustment to your balance sheet, you improved your cash flow by $250 per month, reducing your shortfall from $1,450 per month to $1,200 per month. You still have a budgetary shortfall, and there is more work to do, but you have made a positive change already and without much pain.

Review your existing debts to see if they can be refinanced or restructured to reduce interest or payments or to improve tax efficiency

In our example, we have several debts that can potentially be restructured to improve cash flow. First and foremost, since the house is worth $330,000 and the total debt outstanding against the house is $200,000 ($180,000 on the mortgage and $20,000 on the HELOC), we have an opportunity to do a cash-out refinance.

Refinancing a home can be a cumbersome and expensive process. However, if you have a good credit score, it is still generally possible to borrow up to 80 percent of the value of your home favorably.

For our example, let's assume that you could borrow up to $264,000 against the house in a single fixed 30-year mortgage. Let's also assume that we can get a mortgage at 5 percent, and that the cost to refinance is $4,000. The $264,000 would pay for the $4,000 closing costs and would pay off the $180,000 mortgage and $20,000 HELOC, leaving $60,000 to pay off some additional debts. Which ones should we pay off first? Generally, the higher rate, nondeductible debt should be paid down or off first. In this case, that means we'll want to eliminate the $40,000 in remaining credit card balances (at 10 percent) and the entire $20,000 of the 401(k) loan (at 6 percent).

Let's adjust our balance sheet to reflect these changes:

Assets

$330,000 – Primary residence
$130,000 – 401(k)
+$30,000 – Savings account

$490,000

Liabilities

$264,000 – 1ˢᵗ mortgage
$40,000 – Student loans
+$20,000 – Auto loan

$324,000

Net Worth

$490,000 – Total assets
–$324,000 – Total liabilities

$166,000 – Net worth

At first glance, you might react negatively to the fact that your liabilities have increased and your net worth has decreased due to the cost of the mortgage refinance. However, when we look at the new income statement, a different picture arises:

Monthly Income

$5,000 – Salary

Monthly Expenses

$1,200 – Income taxes

$1,450 – Mortgage (principal & interest @ 5.5%)

$150 – Mortgage escrow (taxes & insurance)

$400 – Auto loan (principal & interest @ 4%)

$250 – Student loan (principal & interest @ 4.5%)

+$1,500 – Other expenses (food, telephone, utilities)

$4,950

Monthly Cash Flow

$5,000 – Income

– $4,950 – Expenses

$50 – Monthly surplus

In this case, by completing a refinance, cash flow was improved by another $1,250 per month, eliminating the shortfall each month and creating a modest surplus. Also, all the high-rate revolving credit card debt and the unfavorable 401(k) loan are gone.

Naturally, refinancing is not always an option. If it were not available in this case, either due to poor credit or a lack of equity in the house, we would have to skip this step and move to the next step.

Put your existing (or newly refinanced) debts in order by interest rate from highest to lowest to determine where extra principal should be going first

Reducing the principal amount of existing debts with a refinance is a good step toward cash flow, but as we discussed earlier, it does not reduce total debt service or improve net worth. The next step is designed to create a plan to chip away at the remaining debt in a strategic way.

Putting the remaining debts in order of interest rate yields the following list:

> $264,000 – Mortgage (at 5% interest)
>
> $40,000 – Student loan (at 4.5% interest)
>
> $20,000 – Auto loan (at 4% interest)

You might look at this list and determine that the mortgage is the most expensive debt. However, since interest on mortgage balances under $1,000,000 may be tax deductible, the true net cost of that note (assuming a 20 percent income tax rate) is 4 percent. This is calculated by multiplying the stated interest rate (5 percent) by 1 minus the tax rate (1 – 0.20 = 0.80) to come up with the after-tax equivalent cost of the mortgage loan of 4 percent.

So, now the list looks like this:

> $264,000 – Mortgage (at 4% tax-equivalent interest)
>
> $40,000 – Student loan (at 4.5% interest)
>
> $20,000 – Auto loan (at 4% interest)

Every extra dollar of available cash flow (in this case, $50 per month) can be applied to the student loan as an extra payment amount, so you would be paying $300 per month instead of $250 per month toward that balance. Not only will this save you interest, it will pay off the loan more quickly than originally expected. Of course, if your income increases during that time, additional payments can be made to pay it off sooner.

Create a schedule and stick to it

You can find some fantastic software programs that calculate debt reduction plans for households. My favorite is Quicken. You can use a version online for free at quicken.com, or you can purchase the full version of the software at major retailers or online for about $50. After entering all your debts, it will print out virtual payment coupons for you to stay on track.

If you utilize Quicken properly, it is likely the best $50 you'll ever spend in trying to regain control of your finances. Remember, however, that owning this software package is like having a gym membership: if you don't use it, you aren't likely to get results!

In Debt Management 103, we'll take a look at creative solutions for when debt refinancing opportunities don't exist.

POST-COURSE EXERCISE QUESTIONS

1. **TRUE** or **FALSE**: To get out of debt, the first step is to stop spending more than you earn.

2. **TRUE** or **FALSE**: Refinancing can be an effective strategy for getting out of debt more quickly.

3. **TRUE** or **FALSE**: The ability to take an income tax deduction for some types of interest can play a role in debt reduction planning.

4. **TRUE** or **FALSE**: Once one of your debts has been paid in full, you should apply that payment amount as excess principal towards another debt.

5. **TRUE** or **FALSE**: If you're able to make extra payments toward your debts, it is always best to make them to your largest debt balance first.

POST-COURSE EXERCISE ANSWERS

1. **TRUE**. Like the adage that says to get out of a hole you must first stop digging, it is impossible to have negative cash flow and still reduce your debts. Once you are earning more than you spend, you'll be able to put some or all of those excess earnings toward debt principal to reduce your balances owed.

2. **TRUE**. Refinancing debts—especially a long-term debt like a mortgage or certain student loans—can make a positive impact on your debt reduction plan. First, refinancing might reduce the interest rate on some of your debt, which can make minimum payments smaller and allow for excess principal payments to be made more rapidly. Secondly, by refinancing, it may be possible to extend the term on one low rate debt in order to create better cash flow to pay down your other higher-rate debts more quickly.

3. **TRUE**. When determining which debts to pay off first, you want to consider the actual impact on your cash flow, and that means understanding the after-tax costs of each debt. If loan interest is deductible, you'll want to adjust the nominal interest rate in your calculations to determine which has the greater impact on your cash flow. A 6 percent loan with deductible interest might actually be less expensive to maintain than a 5 percent loan with nondeductible interest, so be careful when ordering your debts to understand the actual impact on your finances before setting up your debt reduction plan.

4. **TRUE**. In general, a debt reduction plan works best when you contribute a set dollar amount toward all debts regardless of how many debts remain. Once the highest-rate debt has been paid, take the amount of that payment and apply it as extra principal to the next highest rate debt. This way, there is no adverse impact on your cash flow, and you can get out of debt much sooner.

5. **FALSE**. While it can be tempting to see your largest debt balance as the most damaging to your financial health, it is the debt with the highest after-tax interest rate that should usually be paid down first. The size of the debt matters less than the impact on cash flow and the calculation of adverse interest. For many people, a successful outcome

of a debt reduction plan is one that eliminates all outstanding debts except for a favorable mortgage on their primary home. That might be the largest debt, but it is rarely the most adverse debt.

EXTRA-CREDIT ASSIGNMENT

If you are a homeowner, consider getting an appraisal on your home to see how much equity is available and explore options for a home equity line of credit (HELOC). Start with your present bank or credit union where you already maintain a relationship, but don't be afraid to shop for favorable terms. You don't need to have all of your borrowing with the same institution for any reason, so explore the options and get the best deal you can find.

If you have enough home equity to clean up any adverse consumer debt, consider this strategy as a step toward financial freedom. Note that even if you do not presently need to use the line for debt restructuring, having available credit is an excellent tool for emergencies and opportunities that arise in the future. It is always better to borrow money when you don't need it than when you do, because financial institutions can be hesitant to lend money to people favorably when they are in great need.

Debt Management 103:

CREATIVE STRATEGIES TO REDUCE DEBT FAST

Hey, it's okay. Sometimes you get behind in your classes. Maybe you dropped a course because you didn't like a professor or maybe you had a personal issue that distracted you so you reduced your course load. In that instance, you'd talk to a counselor to find a creative strategy to make up ground. Maybe you add an extra course the following semester or plan to take a course over the summer to get back on track. That's what we're doing in this course—exploring creative strategies to get us where we want to be.

Earlier in your studies, we talked about refinancing loans to get control of debt and that sometimes that option isn't available to us and we need to do some creative thinking.

Some potential solutions to reduce debt without refinancing include balance transfers using alternative creditors, reordering debts for strategic payment, and intrafamily transfers.

Balance transfers using alternative creditors

Earlier this semester, we discussed the fine print and tricky sales practices used by some credit card companies when balances are transferred. That being said, not all balance transfer offers are adverse ones. If you do not have the equity in a home or other real estate property to do a cash-out refinance, the next step may be to explore balance transfers.

If you are paying 10.99 percent on a credit card and you are offered a chance to move the balance to another card at 4.99 percent, there are a few questions that need to be answered before proceeding:

1. Is there a fee for the transfer? Sometimes it can be as high as 5 percent of the balance being transferred.
2. Is there a time limit for the special interest rate? Sometimes it can be for a period as short as three or six months, after which it reverts to a much higher standard rate.
3. Do you have a balance on the card already? If so, you may be paying a higher rate on the existing balance than you will be on the balance being transferred, which means that the higher-rate debt will not be paid down at all until the balance transfer has been paid off in full.

Generally, if there is no fee for the transfer, you can move the balance without much worry so long as the new rate is lower than your existing one.

If there is a fee for the transfer, you need to spread that fee over the period of time for the special balance transfer rate. In our example above, if you have 12 months at 4.99 percent and a 5 percent transfer fee, you are essentially (although not exactly) paying 9.99 percent for the year. As this is still better than the 10.99 percent you are paying currently, it may be okay to make the transfer.

On the other hand, if you have only six months with the special transfer rate, your 5 percent fee is spread out over only half a year, which means you are spending the annualized equivalent of 13.49 percent. This is higher than the 10.99 percent rate you already have in place. As a rule of thumb, if you are transferring balances from one credit card or loan to another, you want the lowest possible rate, with little or no fee, and the longest possible terms for the special rate.

Reordering debts for strategic repayment

As you'll recall, the debt reduction plan involves listing and ordering existing debts from highest interest rate to lowest interest rate, taking tax deductibility into account.

If you have no option for refinance or balance transfers, paying principal strategically can still save you lots of money in terms of interest expenses and can get you free from debt in less time.

For the sake of example, let's say you have the following debts:

In this case, the total debt is $80,000.

$35,000 – Home equity loan (at 7.9% interest-only)

$20,000 – Student loan (at 2.9% interest)

$15,000 – Car loan (at 6.9% interest)

$10,000 – Credit card (at 10.99% interest)

Let's assume that you have been paying a little extra toward principal on all of the loans to try to pay them down sooner as follows:

Home equity loan:
   Minimum payment: $230
   Actual payment: $300

Student loan:
   Minimum payment: $85
   Actual payment: $100

Car loan:
   Minimum payment: $305
   Actual payment: $350

Credit card:
   Minimum payment: $200
   Actual payment: $250

The total required payment each month is $820, but in this example, you are sending payments of $1,000 (an extra $180 per month).

With this payment schedule, it will take **23 years** to get out of debt entirely and the total interest paid on the $80,000 of principal borrowed would be **$43,949!**

Let's put the debts in order and change the way they are being paid to see if there is a difference. We'll assume that the home equity loan is tax deductible because it was used for home improvement purposes and falls within the federal limits for deductibility. In that case, the net cost of a 7.9 percent interest payment is only 6.32 percent if you are paying 20 percent in combined federal and state income taxes. In higher tax brackets, the tax-deductible equivalent is even lower. For more information and to determine your marginal tax bracket, check out the resources at irs.gov or review your most recently filed income tax returns.

Credit card (10.99%)

Car loan (6.9%)

Home equity loan (6.32%)

Student loan (2.9%)

Using the same $1,000 per month that was being used before, here is the new payment schedule for month one:

Credit card:
  Minimum payment: $200
  Actual payment: **$380**

Car loan:
  Minimum payment: $305
  Actual payment: **$305**

Home equity loan:
  Minimum payment: $230
  Actual payment: **$230**

Student loan:
  Minimum payment: $85
  Actual payment: **$85**

The total payment amount is the same but all of the extra principal payment is being sent to the highest tax-adjusted rate note. It seems like a small adjustment and it doesn't cost you anything to make this shift; however, with this adjusted payment schedule, it will take **nine years** to get out of debt entirely and the total interest paid on the $80,000 of principal borrowed would be **$23,139**!

With a simple adjustment to the payment schedule, you saved $20,810 in interest and got out of debt 14 years sooner than you would have with your original plan!

You would still pay the same $1,000 per month, sending all the extra principal payment to the credit card until the balance on the card was paid in full. Then you would continue to pay $1,000 per month but the extra principal would be paid on the loan with the next highest interest rate (in this case, the car loan).

Intrafamily transfers

The last strategy we will discuss is sometimes viewed as a last resort. I see it as a win-win opportunity for family members to help one another.

Let's assume you have a family member who is retired and living on the income from their investments. We'll say that one of their assets is a certificate of deposit at their local bank with a $25,000 balance paying 2 percent.[11]

What if they were to lend that principal to you, in a legitimate interest-only note at 6 percent interest? Your family member would get a raise from $500 per year to $1,500 per year, and you would have the ability to pay off $25,000 toward higher-rate debt and to pay back your retired family members instead of a bank or financial institution.

Now your credit cards and auto loan are paid off in full, and your overall debt payments look like this:

Home equity loan:

    Minimum payment: $230

    Actual payment: **$790**

Intrafamily loan:

    Minimum payment: $125

    Actual payment: **$125**

Student loan:

    Minimum payment: $85

    Actual payment: **$85**

---

11 Bank certificates of deposit are FDIC insured up to applicable limits and offer a fixed rate of return.

Note that your payment each month is still $1,000 and that the home equity loan now has the highest interest rate, so it receives the excess principal each month until it is paid off.

The total interest paid on your debt service drops further and you are debt free even sooner than you would have been without this financial move. Note also that while you are saving money and time, your family members are enjoying a higher interest rate on their savings than the bank was paying them before this transfer.

There are some complicated downfalls to an intrafamily loan, especially if the lending family members need the income and the borrowing family members default on the loan. In theory, this can be overcome with the use of collateral, but in practice, this is a risk that some families are willing and able to take, while others are not.

Congratulations on completing your first semester at Retire U! You'll now be much more confident when you arrive after your much-needed break.

POST-COURSE EXERCISE QUESTIONS

1. **TRUE** or **FALSE**: It is possible to pay your debt down more quickly if you make extra payments strategically.

2. **TRUE** or **FALSE**: Borrowing from a family member can be effective as long as all agreements are honored.

3. **TRUE** or **FALSE**: It is usually better to make extra payments to your highest-rate debts first.

4. **TRUE** or **FALSE**: It is never a good idea to pay a balance transfer fee to move a debt balance from one credit card to another.

5. **TRUE** or **FALSE**: It is always better to have fixed interest rates on your debt.

POST-COURSE EXERCISE ANSWERS

1. **TRUE.** As illustrated in this course, simply sending extra principal to debts in a random or arbitrary way will not have the same impact as a strategic, scheduled repayment plan. To pay debts down more quickly, use the strategies discussed in this course.

2. **TRUE.** Borrowing from friends or family can be a very slippery slope and can cause lots of relationship damage unless the loan is a legitimate one that is immortalized in writing and followed by all parties. If intrafamily loans are honored, each party can benefit from the outcomes. The lender may get a higher income (in addition to some satisfaction for assisting a loved one in need), and the borrower may get reduced payments, a cleaner credit report, and a sense of optimism that debt reduction is underway in earnest.

3. **TRUE.** Usually this is the case, although not always. Unless there is a compelling reason to pay off a lower-rate loan early (due to an unusually high minimum payment requirement or the need to prepare to reuse collateral in another way in the future), it is generally better to pay the highest-rate debts first and to reduce the carrying costs of high-interest debt.

4. **FALSE.** There are times when paying a balance transfer fee can still be a sound financial strategy. As long as you transfer a balance whereby the total cost of a year's interest (the new rate and the balance transfer rate combined) is less than the current rate of interest on the existing card, there might still be meaningful cost savings. Just don't forget the impact of the balance transfer fee when comparing offers for balance transfers.

5. **FALSE.** The benefits of variable or adjustable rate loans must be weighed carefully with the certainty of fixed-rate loan payments before a decision can be made. There are examples when variable-rate debt can be more favorable. For example, if you plan to move from a home in the next five years, a mortgage with a lower rate for the initial five years and an adjustable rate thereafter might be more cost effective than a 30-year fixed-rate mortgage at the time of financing. You also need to consider the trends in interest rates in general. In

a low interest rate environment, it is usually better to lock in a fixed rate for borrowing to avoid increases in the future. However, in a high interest rate environment, using a variable rate note might allow you to experience rate decreases over time without the cost and hassle of a refinance.

EXTRA-CREDIT ASSIGNMENT

If you completed your extra-credit assignment at the end of Debt Management 101 and you have your full inventory of debts, this assignment will be relatively easy. For this course's assignment, you now need to order your debts (as demonstrated in this chapter) and to determine a schedule for your debt reduction plan.

You can use a software program to assist you or you can accomplish this manually. Commit to a certain dollar figure to apply to debt every month that is greater than the sum of the minimum payments due. And apply all of that excess money each month to the principal on your outstanding debt with the highest after-tax interest rate.

SECOND SEMESTER

Now that a few of your core courses are under your belt and you're feeling more confident and comfortable on campus, you're ready to start choosing a few elective courses.

In this semester, we'll continue our discussion on cash management, we'll begin the risk management and protection coursework, and we'll introduce the financial planning curriculum.

Course Schedule for Freshman Year—Second Semester:

- Risk Management & Protection 101: Building the Moat Around Your Financial Castle
- Cash Management 102: Budgeters Rule the Financial School
- Financial Planning 101: Advisor Secrets You Need to Know
- Financial Planning 102: Where You're Going Begins with Knowing Where You Are

Risk Management & Protection 101:

BUILDING THE MOAT AROUND YOUR FINANCIAL CASTLE

When you have assets worth protecting, it's time to dig your moat. This isn't just for your castle itself. Your moat must protect the castle, its contents, and its inhabitants from disasters or "invaders" of all types.

The term "risk management" is not a euphemism for "insurance." Several risk management techniques do not involve insurance coverage, including establishment of an emergency fund and maintaining appropriate legal documents. There are other techniques relating to asset titling, beneficiary designations, and estate and trust planning, which we will cover in future courses.

While this course deals with some of the insurance-based solutions for risk management in a financial plan-and all insurance solutions are a form of risk management-know that not all risk management solutions involve or require insurance. The primary purpose of insurance is to insure against only those risks *you cannot bear*. You don't need to insure against every conceivable risk, only those that would cause you hardship if they weren't covered.

Most families need to consider, at one time or another during their lives, these seven primary types of insurance:[12]

1. Automobile insurance
2. Homeowners or renters insurance
3. Liability insurance (personal and professional)
4. Disability insurance
5. Long-term care insurance (LTCI)
6. Medical insurance
7. Life insurance

We will address all of these insurance types in this course with the exception of long-term care insurance, which will be covered in detail during a course dedicated to planning for long-term care during your junior year.

Insurance may not be the most fun topic to discuss and it's rarely bragged about at the company water cooler, but in an ideal financial plan, the insurance component can't be overlooked. It should usually be completed prior to the savings, investment, retirement, tax, or estate planning components of the plan.

Automobile insurance

Auto insurance is one of the elements that falls under the name "property and casualty," along with homeowners, renters, and liability coverage. While there are additional features of boat, RV, and motorcycle insurance, and other less common types, we are going to focus on the most prevalent ones.

The most dangerous activity in which most of us participate (at least regularly) is driving. There are few greater sources of damage or liability than when we get behind the wheel of our cars or trucks. As a result, the proper coverage is critical to protecting our financial well-being. Laws vary from state to state, but generally, the state-imposed minimum coverage level is insufficient to cover the risks we face when driving.

Three primary limits on automobile insurance define the amount of coverage provided by your policy, and they can be found on the declarations

---

12   This material neither constitutes nor is intended to constitute an offer or an agreement to provide insurance coverage; it is intended to provide general information and is not necessarily a complete description of all terms, exclusions, and conditions applicable to products and services.

page. The first is a property limit. The second is a liability limit, generally for your actions and for those of uninsured or underinsured drivers with whom you come into contact. The third is your retention limit (or deductible) for both comprehensive and collision claims.

Property limits are designed to cover the physical value of the automobiles involved in an accident. While these are important, the far larger threat to your financial security is found under the liability section, which covers you in the event of a lawsuit stemming from an incident while you or a family member is driving your car. In some states, the minimum liability coverage is $50,000 or so. However, when someone is injured or killed in an auto accident, they (or their family members) don't sue for $50,000. They often sue for millions of dollars. Therefore, I generally suggest at least $500,000 of liability coverage as well as a property limit of $100,000 on these policies.

The deductible amount is the amount that is not paid by the insurance company in the event of a claim and is paid out of your pocket before any insurance proceeds are paid. For most people, a $250 deductible is reasonable for comprehensive claims (resulting from dings and scratches and cracked windshields) and a $500 or $1,000 deductible is suitable for collision claims (resulting from an auto accident).

Setting your deductible higher will lower your premium but will also create a greater impact on your emergency fund in the event of a loss so this isn't just a minor detail of the policy. You want your deductible low enough that you could handle a loss but high enough that you're not paying unnecessarily high premiums.

Remember that a ding or scratch might be annoying but is unlikely to impact your financial life so only insure for risks you cannot bear. Don't pay extra premiums for first-dollar coverage for the little things.

As automobile insurance usually renews automatically every six or 12 months, it's a good idea to explore a few insurance carriers periodically to make sure you have a competitive policy and premium. If you have any accidents or tickets on your record, it can be difficult or expensive to change carriers.

Note that some insurers will insure only preferred risk drivers (i.e., those drivers with the best records). If that describes you and your family, you'll want to be with one of those companies, if possible, to get the best available coverage at the most competitive rate.

Lastly, when you have teenage drivers in your household, you can expect your premiums to be very high. You may want to explore multiple insurance carriers, as some will cover teenage drivers more favorably than others.

Homeowners or renters insurance

The two primary types of insurance for your home and personal property are homeowners insurance (if you own your home) and renters insurance (if you are a tenant).

Renters insurance is designed only to cover your personal property and to provide a liability limit for you. You do not need to insure against damage to the physical structure, as the owner of the house or apartment must do that. Property limits will vary widely depending on the value of your belongings (furniture, televisions, clothing, etc.) but generally should be a high enough number that in the event of a disaster you can replace everything you own and start over.

Homeowners insurance will vary based on whether your home is a single-family house, a townhouse, or a condominium.

In a single-family house or townhouse, as we discussed when we covered mortgages, your mortgage company will require you to make a deposit into your escrow account each month to fund your homeowners insurance policy premiums each year. They want to make sure that you have paid your premium because they don't want to see the collateral backing their loan to be destroyed without proper protection.

Your homeowners policy will have three primary areas insured—dwelling, property, and liability. The dwelling is the physical structure of the house. It needs to be insured at a level such that if you experience a total loss, you could have the structure rebuilt. The dwelling limit does not necessarily need to be as high as the fair market value of your property because you are not insuring the *land* upon which the dwelling is built; you are only insuring the dwelling itself.

The most important feature of dwelling coverage is to make sure that you have full replacement cost coverage. That way, if the insurance company recommends $200,000 of coverage for you but it costs $300,000 to rebuild your home, it becomes the insurance company's problem and not yours. Without full replacement cost coverage, you could accidentally be setting yourself up for a large deductible when you face an out-of-pocket overage amount ($100,000 in the example above) in the event of a claim.

Note that policies often have very important exclusions that may require you to buy additional endorsements or even separate policies. For example, most policies will *not* cover damage by flood and many will exclude hurricanes, tornados, and the like, depending where you live. If you are in an area defined as a flood plain, you'll need to explore federal flood insurance in addition to your homeowners policy.

Other exclusions are company specific or state specific, so read the policy very closely and ask your agent as many questions as necessary to make sure you have the protection you need.

The property coverage under a homeowners policy, like under a renters policy, is the value of your "stuff." One note of caution about the property coverage—many policies have limits on certain types of property like artwork, jewelry, and collectibles. If you have any of these items in your home worth more than $3,000, you'll want to get excess scheduled personal property coverage under your policy and to have each item appraised and listed by name and replacement value on your declaration page.

Some companies will include the scheduled personal property coverage in the same homeowners policy, while other companies will write it as a separate policy (called inland marine coverage) with its own declaration page.

While lots of endorsements are typically available to add to your homeowners or renters policy, the one that you will want to accept regardless of your personal situation is the rider for identity theft and fraud. In rare instances, this coverage may be in the basic policy but with most companies you must add it as an additional coverage. These riders are very inexpensive ($25–50 per year) but they can save the day if you're are a victim of identity theft or a similar crime by assigning a case manager to help you navigate a very complicated and frustrating process and by providing funds for lost wages or travel expenses incurred in cleaning up your fraud-damaged credit.

If you own a condominium, you will have some very tricky and important rules to consider. You'll want a copy of the master policy to find out what is covered by the condo association and what you need to cover on your own.

Generally, anything inside your walls is your responsibility and anything from the walls outward is the responsibility of the master policy. However, imagine the situation where you live on the second floor of a condo building and your icemaker leaks and floods your neighbor's unit on the floor below. You need to make sure that you are protected so ask the tough questions of your insurance agent.

Make sure to discuss amendments and alterations coverage if you were to upgrade anything in your unit—carpet, cabinets, fixtures, etc. The master policy might only cover contractor-grade fixtures.

Also, ask whether your policy covers the master policy deductible if a loss were to start in your unit and impact one or more of your neighbors' units. That deductible can be $10,000 or more, which could be a very expensive and unpleasant surprise down the road.

Like the automobile policy, your homeowners policy will have a deductible, which you can choose within certain parameters. Setting your deductible higher will lower your premium. For some homeowners, a deductible of $500 or $1,000 will be necessary. However, if you have significant cash reserves, consider a deductible of $2,500, or even 1 percent of your dwelling coverage, to lower your premium.

You'll want to avoid filing small claims, as they can impact your premium rating. It's better to deal with the small events out of pocket and to keep the insurance for the big things. Remember: the primary purpose of insurance is to pass risks you *cannot* bear.

For liability limits on both homeowners and condominium policies, I suggest that the limit be high enough to allow you to add excess liability insurance (discussed next). Check with your agent and find out that limit—it is usually either $100,000 or $250,000 but it can be higher.

Liability insurance (personal and professional)

We have already discussed the liability limits that will be included in your automobile and homeowners or renters insurance policies. However, one of the biggest risks to financial security is the risk of being named in a lawsuit. One way to protect yourself and your family is with an excess liability umbrella policy.

As the name implies, the umbrella policy goes over and above your home and car coverage. The umbrella is bought in increments of $1,000,000 and is relatively inexpensive because it only provides coverage once the liability limits of the underlying policies have been exhausted.

I generally recommend $1,000,000 as a baseline and then the coverage can be increased as your net worth grows.

These policies are not only for the wealthy. They can also be useful for families with high income, even if their net worth is modest. A large lawsuit can decimate you financially in two ways—one is having your assets used to pay a claim and the other is having your wages attached to pay a judgment, which is a risk worth insuring at almost any income level.

Talk to your insurance agent or company who handles your home and auto coverage about adding a liability umbrella policy. Often, to obtain an umbrella policy you must have all three policies with the same company. As a rule, carriers provide multi-policy discounts so keeping your property and casualty insurance with the same company is usually a good idea, whether you opt for the umbrella or not.

Professional liability coverage is often industry specific. The most common types of professional liability coverage are malpractice insurance, errors and omissions (E&O) insurance, and directors and officers (D&O) insurance.

Malpractice is a commonly required coverage for physicians and lawyers, while E&O is the type of insurance often carried by financial advisors and accountants. D&O is designed to protect officers and other board members of public companies and nonprofit institutions, trustees of educational institutions, and others serving in an advisory capacity from liability due to mistakes made in those roles. Usually D&O is provided by the company or other institution on behalf of their board members, while malpractice and E&O can be provided for employees at employer expense but is usually paid for by subcontractors and practice owners personally.

As you might imagine, the cost of the coverage will be determined largely by the likelihood of being named in a lawsuit and the typical size of a claim in your profession. For example, the malpractice insurance for a heart surgeon or OB-GYN will be more expensive than the malpractice insurance for a general dentist.

Disability insurance

If you had a goose that could lay golden eggs, would you insure only the golden eggs or would you also insure the goose? We've talked at length about insuring your property. However, for working people, the largest single financial risk that can most quickly destroy personal savings and create debt or insolvency is to become suddenly unable to work. While we don't like to picture ourselves disabled, illnesses and injuries are a fact of life, and we need to be as prepared as we can, even if we hope we never need the coverage.

For many working Americans, disability insurance is provided through their employers in a group policy. Typically, there are two types of disability coverage—short-term disability (STD) and long-term disability (LTD).

STD is usually limited to 90 or 180 days and is designed to provide a paycheck while you recover from an illness or injury. Some STD policies will also provide benefits during maternity leave. These policies are either employer-paid group benefits or individually paid voluntary benefits. Benefits are usually paid weekly and are capped at either a dollar amount or a percentage of salary. A typical limit is 60 percent of your salary up to $1,000 per week. The benefits are generally free from income tax because any premiums paid are not tax deductible.

LTD is by far the more important of the two coverage types for most individuals to carry because LTD is designed to replace a portion of your income for many years. Like STD policies, the benefits under LTD are usually capped at 60 percent of your salary up to a set limit (often $5,000 or $10,000 per month). Most policies will provide monthly benefits up to a dollar limit or salary percentage until age 65 or for five years, whichever is longer. It is very important to pay premiums with after-tax dollars (i.e., not to take a tax deduction) so that benefits paid in the event of a claim will be free of income tax.

For someone without an employer-provided group disability policy or someone with an income above a group policy's benefit limit, individual policies can be obtained. The process usually requires full medical and financial underwriting, including a paramedical exam, a review of your recent paycheck, and one to two years of your tax returns.

For professionals, it is very important to get coverage that defines being disabled in terms of being unable to engage in your *own occupation*. This language can be found in the definitions section of a disability policy and is perhaps the most important paragraph in the whole policy. If you are a surgeon or a concert pianist, for example, you could become fully disabled by slamming your hand in a car door if it kept you from performing surgery or playing the piano. If the contract has language about "any occupation," you are only disabled if you can't work at all in any job, sometimes with little or no regard to as how much your income has been reduced.

Lastly, if you are buying a policy for yourself, there is another important distinction regarding the policy premiums that can be very tricky. If a policy is guaranteed renewable, it means that you cannot have it cancelled by the insurance company except for your failure to pay a premium. However, it does *not* mean that your premium amount is guaranteed to remain the same.[13]

To have a premium that cannot be increased by the insurance company, the policy must be noncancelable and guaranteed renewable. This is a question to ask your financial advisor or insurance agent to make sure you know exactly what the insurance company can and cannot do with your premium rates.

Since benefits are generally not taxable, if you are able to get 60–70 percent of your income insured, that is usually enough for LTD.

Medical insurance

Although individual health insurance exchanges exist across the country, medical insurance is still dominated by a model that is employer-centric. That means that in most cases, someone must have an employer who offers coverage to obtain it favorably and without personal underwriting. For better or worse, that means that when you are looking for a job or making

---

13 All guarantees subject to the claims-paying ability of the issuing insurance company.

a career move, the employee benefits (including health insurance) may be as important as the discussion about salary or wages.

Medical insurance tends to be very expensive if you obtain it on your own or if you work for a for-profit company. Only those employed by the government or by a small percentage of private companies can get medical insurance without it being an onerous expense for their family.

While even uninsured individuals have access to emergency and hospital care, it is very uncommon for the uninsured to be able to get favorable access to physicians or preventative care so carrying medical insurance is a necessity.

If your employer (or your spouse's employer) offers health insurance benefits, I urge you to accept coverage. If there are multiple plan offerings, read them carefully and ask your financial advisor or benefits coordinator to help you select one.

If your employer does not offer you coverage, explore individually underwritten plans or state-mandated plans to make sure you have at least catastrophic coverage. In the US, many bankruptcies are declared each year due to a medical emergency, and health insurance can help you avoid being part of that troubling statistic.

You can choose from many types of plans, and the costs and benefits can differ greatly. This is also a rapidly changing area of insurance so your options from one year to the next might be very different.

Some plans allow for benefits only within a network of physician providers or charge higher copayments to the insured for using a provider outside of that network. Some plans have low deductibles and cover almost all medical expenses. Naturally, those plans tend to be very expensive.

As a way to reduce premium costs and a means to have consumers shop to find better pricing on their care options, health savings accounts (HSAs) were created in 2003. HSAs allow people covered by high-deductible health plans (HDHPs) to receive tax-preferred treatment on money saved for medical expenses. The primary benefits of an HSA include the ability to make contributions that are currently fully income-tax deductible at the federal and state level up to the limits set annually.

As of 2020, high-deductible health insurance plans, which are HSA-qualified (those plans with deductibles of at least $1,400 for individuals or $2,800 for families), allow contributions to an HSA. The annual contribution limits in 2020 are $3,550 for individuals and $7,100 for families. An additional contribution of $1,000 can be made if the insured is over age 55. If an employer is making contributions on an employee's behalf, the employer contribution counts toward those annual limits and is not in addition to those amounts.

The HSA can be held with any bank that offers them and is usually funded by payroll deduction, although some employers do make contributions on behalf of their employees as well.

In addition to the tax deduction for money going in, HSA money can grow tax free indefinitely. There are no 1099s generated, no capital gains, and for qualified withdrawals, no income tax on distributions, whether they are made to a medical provider directly or sent as reimbursement to the account holder.

Although a financial institution usually requires a minimum account balance (often $2,000 or so) before funds in an HSA can be invested, the HSA fund doesn't have to sit in cash savings. The money can be invested in mutual funds like any investment account and can grow without capital gains. So long as the money is used for qualifying health expenses—whether in this year, next year, or 15 years—there are no income taxes on the withdrawal.

Unlike a flexible spending account for healthcare (FSA), with which the HSA is often confused, the HSA is an account for medical expenses that you can roll over from year to year. Because 50 percent of all medical expenses is incurred in the last six to 12 months of life, this ability to grow the account is very attractive. The funds can also be allowed to grow and then used toward premiums for long-term care (LTC) insurance when the time comes.

In the event you're fortunate enough never to need the money for healthcare, once you have reached age 59½, you can take HSA distributions similar to withdrawals from traditional IRAs. In this case, you will pay ordinary income taxes but no penalties. There are no required minimum distributions (RMDs) from an HSA, so the account can be held for a lifetime and inherited by an heir.

The rules for HSAs detailed here are the federal rules. Some states now have additional rules that apply to their tax filers, including limitations or disallowance of tax deductibility or deferral, so check your home state's statute or ask a financial or tax advisor for guidance.

The HSA truly offers the best of all worlds—tax-deductible contributions made by payroll deduction, tax-deferred growth, tax-free withdrawals for qualified medical expenses, and flexibility in the event the funds aren't needed for healthcare. For more information on the federal HSA provisions, visit the IRS website.

Life insurance

Few financial products are as misunderstood as life insurance. In addition to the benefit offered when an insured person dies, life insurance offers lots of wealth creation, preservation, and transfer strategies and many creative tax and business planning uses. Let's begin with the basics.

When you take out a policy you must have insurable interest, so you need permission from the insured and a reason why you're applying for the policy. Generally, while there is no specific contribution limit, you can only qualify for a policy with a death benefit designed to replace the human life value of someone who dies. For a working person, that means that life insurance can be structured to make sure that your paychecks keep coming to your family, even if you are deceased.

As a rule, someone young and single (without children) does not need life insurance. There are lots of reasons why they might *want* life insurance but they do not *need* it. That is because no one will suffer *financially* in their absence. The same can be said about a retiree so long as the retirement savings is sufficient in size and is protected from other risks, like long-term care, liability, inflation, and estate taxes.

If life insurance replaces a working person's income should they die prior to retirement, how do you calculate that replacement value? If you earn $60,000 per year and want to replace your entire income, what amount of money sitting in a bank or other financial institution would be required to draw $60,000 per year without spending down principal?

If you draw 4 percent from the account each year, you will need $1,500,000 in an account to provide $60,000 annually. If you don't have an account that size, life insurance can make up the difference in your absence so that your family can continue their lifestyle even after you are gone.

You can choose from many kinds of life insurance, but the two basic types are either term or permanent policies.

As the name implies, term insurance is designed to be temporary. If you are 35 years old and want to have life insurance until you graduate into retirement at age 65, you may want to explore a 30-year term policy. If you die before you retire, your family gets the lump-sum death benefit, puts it in a financial account, and can continue to draw your salary. If you live to 65, the term insurance expires, and you will need to rely on your retirement savings and investments to keep receiving your income each year.[14]

Permanent insurance differs from term insurance in that it is designed to pay a claim when you die, regardless of your age. There are several different types of products on the market, and new products are being introduced all the time. I will do my best to summarize the main types here, but I urge you to make sure you thoroughly understand a life insurance product before buying it.[15]

The main types of permanent life insurance are as follows:

- Whole life
- Universal life
- Variable life
- Variable universal life

While there are other hybrid contracts, some of which are linked to returns of an equity index or to ancillary long-term care benefits, these are the primary four. I will describe each one, including the uses and pros and cons of each, as well as a brief history of how the products were developed to give them some context.

---

14   All guarantees are based on the financial strength and claims-paying ability of the issuing insurance company, who is solely responsible for all obligations under its policies. Products and services may not be available in all states.

15   There are considerable factors that need to be considered before replacing life insurance, such as, but not limited to, commissions, fees, expenses, surrender charges, premiums, and new contestability periods. There may also be unfavorable tax consequences caused by surrendering an existing policy, such as a potential tax on outstanding policy loans. Please discuss your situation with your financial advisor.

Whole life insurance

The concept of whole life insurance has been around for ages. At one time, it was the only alternative to term insurance. Most of the policies were issued by mutual life insurance companies—those that are owned by, and for the exclusive benefit of, their policyholders. They typically pay dividends on their whole life policies to policyholders based on the underlying performance of the company's general accounts because they don't have traditional stockholders or other company owners to reward when they are profitable.

With whole life insurance, just about every feature of the policy is guaranteed contractually—the premium, the cash value schedule, and the death benefit. The dividends, if any, are not guaranteed but the top carriers have had a strong history of paying them.

Today, there are very few mutual insurance companies left, which means very little choice in the whole life marketplace. Many companies have demutualized, which means that they went public and allowed stockholders to own the company instead of policyholders. In these cases, policyholders were given some stock based on their policy ownership, but in my opinion, this process never worked out well for the policyholders. Now when those companies pay dividends, they must pay their stockholders before their policyholders. The good news is that there are still a few very strong mutual companies writing high-quality whole life insurance policies.

Because whole life has built-in guarantees on most features, it can have higher premiums than other types of permanent insurance. However, it can also be designed to grow cash values and can be a permission slip to spend other assets down, knowing that heirs (or surviving spouses or partners) will receive a predictable death benefit.

Whole life can be structured to have premiums paid for life or for a specific number of years, which must be seven or more for tax reasons. Life insurance policies bought with premiums for fewer than seven years have a special place in the tax code that is not favorable, being dubbed "modified endowment contracts" instead of "life insurance" by the IRS. There are other cases in which that can also occur. If you want the cash value to build up in a tax-deferred and potentially income tax-free way in the policies, it is critical to make sure when you buy one that it is not a modified endowment contract.

In some ways, whole life insurance is the most powerful but least understood tax avoidance tool available. To me, whole life insurance operates like a Roth IRA but with no contribution limit and with an added death benefit. Multiple tax and liquidity benefits and planning opportunities result from owning whole life insurance, such as:

- **Tax-deferred growth:** When you make contributions—that is, you pay your premiums—there is no tax deduction. However, the cash value will grow income tax free for life, and when the death benefit is eventually paid, it will be received income tax free as well.

- **Access to cash value during lifetime:** You can access the cash value in a whole life policy during the lifetime of the insured in several ways. In most cases, this takes the form of supplemental retirement income or collateral for access to working capital. Withdrawals made from whole life policies are generally income tax free up to basis and collateral for a policy loan up to the full cash value amount.

One of unique features of whole life insurance is that it is a phenomenal source of collateral. You can borrow against your own cash value favorably while you are alive. The current interest rate on a whole life insurance loan is about 8 percent. And before you say, "But wait, that's a high rate!" recognize that the loan is **not** a withdrawal from the cash account.

The cash account stays fully funded on a contractual basis and the loan is a separate agreement. So the cash value in the policy continues to grow, as expected, even if you borrow against it. For example, if your policy earns a 5.5 percent dividend and you're paying 8 percent to borrow against it, your net cost for the loan is just 2.5 percent. Interest payments are often optional—they can be paid in cash or can utilize cash values in the policy to pay them—and principal payments are always optional. There is no limitation on the time a loan may be outstanding. Lastly, if you die while the loan is outstanding, the amount of death benefit paid is simply reduced dollar for dollar by the outstanding loan balance.

When prevailing interest rates are lower than the stated loan rate in the policy, it is also possible to collateralize the policy's cash value by using a cash value line of credit (or CVLOC). These can be issued to 95 percent of the cash value in a whole life policy and are often at or slightly below prime interest rates. Done properly, they are interest-only variable lines that can be used and reused as needed over time. Most have no application fee or annual fees so you only have to pay interest on outstanding balances.

While whole life insurance should *not* be considered as a source of education savings and you should stick with 529 plans or other investment vehicles for that purpose, in most cases the cash value in whole life insurance is not included on financial aid forms. As with a retirement plan, they do not qualify as assets you have to declare when looking for financial aid. Note that many private schools will ask about cash values to determine financial aid, even though for college the FAFSA (Free Application for Federal Student Aid) does not.

An ideal way for married people to use whole life insurance is as a social security offset. Let's take an example in which both spouses are of age to collect social security retiree benefits. One spouse was a high earner and is now getting a $3,000-per-month benefit; the other is getting a $1,500-per-month benefit. When one of the spouses dies, the surviving spouse will keep the larger of the two benefits (in our example, $3,000 per month) but will lose the smaller payment.

By having whole life insurance on both spouses, it allows the surviving spouse to collect the death benefit from the deceased spouse, making up the lost income equivalent to the smaller social security payment. It also gives the surviving spouse the ability to spend the cash value on his or her own policy, since the death benefit is no longer needed for a surviving spouse. In this way, the policy can replace the lost income effectively.

When you buy a whole life insurance policy, you are contractually obligating yourself to make contributions every year in the form of premiums. In return, the insurance company is on the hook not only to provide you with accessible cash value—the living benefit of having the policy—but also with a death benefit, both of which have guaranteed schedules of growth.

Because the premium is not optional but is required for a specific number of years, make sure that you can fund a plan through to completion before initiating a policy. The biggest mistakes I've seen involving whole life insurance are due to insufficient or incomplete funding or surrender of a policy during the insured's lifetime.

My parents had the foresight to buy whole life insurance on my life when I was a teenager. As a young adult, they transferred the ownership of the policy (and responsibility for the premiums) to me. Twice in my adult life I have used the cash value in that whole life policy (and others that I've acquired subsequently) to create additional opportunity and wealth.

The first time I used my cash value was when I bought my first home at age 25. The cash value in the life insurance policy provided the down payment for the home so that I was able to qualify favorably for a more manageable mortgage. The policy loan was paid off gradually over the next few years as I was able to do so. Importantly, having the life insurance policy allowed me to buy a home I may otherwise have had trouble affording, and the home sold 10 years later for a profit. Essentially, I can track some growth in our family's personal balance sheet due to the utilization of the whole life insurance cash values.

The second time I used the cash value in these policies was to generate enough capital to start a business. In 2003, when I launched Brotman Financial Group, I had to lease office space and equipment, hire employees, buy furnishings, and maintain enough working capital to get off the ground. Not a single bank was willing to lend money to a start-up business—even before the global financial crisis. In fact, most banks won't even consider a line of credit for a small business without two years of income tax returns and profit and loss statements. The life insurance policy provided the cash value to start a company, which now many years later is a growing and thriving enterprise.

Today, we have banking relationships and lines of credit with the same banks that wouldn't even speak with us in 2003. In fact, we now have various banks compete for our business regularly. The life insurance loans have been paid off and the cash value is ready to be called upon again in the future—whenever access to the funds is needed for personal or business use.

Universal life insurance

For decades, whole life insurance was the core product of the insurance industry. Then in the 1980s, interest rates in the US were so high that whole life was perceived by some as noncompetitive relative to banking products like certificates of deposit. In a reactive way, and nearly in a panic over losing market share to banks, universal life was born.

With universal life, the growth in the policies became interest rate sensitive. The death benefits were still guaranteed but the premiums were not. So, if interest rates went up or stayed high, policies built more cash, whereas if interest rates dropped, the policies would not build enough cash to maintain their premium schedules and more money would be required by policyholders to continue the policies.

This meant that some of the risk that people were trying to transfer by buying life insurance was now squarely back on the policyholders. However, consumers sometimes have very short memories and the belief was that interest rates would *always* stay high and that these policies were a better way to build wealth than whole life. They were often illustrated showing projections based on 12 percent interest rates.

In the decades that followed, rates came down. The policyholders who thought they had permanent insurance with level-scheduled premiums instead got premium notices many times higher than they expected and many of the policies were lapsed prematurely. It was, in a word, a disaster for some families.

Due to various court cases and litigation, universal life policies being issued today can have secondary no-lapse guarantees on them, meaning that it is now possible to get a guaranteed premium and a guaranteed death benefit and to have the cash value interest rate sensitive. These contracts now allow buyers to choose the age at which the policies will cease to be guaranteed—and the longer the guarantee, the higher the premium.

I see examples of when universal life can be an appropriate solution and recommend it on occasion for trust-owned insurance for estate planning or wealth replacement and in business cases when cash value is unimportant or could be detrimental to the planning scenario. Because there is not a guaranteed cash value schedule, the premiums are lower than those for a whole life policy.

To me, universal life is like term insurance extended for a longer term up to and including your entire lifetime. It offers very few living benefits, but from a pure cost standpoint, there is no less expensive way to guarantee a death benefit for life.

Variable life insurance[16]

Just as the 1980s meant high interest rates and the insurance companies reacting with universal life, the 1990s meant a raging bull market for equities. Again, the life insurance industry was afraid of losing market share—this time to the brokerage firms rather than the banks.

Variable life insurance was created to provide a way to have a self-directed investment account inside an insurance policy. The death benefit was still guaranteed but as with universal life, the premium was not guaranteed. Instead of being related to interest rates, it was related to stock market fluctuation. Again, because consumers have short memories, illustrations were shown reflecting 12 percent (or higher) annual rates of return for the underlying portfolios, despite owning very expensive subaccounts with historic equity returns (net of expenses) lower than those shown.

To the buying public, this was the *new* economy where stock markets could only go up. I can still see the various financial magazine covers in my mind reading, in essence, "Your neighbors are getting rich; why aren't you?"

Fast-forward to 2000 and the bursting of the technology stock bubble. How do you think these policies performed? In many cases, they lost nearly

---

16   Variable life insurance products, which are subject to market risk including possible loss of principal, allow the contract holder to choose an appropriate amount of life insurance protection that has an additional cost associated with it. Care should be taken to ensure these strategies and products are suitable for your long-term insurance needs. You should weigh your objectives, time horizon, and risk tolerance as well as any associated costs before investing. Also, be aware that market volatility can lead to the possibility of the need for additional premiums in your policy. Variable life insurance has fees and charges associated with it that include costs of insurance that vary with such characteristics of the insured as gender, health and age, underlying fund charges and expenses, and additional charges for riders that customize a policy to fit your individual needs. The subaccounts in variable insurance products fluctuate with market conditions and when surrendered the principal may be worth more or less than the original amount invested. All guarantees are subject to the claims-paying ability of the issuing insurance company. Guarantees do not apply to the investment performance of any variable accounts, which are subject to market risk.

half their value and premiums skyrocketed. For policyholders who didn't want to pay the higher premium, they had to reduce their death benefits or surrender policies prematurely.

I confess that the illustrations for variable life looked impressive. For very young people who wanted (as opposed to needed) the life insurance coverage, they provided a tax-favored investment vehicle with a death benefit. However, for people over 35 or so, instead of passing risk, they chose to bear it and to tie it to investment returns.

For most people who need life insurance benefits, I still don't believe that variable life is a viable option. To me, the safer your life insurance is, the less conservative you may need to be with your other investments, and that is a strategy that makes more sense than tying insurance benefits to the investment markets.

Variable universal life insurance

In this product, designed to be a hybrid between universal life and variable life, neither the death benefit nor the premium is guaranteed. To me, this barely qualifies as life insurance anymore and is starting to look like a tax shelter with an incidental death benefit. I cannot think of a single appropriate use for this vehicle in risk management; I see it only as an investment and that is not what life insurance is about. Insurance is about passing risk and on these policies, the owner bears all the risk. That simply fails to merit the name "insurance" to me.

POST-COURSE EXERCISE QUESTIONS

1. **TRUE** or **FALSE**: All risk management strategies involve the purchase of insurance.

2. **TRUE** or **FALSE**: You want your insurance policies to cover all the risks you might face in life.

3. **TRUE** or **FALSE**: There are more reasons to buy life insurance than just the death benefit.

4. **TRUE** or **FALSE**: Disability insurance is usually provided by employers to replace 100 percent of each employee's salary in the event of an accident or illness.

5. **TRUE** or **FALSE**: While term life insurance is designed to be temporary, all forms of permanent life insurance have death benefits that are guaranteed for life.

POST-COURSE EXERCISE ANSWERS

1. **FALSE.** All insurance is a form of risk management but many risk management strategies exist that have nothing to do with the purchase of insurance products.

2. **FALSE.** You want to pass the risks you cannot bear to your insurance companies. Lots of risks would have a small enough impact that you could bear to handle them on your own. Only buy insurance to cover the risks that would harm you meaningfully if the insurance wasn't placed in force.

3. **TRUE.** Life insurance is not called "death insurance" for a reason beyond semantics. Life insurance is designed to replace your human life value and has advantages well beyond the death benefit, including those related to tax savings, wealth accumulation and transfer, liquidity, and creditor protection. The death benefit is only one reason to insure your life.

4. **FALSE.** Many employers provide disability insurance as a part of their basic employee benefits or as an available voluntary benefit, but usually the salary replacement is between 50 and 70 percent and is often capped at a specific maximum benefit. Structured properly, disability insurance benefits should be paid income tax free so 70 percent coverage provides the tax-free equivalent of your entire salary, assuming a 30 percent combined tax liability. If your employer-provided plan is capped and your replacement coverage is less than 70 percent, you may wish to explore additional coverage separate from your employer's plan.

5. **FALSE.** It is true that term life insurance is designed to be temporary but various types of permanent life insurance have differing provisions and not all of them provide death benefits guaranteed for life. In general, only whole life insurance or universal life insurance with a secondary no-lapse guarantee will provide for a death benefit that is guaranteed as long as you live (assuming all premiums are paid in full and on time).

EXTRA-CREDIT ASSIGNMENT

Having a complete financial plan means having a complete risk management plan as a key component, and no risk management plan can be complete without thorough insurance planning.

Your assignment is to review all of the insurance coverages discussed in this course and to consider utilizing a financial advisor to help you determine the adequacy and completeness of those coverages. If there are risks being covered that do not need to be covered, you can begin reducing or eliminating superfluous policies; while if there are risks you cannot bear that aren't covered, you'll want to start improving the moat around your financial castle with appropriate insurance solutions.

Cash Management 102:

BUDGETERS RULE
THE FINANCIAL SCHOOL

Of all the concepts related to financial planning, the one that seems to cause people the most discomfort is budgeting. The idea of someone telling you what you can or cannot spend is so unpleasant that many people simply shut down at the thought. Imagine being told by someone what your grocery budget was for the month and trying not to go over it. In some ways, a budget is to financial planning as a diet is to personal fitness; no one likes either concept, as they are both hard to follow and maintain.

The purpose of budgeting, however, is not to tell you what you can or cannot spend or what choices you need to make when you open your wallet or pocketbook. The goal is to give you the tools you need to be successful and to make a few suggestions that you can decide to use as you see fit.

Think of these tools as you would think of your school supplies. You'll need pencils, pens, paper, and a calculator in your backpack to be prepared for class.

There are four steps to making income last by keeping expenses under control:

1. Keep excellent records of your spending.

2. Communicate with your spouse and other adult members of your household to prioritize expenses.
3. Use a notebook, spreadsheet, or software program to create a budget and stick to it as closely as possible.
4. Set a goal to have money leftover at the end of every month.

Keep excellent records of your spending

When it is time to complete your tax returns every spring, do you find that you have the records you need to complete them with minimal time and effort?

If you need to get warranty service on an appliance or you choose to return a product you've bought, do you have the receipts and documentation handy?

For many households, record keeping is a shoe box on the dresser or a pile of receipts on the kitchen table. And yet, record keeping is the single most important organizational step toward making income last.

You can use a single file drawer for your household to keep all your records for the present year. You can use folders by month for receipts and spending and other folders for categories like bank statements, insurance, paystubs, etc. If you'd prefer, you can also just take a picture with your phone and store it in a directory on your computer or in the cloud.

Once the year is over, box up the records and store them in a well-marked and easily accessible location. If you're using an electronic system, back up the year's records and archive them. I recommend storing almost all records for seven years. The only items I keep longer are income tax returns, property deeds and titles, legal documents, and cost basis history for investments, including real estate.

Every January, when your records are boxed up for the prior year, you can review and shred most of the box from seven years earlier, saving only those few items that are still relevant.

Communicate with your spouse and other adult members of your household to prioritize expenses

When couples and families communicate well about money, lots of disagreements and hurt feelings can be avoided entirely.

I recommend that families spend time reviewing finances together on a regular basis. That can be weekly, monthly, or less frequently so long as everyone agrees on the schedule. In addition, I strongly encourage both spouses to attend meetings with financial advisors and accountants so that the conversations regarding finances are open ones.

Make sure that both spouses are using the same record-keeping system so that there is no confusion and so every adult in the household can find what they need when they need it.

You may also want to keep a miscellaneous category for minor cash expenses so you won't feel compelled to enter every cup of coffee. It can be stressful to remember to track the minor everyday expenses and if you have healthy cash flow, it simply isn't necessary.

There is no single best way to handle household bills. Sometimes one spouse or the other handles them all, and sometimes spouses divide and conquer, where each is responsible for certain household bills each month. Whatever works for your household is fine so long as you communicate openly with one another along the way.

DON'T BANK ON IT

Even with open communication, problems can arise when both spouses use their debit or ATM card for the same bank account. I recommend that most married couples maintain two primary checking accounts, both of which are titled jointly. Each spouse is the primary account holder on one account and the secondary account holder on the other. Each spouse keeps a personal checkbook and has a personal ATM card. Since both accounts are jointly titled (and with the same bank), transfers between the accounts are generally easy and free and that allows for conversations about which spouse is paying which bills and from which account.

Use a notebook, spreadsheet, or software program to create a budget and stick to it as closely as possible

I encourage households to use a software program to create a budget and to track progress from month to month and year to year, and the software I recommend is Quicken. You can use the software to download credit card charges and investment returns and to write checks and pay bills online, or you can simply use it as a computerized checkbook. The extent of your usage is up to you, but I find you'll do more and more with the software as you become more comfortable with it.

If you are not tech savvy or if you prefer a longhand copy, you can use a basic notebook. One page can be used per month with two columns—one for the inflows (money in) and one for the outflows (money out) of your household. You can also use one page per budget category or any other system that makes sense to you.

The important thing is to create a budget within your means and to do what you can to stick to the bottom line.

Outflows are divided into four primary categories: fixed expenses, variable expenses, discretionary expenses, and long-term savings and investments.

Fixed expenses are those that do not change from month to month and are therefore predictable. Your rent or mortgage payment, auto insurance, and loan payments are good examples of fixed expenses.

Variable expenses are those that reoccur on an ongoing basis but for amounts that vary. For example, you may go to the grocery store every week but your bill differs from week to week.

Discretionary expenses include those that are generally considered optional in the household budget. Spending on vacations and recreation tends to fall in this category. Since many of these expenses are major, it is best that you set a goal to have a specific amount of money by a specific time and set the funds aside on a regular basis to reach that goal.

As you learned in Cash Management 101, ideally you will pay yourself first and prioritize your long-term savings and investments such that all of your expenses can be covered by the amount *leftover* after making your scheduled contributions.

Set a goal to have money leftover at the end of every month

If your budget is such that you are not yet able to pay yourself first, at least make sure that your cash flow is positive. In Debt Management 101, we addressed the implications of negative cash flow and strategies to combat it. If you set aside whatever is leftover at the end of the month and call it your savings plan, it is at least a good first step until you are ready and able to pay yourself first.

MAKE SURE TO KEEP SCORE

Now that you have designed a budget, it is time to set up a system to track your progress. There are three steps in setting up the framework to follow the money:

1. Utilize your budgeting system to track spending and mark your progress.
2. Notice trends and cycles that impact your month-to-month cash flow.
3. Adjust your budget as needed, to keep spending within your income limitations.

Each of these steps is critical in making sure that you have collected the right data in the right way to make it useful for you. This exercise is a waste of time and effort unless you make a commitment to do it wholeheartedly and accurately.

Utilize your budgeting system to track spending and mark your progress

Getting started is as simple as turning the page of your notebook or starting to enter data into your software package. In this case, each account needs its own page: bank accounts, home and auto loans, mutual funds, credit cards, and even property values like your home or business.

Your simple balance sheet is nothing more than the aggregated total of your asset accounts minus the aggregated total of your liability accounts. In this system, each account will have a page of the notebook or spreadsheet or will be entered as a distinct account in Quicken or some alternate software solution.

Once you have the accounts set up, you'll need to use this system to list all transactions for each account. If you charge baseball tickets on your credit card, it gets listed as a debit on your credit card account; if you make a withdrawal at the ATM, it gets listed as a debit on your checking account; etc. These account pages are basically checkbooks for each of your accounts, even if they do not have checks.

Sometimes an entry needs to be listed twice. If you make a payment to your credit card from your checking account, the activity gets listed on both pages—as a debit from the checking account and as a matching credit into your credit card account. Note that one of the other reasons why I prefer the software solution to a manual system is that it will prompt you for offsetting transactions.

Although I find the tutorials on the various software packages helpful, if you are having trouble setting up this system on your own, you can call on your financial advisor or CPA to assist you. The setup will take a few hours but the result will be an organizational system that keeps you on track.

Each income or expense needs to be assigned a category. For example, a trip to the grocery store might be called "food: groceries" and a dinner out at the local restaurant might be called "food: dining out." Categorizing items this way means that you'll be able to run a report showing all expenses for food (the category), which would include both dining out and groceries (the subcategories) or a report showing only one or the other for any particular time frame. Note that income items will also get categorized, such as salary income, gift received, or interest income.

Notice trends and cycles that impact your month-to-month cash flow

Once you have mastered the data entry, you will be able to use it to run reports. If, for example, you want to know what your total cash flow has been for the first three months of a given year, you can run a report showing all income items and all expenses for that time frame.

You can also run reports or create graphs showing your net worth and how it has changed over time. You will get great satisfaction from a graphic showing your debts decreasing and your assets increasing to give you positive net-worth growth. They say a picture is worth a thousand words; this one is potentially worth thousands of dollars, as it helps you stay on track.

Adjust your budget as needed, to keep spending within your income limitations

This system will allow you to match up your budget with your actual earnings and spending to see how you are doing from month to month and year to year. Then you can tweak budget line items—for example, deciding to spend less on dining out or determining that you can afford to put extra money each month toward your debt principal or your vacation fund.

Over time, you will be able to see many years of history and that will become priceless in your quest to reduce debt and begin building and accumulating personal wealth.

DON'T BEAT YOURSELF UP

If you have created a budget and you suddenly have a medical emergency, a home repair expense, or some other unpleasant financial surprise, recognize that it happens. In a perfect world, your plan will include an emergency fund to handle these surprises. However, a budget-busting expense will still impact your cash flow. If you build in some wiggle room for miscellaneous expenses, that can help you deal with them more effectively when they arise.

POST-COURSE EXERCISE QUESTIONS

1. **TRUE** or **FALSE**: One critical component of cash management is making sure you have a budget that is planned down to the penny.

2. **TRUE** or **FALSE**: As long as you're making more than you spend, a budget isn't necessary.

3. **TRUE** or **FALSE**: Budgeting can be done manually or with the help of financial software.

4. **TRUE** or **FALSE**: It isn't necessary for all adult members of a household to discuss and agree on a budget.

5. **TRUE** or **FALSE**: Any budget needs to be flexible enough to handle surprises—either unexpected windfalls or major expenses.

POST-COURSE EXERCISE ANSWERS

1. **FALSE.** In most cases, it is not necessary to track where every penny goes. If you use a credit or debit card for minor expenses, it may be easier to be accurate than if you pay cash. A simple category for miscellaneous expenses can be used for cash expenditures and tracking your ATM withdrawals without the need to write down every cash expense.

2. **FALSE.** Almost everyone can benefit from at least a basic budget. If you are paying yourself first and saving and investing enough to cover all of your long-term goals, it may be possible to skip the full process, but some record keeping and trend watching make the budget itself valuable, even if cash flow isn't an issue.

3. **TRUE.** This is based solely on your preference and your comfort with technology. To me, the use of software is a best practice but it is by no means the only way to budget.

4. **FALSE.** Even if only one spouse or partner is handling the bill paying and record keeping, it is helpful for financial and psychological reasons to have open communication on all money topics and decisions, including budgeting and cash flow.

5. **TRUE.** Just like an ideal financial plan needs to work *no matter what happens*, an ideal budget should include enough of a cushion to handle most unexpected events, if possible.

EXTRA-CREDIT ASSIGNMENT

The extra-credit assignment is to create a budget, if you don't have one, or to computerize your budget if it already exists and is manual. Track your income and expenses diligently for three months to get a sense of your current cash flows. Then use the data from your checkbook, credit card statements, bank statements, software program, or other system to get a sense of where you stand currently. Then use that data to create (or update) your budget to ensure that you have maximized your cash flow. If possible, use this exercise to find a way to increase your long-term savings and investment plans by paying yourself first too!

Financial Planning 101:

ADVISOR SECRETS YOU NEED TO KNOW

In college, you may have been assigned a freshman advisor or other counselor to assist you in selecting your courses. For our purposes, your Certified Financial Planner™ practitioner is your counselor, and your coursework has been determined in a linear way to help your knowledge base accumulate strategically.

Certified Financial Planner™ practitioners abide by seven practice standards for the financial planning process, as established by the CFP® Board's Code of Ethics and Standards of Conduct and published at cfp.net. Those seven practice standards are as follows:

1. Understanding the Client's Personal and Financial Circumstances
2. Identifying and Selecting Goals
3. Analyzing the Client's Current Course of Action and Potential Alternative Course(s) of Action
4. Developing the Financial Planning Recommendations
5. Presenting the Financial Planning Recommendations
6. Implementing the Financial Planning Recommendations
7. Monitoring Progress and Updating

However, before an advisor can begin your financial planning process, you have to know how to select an advisor right for you and your personal and financial situation and objectives. And just as Dorothy had to look behind the curtain in The Wizard of Oz, as you, too, need to look into some key differentiators to find out if the financial "wizard" you're interviewing is right for you.

ESTABLISHING AND DEFINING THE RELATIONSHIP

Before engaging the services of a financial advisor, it is important to establish and define the scope of the engagement. That means interviewing one or more potential advisors by asking lots of differentiating questions and comparing the answers. Some of the questions you might want to ask include:

- What services does the advisor provide personally?
- How often will the advisor meet with you?
- How much communication can you expect on an ongoing basis?
- Does your advisor have other team members who are available to you?
- Who are the typical clients of this advisor or firm?
- What is the advisor's planning and investment philosophy?
- Does the advisor represent specific companies or products?
- How does the advisor select specialists?
- Will you have online access to your planning and accounts?
- Does the firm expect to grow, and how might that impact your relationship moving forward?
- What is the cost of doing business with this firm?
- Does the firm utilize a commercial custodian or other entity to safeguard client assets?

Let's look at the way the answers to these questions may influence your decision to select an advisor or firm.

What services does the advisor provide personally?

You'll want to know if the advisor provides recommendations on all the components in a comprehensive plan or only on a few areas. If the advisor is a stockbroker, for example, the scope of your relationship might be limited to your investment or retirement portfolio.

In most cases, you'll want to work with someone who can bring your entire plan into focus and can aid in the execution of that plan.

How often will the advisor meet with you?

This is really a personal preference question and is often a function of the complexity of your personal finances. However, you do want to establish this up front so that you aren't surprised six months into the engagement.

I know some investment firms that hold portfolio reviews as frequently as once per quarter, while others only meet with their clients on an as-requested basis. I believe that the ideal meeting schedule is one full annual strategy meeting, along with a year-end tactical planning call for time-sensitive decisions that need to be made by December 31. Your advisor or firm should also be available throughout the year when challenges or opportunities arise.

How much communication can you expect on an ongoing basis?

In addition to personal meetings or telephone calls, what other communication can you expect from your advisory firm? Some firms limit their correspondence to monthly or quarterly statements, while others mail out regular newsletters or performance reports or send periodic e-mails with market news or planning ideas. Some host seminars for the public, while others limit their speaking engagements to private client-only affairs.

Ideally, an advisory firm should try to communicate frequently without being overwhelming, perhaps with a brief weekly e-mail and monthly electronic reports in addition to basic statements and confirmations. For any advisory firm it is a delicate balance and one that is ever-changing based on the makeup of the firm's clientele.

Does your advisor have other team members who are available to you?

Knowing the size and depth of the firm's team will be critically important to you, especially if you value frequent communication. In some firms, a single assistant may be servicing the clients of six or more advisors, while in other firms there may be a team of licensed professionals ready to assist with your planning.

If your advisor shares an assistant, you are likely with an organization that only handles some small portion of the financial planning process.

I believe that the ideal ratio is two assistants or staff members for each advisor to make sure that there is depth at every position. That way, if an advisor is in a meeting or out of the office, clients can continue to interact with the team and get most questions answered or needs met.

Who are the typical clients of this advisor or firm?

It is important to have a sense of who the advisor's other clients are to make sure you are a good fit. You'll want to know if you'll be a firm's biggest client—or smallest one. You may also want to know, for example, if you'll be a 34-year old client at a firm specializing in planning for senior citizens.

In our firm, we work with multigenerational families, usually engaging with clients who are 45–60 years old and who have to worry simultaneously about caring for aging parents while educating children or grandchildren, all while hoping to reach financial independence themselves someday. Other firms have their own niche clientele and ideally you want to find a firm specializing in clients who are a lot like you.

What is the advisor's planning and investment philosophy?

It is best if your advisor's philosophy and yours are in harmony. For example, if you are risk averse, you may not want to work with an advisor promoting his or her short-term stock-picking success. Does your advisor believe in a buy-and-hold strategy with passive management or try to time markets or make frequent tactical changes? Does the firm favor a more offensive or defensive posture to planning? How do those variables correspond with your objectives?

All of these questions will help you determine if the potential firm is a good fit for you and your family on a personal level. However, these questions will not determine if the advisor is good or bad at what he or she does. Again, it is about personally matching your preferences with an advisor's strengths or specialties.

Does the advisor represent specific companies or products?

It can be difficult to know if you are getting objective advice when an advisor's compensation is driven by product sales. Whether the advisor's recommendation is to buy a mutual fund, an annuity, or an insurance product, or even to hire a proprietary money manager, it is a potential conflict of interest upon which you should request disclosure in advance of engaging in the planning relationship.

When you decide who to hire to help you manage your finances, I believe you should do everything in your power to make certain that your advisor is always representing your best interests. The up-front disclosure of potential conflicts of interests does not preclude objectivity in rendering advice. However, if the advice you receive is heavily or entirely reliant on proprietary products, you may want to seek a second opinion prior to engaging.

How does the advisor select specialists?

Because the financial planning process will often involve a team of specialists, you need to know how your potential advisor chooses other professionals to work with you and if he or she is willing to work with your existing professionals.

These specialists may include accountants, attorneys, financial institutions (like banks or credit unions), insurance agents, real estate agents, mortgage brokers, money managers, and others.

Think of your financial planning firm as your general contractor and the specialists as the subcontractors. The outcome of your work with this firm can often rely on the quality of the specialists they (or you) choose.

Ideally, you want an advisor who will work with your existing specialists or who can make referrals to ancillary professionals who are considered experts in their fields and who will not be reliant solely on in-house specialists or staff. You should never be required to use any specific specialist to maintain a relationship with your advisor.

Will you have online access to your planning and accounts?

This is increasingly becoming a moot point, only because having online access to accounts is not as much an option as it is a necessity in today's world. However, it is worth asking what type of access is available, what systems maintain the data, and what security measures are in place to protect the online data. You may also want to ask if the data generation and storage is completed in-house or by a third-party vendor.

In our firm, we use a third-party vendor for online access for two main reasons. First, it allows us to focus on financial planning instead of being a technology firm. Second, it allows our clients to know that an independent third-party custodian is maintaining the integrity of the data.

Does the firm expect to grow, and how might that impact your relationship moving forward?

This is a very important point and one that is frequently overlooked. If your advisor builds a solo practice to the point that he or she can no longer service clients effectively, communication breakdowns are possible. In addition, you may not want to be handed off to another advisor in a firm if it effectively ends the relationship you had with your own trusted advisor.

The future of the financial advisory business is captured in the term ensemble practice. This term has generated volumes of professional articles and books but it is generally accepted to mean a firm with clients serviced by multiple planners, rather than having a relationship exclusively with one.

Working with an ensemble practice has benefits for clients, as it provides depth of knowledge, continuity and convenience of advice, collaborative professional advice generation, and a deeper relationship with a team of people. It also has benefits for advisors, who can leverage one another's strengths and can create professional synergies that a solo practice cannot replicate.

What is the cost of doing business with this firm?

Before you enroll in college, it is important to know all of the costs of attendance: tuition, room, board, books, travel, and other expenses.

In the financial planning world, there are several ways in which advisors are compensated and they are regulated by the types of licenses held by the advisor, not by his or her professional designations. Only registered representatives or investment advisory representatives can earn fees for investment advice or commissions on financial products.

Planners and their firms can be paid in several different ways:

- By a flat project or engagement fee
- By an hourly or other time-based fee
- By an annual (or periodic) retainer fee
- By a fee expressed as a percentage of assets under management
- By commissions for making transactions

If you are paying fees for planning services, generally you need to know if there are fees associated with each meeting or conversation or if the services are bundled.

While none of these compensation arrangements is good or bad per se, I believe that the best way to get comprehensive advice is on a fee basis or based on a percentage of assets under management. That way, a client pays a firm to perform analysis and provide recommendations that are not tied solely to the sale of one or more products.

Does the firm utilize a commercial custodian or other entity to safeguard client assets?

The safeguarding of client assets is something that should be a given with any financial firm. However, in the wake of various scandals (such as Bernie Madoff), the security and validity of client accounts is being called into question like never before.

Most financial firms employ a clearing firm to handle the safeguarding and segregation of client assets and to take them out of the hands of the advisors themselves. Essentially, it provides a client with the comfort of third-party oversight for the custody of their assets. There are a number of large clearing firms in the U.S., with the most notable ones being National Financial Services (NFS, LLC), Pershing, and Charles Schwab.

Note that some very large firms are self-clearing, which means that they are the custodians for their own client assets. As long as these are legitimate firms, it is neither a good nor bad arrangement, it is just a way of doing business. Either way, you should never be asked to write a check directly to your advisor nor should your advisor ever accept cash from you.

Your advisor and financial planning firm has legal responsibilities not to comingle assets amongst multiple clients and not to lend money to or borrow money from a client. There is a laundry list of other restricted activities, any of which should raise a red flag for consumers. For more information, you can check out the regulatory websites for FINRA or the SEC.

The responses to these types of questions will help define what you are personally seeking from an advisor so you can determine how you want to proceed and can evaluate the responses based on your needs. An advisor's response to these questions will help you determine if the potential firm is a good fit for you and your family on a personal level. Note that these questions will not determine if the planner is good or bad at what he or she does. However, they will help personally match your preferences with a suitable advisor for you.

WHAT YOUR ADVISOR WANTS FROM YOU

You have learned what you should expect from your advisor in establishing and defining the relationship, but what about what your advisor might expect from you? Let's discuss some of the items that you'll want to explore to determine what your role in the engagement might be:

- In most cases, to do an excellent job of financial planning, an advisor will expect you to be forthright with your financial picture and open to discussions about sensitive issues, like family medical history, interpersonal family relationships, and so forth.

- If you are married or in a committed relationship, it is generally important to have both individuals at each meeting so that everyone is on the same page. I have seen many financial-planning conversations turn in dramatically different directions when both partners are asked the same question and give different answers. For example, I remember asking one couple how long they planned to stay in their present home. The husband said, "Indefinitely" and the wife said, "About 12 months." They just looked at each other, dumbfounded at how they had no idea the way the other felt on the subject. I turned to the husband and delicately advised him to get some boxes ready for the big move!

- It may also be necessary for you to gather documents, contact former employers, make changes to employee benefits, or take other steps to keep the plan accurate and current. Oftentimes, clients find the up-front work to be a bit onerous, but once the planning process has been implemented, most of the ongoing work falls squarely on the advisor's shoulders.

This concludes the section on establishing and defining the client-planner relationship.

POST-COURSE EXERCISE QUESTIONS

1. **TRUE** or **FALSE**: If you choose to engage with a financial planning firm that operates as an ensemble, you might have more than one person providing you with insight and advice.

2. **TRUE** or **FALSE**: Knowing a prospective advisor's investment philosophy might help determine if that advisor is a good fit for you.

3. **TRUE** or **FALSE**: Once you have a financial plan in place, you'll want to review and adjust it regularly.

4. **TRUE** or **FALSE**: All financial advisors are compensated in the same way.

5. **TRUE** or **FALSE**: An independent third-party custodian might provide better investment returns than a self-clearing firm.

POST-COURSE EXERCISE ANSWERS

1. **TRUE.** One of the characteristics of working with an ensemble firm is the ability to work with a full team of advisors, each of whom can play roles in developing, presenting, and monitoring your financial plan.

2. **TRUE.** If possible, you will want to have harmony between your investment philosophy and your advisor's. For example, if you want a defensive asset allocation and a prospective advisor is a stock picker, that might not be an ideal advisor for you.

3. **TRUE.** Your financial plan should never sit on a shelf and collect dust. For one reason, the plan can become obsolete quickly with just a few small changes due to income, expenses, health, tax law, or other factors. Just like your annual physical exam with your doctor, an annual strategy meeting with your financial advisor to keep your plan on track is a worthwhile endeavor and can help you on your path to financial independence.

4. **FALSE.** There are several distinct methods of compensating a financial advisor and dozens of combinations, including the use of two or more of those compensation methods to create a hybrid solution. While no method is good or bad, it is very important to understand how your advisor is compensated and how that may impact decision-making or the objectivity of recommendations.

5. **FALSE.** The choice of a custodian to hold your assets and to provide statements, tax documents, and online access has nothing to do with investment returns or performance. The reason to consider a firm that uses a third-party custodian is to have an extra layer of oversight on protection in terms of your account security and validity.

EXTRA-CREDIT ASSIGNMENT

The extra-credit assignment for this course is dependent on whether or not you already have a professional engagement with a financial advisor.

If you have a financial advisor currently, ask him or her the questions addressed in this course. If you are unsatisfied or uncomfortable with any of those answers, consider getting a second opinion.

If you do not yet have a financial advisor, ask your friends, family members, colleagues, or other legal or tax advisors for one or more names of their trusted advisors and begin the process of interviewing a few to find the right fit for you.

Completing this extra-credit assignment may not ensure that you find the right advisor for you, but it will certainly assist in beginning the process of engaging a professional appropriate for your financial and personal situation.

Financial Planning 102:

WHERE YOU'RE GOING BEGINS WITH KNOWING WHERE YOU ARE

When students arrive on campus, they are at different stages of academic readiness. Some have subjects in which remedial prerequisites will be needed, while others have advanced placement or other college credits already on their transcripts when they arrive for freshman year.

The concept of financial readiness is similar. Some people reading this book have significant personal debt and are living paycheck-to-paycheck. Others have built significant wealth and want to use it wisely and preserve it for future generations. The destination for all types of readers is the same: graduating into a financially independent retirement.

While envisioning our destination is always exciting, the first step in any journey is determining the launch point. This helps us explore various trajectories and ultimately to decide on an optimal path from A to B.

Here are seven things you need to measure before you start making any changes to your financial plan:

1. Do you have positive or negative cash flow?
2. Do you have adverse debt?
3. Do you know your net worth?

4. Do you know your *liquid* net worth?
5. Do you have a suitable emergency fund?
6. Do you have contingency planning in place?
7. Have you set your planning goals and objectives, and do you know if you are on track to meet or exceed them?

At first glance, you will notice that absent from this list are questions dealing with any specifics—about portfolio holdings or design, insurance products, investment philosophy, or the institutions you use for banking, investing, or insuring. That is because those details are not nearly as important to the success of a plan as the basics. Owning a hot mutual fund or stock is not the same as having a financial plan. Neither is having a fixed mortgage versus an adjustable one, owning gold bars, or using whole life insurance. All of these are tools but they are also the *noise* that can prevent people from making plans. Sometimes it can seem too overwhelming to fight through that noise so inertia sets in and no progress is made.

For now, let's talk about the foundations—these seven questions—and then we'll come back to the specific tools that can help make your plan a reality.

Do you have positive or negative cash flow?

Cash flow is the illustration of money being earned and money being spent. If you are spending more than you are earning, you have a fundamental problem that needs to be addressed before any planning can be done. Think of it as plugging the hole in the bottom of your bucket before trying to fill it up.

There are several solutions to this problem and on the surface they are obvious: Make more money and/or spend less money. However, it is rarely that simple. You could seek a promotion, or a new job, or you could take a second job. It may also be that going back to school to learn new skills or to finish your degree could lead to higher earning potential. That is an excellent way to do it, but it will take significant time and will require some planning (not to mention the possibility of some tuition expenses!).

It may also be that you can increase your income in a more passive way— by investing in income-producing bank accounts or securities, for example. If you have funds in a savings account earning 0.25 percent and can move them to a certificate of deposit earning 2 percent, it will create more income. Of course, it may also create a lack of liquidity or fees and penalties if used incorrectly.

It is also not likely to change your negative cash flow into positive cash flow by itself. Investing for income (or yield) can be a suitable strategy for some investors but not for others. In fact, some financial vehicles may be more (or less) appropriate for your specific needs for a variety of possible reasons beyond the scope of this book.

As it is often difficult to increase your income overnight in an amount suitable to change a cash flow imbalance, you'll need to look at what you are spending and try to make some meaningful change in that area. While I am not suggesting that you impose a strict budget upon yourself, I do suggest that you *track* where the money is going and aim to make meaningful changes where you can.

It might mean refinancing a debt or eating at restaurants less frequently, or it might mean curtailing a habit related to shopping or four-dollar cups of coffee. It might also mean looking for less expensive housing options or automobiles or exploring public school options rather than private school options for kids.

Every situation is unique, and once you track your expenses, you'll have a better idea of where the money is going.

Do you have adverse debt?

No discussion about wealth building can be complete without a discussion on debt. In brief, debt is a great leveler of dreams and costs a lot of American families sleep at night. In the simplest of terms, if you can't afford something, *don't buy it*. I know that will be lousy for the US economy in terms of consumer confidence and output by retailers and manufacturers but your own economic recovery from debt must come first. If you can't afford it, *don't buy it*.

Not all debt is bad debt. A mortgage on a home, rental property, or office building creates leverage and can be a good way to buy an asset that becomes the collateral and allows for financing. Student loans can be acceptable debt if the terms are favorable and if your degree results in higher earning potential for a lifetime.

However, credit cards, department store cards, and other consumer debt are categorically *bad debt* and should be avoided as much as possible. Even car loans should be avoided (or postponed as long as possible) and should only be undertaken if the resulting payment won't too adversely impact your cash flow or render your savings and investment goals unreachable.

Do you know your net worth?

Your net worth is a relatively simple calculation: Add up all of your assets and then subtract all of your liabilities. For example, if your house is worth $500,000 and you have a mortgage balance of $200,000, it will add $300,000 to your net worth. Your assets include everything you own—houses, bank accounts, investment accounts, cash value in your life insurance, retirement plans, artwork, jewelry, etc. Likewise, your liabilities include everything you owe—mortgages, equity lines, car loans, student loans, credit cards, margin loans, etc.

One of the key objectives in financial planning is to calculate the amount of money you need to save to retire. Before trying to determine your *target* net worth, you need to identify your *current* net worth. Like the "You are here" sticker on a mall kiosk map, in order to get where you're going, you've first got to establish where you are.

As you become wealthier, knowing your net worth becomes increasingly important, primarily for tax purposes. When you and your spouse or partner die, before assets can be distributed to your children or other heirs, the government steps in with their calculators and decides how much of your property to confiscate prior to allowing the next generation to enjoy it. If this sounds harsh and a bit ridiculous, it is. Nonetheless, the federal government and many state governments have their hands in your pockets beyond the grave. With careful estate planning, you can eliminate or offset this risk, and we'll talk a bit later about selecting an attorney who can assist you with this process.

Each year, the federal government announces a limit that allows individuals and married couples to leave property to heirs without federal estate taxes coming due. As of 2020, federal estate taxes are a moot point for the majority of American families. If you are in the small minority who still face the imposition of federal estate taxes, there are strategies that you can employ through the use of your financial, tax, and legal advisors to eliminate, reduce, or plan for them.

Note that as of 2020, 14 states and the District of Columbia impose an estate tax, six states impose an inheritance tax, and Maryland and New Jersey impose both. Most of the states that levy these taxes have much lower limits on wealth transfer and tax rates as high as 20 percent so you'll want to consult your legal and tax advisors for state-specific limits and rules.

While even the state-level exemptions sound large enough to exclude most households, because the death benefits paid by life insurance count in the calculation, these taxes impact more households than you might suspect.

The rules are very complicated and change constantly, so you'll need to make sure that you have a qualified estate planning attorney to work with you and your financial advisor to mitigate this potential taxation as much as possible.

Do you know your *liquid* net worth?

I consider this question to be more important than the last for most families. That is because liquid net worth measures the resources that can be used to create spendable income right away, whereas the overall net worth includes those resources that might require encumbrance or sale before they can create income, which might take time, cost money, or be impossible to accomplish for various reasons.

For people over age 55, liquid net worth is generally your net property not including your primary residence, vacation home, closely held business interests, or rental real estate. For younger people, we generally also exclude retirement plans from a liquid net worth calculation, as they cannot be utilized favorably at that time. Even for people aged 55–59½, there are restrictions on the use of qualified retirement accounts and IRAs. Therefore, we may exclude them from a calculation unless early retirement is being seriously considered.

A sustainable withdrawal rate is defined as a percentage of your working assets that you can withdraw each year without placing so much pressure on your principal as to risk running out of money. Choosing a sustainable withdrawal rate is a very important and challenging task. I have seen lots of so-called Monte Carlo simulations for retirees that illustrate the odds of outliving their money. They show a perfect scenario until age 87 but with complete poverty awaiting them on their 88th birthday. To me, that is not sound planning.

Although our present health, family history, and personal habits may provide some indication, we do not definitively know how long we're going to live. To me, the only plan that makes sense is one that provides for adequate resources throughout the human life span and that is most likely to leave funds behind for heirs or charities.

There are many schools of thought on withdrawal rates. These rates reflect the percentage of annual withdrawals taken against a principal sum, irrespective of whether there are enough earnings or growth to warrant that withdrawal over each period. In other words, if a withdrawal rate is 4 percent, for every $1,000,000 in liquid net worth (sometimes referred to as working assets) there will be $40,000 in withdrawals taken from that account each year.

In an ideal world, to be more comfortable regarding the likelihood of maintaining a lifetime of principal, a rate of 3 percent would be used. However, in our planning with clients, the world is seldom ideal. Any rate higher than 5 percent creates significant risk of running out of money during your lifetime and requires some additional planning to resolve.

When undertaking planning for sustainable wealth, we will only use those assets that will predictably be working assets (liquid net worth) in determining the answer to the question, "How much do I need to retire?" We'll need to quantify that for you before you can possibly graduate into retirement.

Do you have a suitable emergency fund?

Having an emergency fund of readily available cash is an important step toward financial independence. It is also a good way to make sure you aren't losing sleep at night. I've seen the required size of that emergency fund articulated in various rules of thumb by the media and other professionals and organizations.

Rules of thumb are unreliable tools because every situation is unique and one size never fits all. However, for households with dual incomes (when the two incomes are similarly sized), we tend to use three months of expenditures, net of taxes, as the emergency fund target. For a household with only one income or with enough income disparity that there is a clear breadwinner, we tend to use six months as a barometer.

The reason for this difference is that while it is possible to insure against many risks in our planning, we cannot effectively insure against loss of a job. Unemployment benefits are inadequate for most households so resources will need to be available during a period of unemployment or underemployment. If a sole breadwinner becomes unemployed, it is a serious blow to the household. If one of two equal breadwinners was to become unemployed, it would require only half of the emergency fund draw, which means that three months of overall net expenditures can last for six months if only half of the amount required to pay the bills is taken from the fund each month.

For retirees, we will often set the emergency fund target higher—as much as one to five years of expenditures—to make sure that in volatile market conditions or interest rate environments, big decisions can be postponed or timed to minimize the need for selling securities at an adverse time to cover monthly expenses in retirement.

Your situation will be unique in all ways, including this one, so if your personal circumstances or comfort level varies from these ranges, let your advisor know and your plan can be adjusted accordingly. The risk of maintaining too small an emergency fund is clear—the need for immediate capital may require transactions, fees, taxes, or penalties if there isn't enough easily accessible cash. On the other hand, the risk in maintaining too large an emergency fund is more of a hidden cost—the *opportunity cost*—which means that you are sacrificing potentially higher returns in exchange for a larger cash holding. Naturally, you're also minimizing the risk of loss of principal with those funds, which is why I maintain that every situation is unique and rules of thumb are insufficient rationales for financial decision-making.

In an earlier course, we discussed virtual moats around your financial castle and there can be several, starting with your emergency fund. You'll want to start with a simple savings account or money market. You may want to include other available funds like short-term bonds, bond mutual funds or exchange-traded funds, or even available funds on your home equity line of credit or securities-backed line of credit. We'll talk more about where to hold your emergency fund in future courses.

Do you have contingency planning in place?

During your sophomore year, you're going to cover risk management in greater detail. For now, understand that the only *ideal* financial plan is one that works *no matter what*. If there is unemployment, illness, disability, premature death, lawsuit, divorce, extreme longevity, and/or cognitive impairment, the plan *must* be prepared to handle it. Otherwise, the plan is set to fail under various circumstances and isn't ideal.

People choose not to take all of the risk management steps we suggest for various reasons. Some of them are legitimate limitations based on individual circumstances, while others can be rationalizations. However, it is your personal advisor's role to inform and yours to decide. Should you elect to self-insure or ignore various contingency plans, you are accepting a risk instead of passing it to an insurer, and the plan will only be a good one as long as that risk is avoided or its impact is minimized.

Have you set your planning goals and objectives, and do you know if you are on track to meet or exceed them?

At this point, you have your current net worth statement, you've completed your contingency planning and you have positive cash flow to support your wealth creation efforts. You may even know your target net worth for retirement. But do you know if you are on track to get there within the time frame you'd like?

Depending on your age and income level, you are likely to find that your target net worth is larger than you ever imagined. That is due to the extreme impact that inflation has on the value of a dollar, making future dollars less valuable than current ones. As a result, it takes far more future dollars just to maintain your present lifestyle down the road.

As a simple example, if you determine that you need $100,000 per year in today's dollars to replace your income (net of savings but before the impact of taxes), and plan to retire in 25 years, here are the numbers:

In today's dollars, with a 4 percent maximum withdrawal rate, you would need $2,500,000 to create $100,000 per year. However, if we adjust for a hypothetical 2.6 percent inflation rate, the $100,000 per year in 25 years is almost $190,000 per year. With that same maximum 4 percent withdrawal rate, it means you would need $4,750,000 in principal to withdraw the $190,000 in your first year of retirement 25 years from now to live *exactly* as you could on $100,000 today.

There is more to the calculation than that simple example, but the point of the exercise is to show the impact of inflation on your target net worth and why it sounds so big. In that example, if you had $3,000,000 in working assets *today* (less than your target number of $4,750,000) and only needed $100,000 per year to live comfortably, you would be financially independent based on our definition and would likely not need to work another day in your life.

On the other hand, using your 4 percent withdrawal assumption, having that same $3,000,000 in working assets *25 years from now* would mean having only $120,000 of your targeted $190,000 annual lifestyle. That means you'd have only 63 percent of your pre-retirement income and would either have to work part time to close the gap, adjust your lifestyle dramatically, or postpone retirement for potentially a long time.

We'll address in future courses strategies for how to close the gap between your *current* retirement projection and an *ideal* one.

This concludes the first year of your Retire U experience—congratulations on making huge progress already!

POST-COURSE EXERCISE QUESTIONS

1. **TRUE** or **FALSE**: All debt is bad debt.

2. **TRUE** or **FALSE**: Your home equity line of credit can be a suitable source of emergency funds.

3. **TRUE** or **FALSE**: Once you retire, you won't need to worry about inflation anymore.

4. **TRUE** or **FALSE**: All assets can create income in retirement.

5. **TRUE** or **FALSE**: Starting to build wealth is as simple as spending less than you make.

POST-COURSE EXERCISE ANSWERS

1. **FALSE.** Some debt is used as leverage to allow for the financing of real estate, closely held businesses, or other assets that may grow in value. As a rule, consumer debt is bad debt but all debt is not necessarily bad.

2. **TRUE.** While your home equity line of credit (HELOC) should not ideally be the first place to go for funds in an emergency, having readily available credit is helpful in having a "sleep at night" fund. Generally, you want to have available cash assets in savings and/or liquid certificates of deposit or short-term bonds or funds before you would consider using your HELOC, but it is, in fact, a suitable source of funds in an emergency.

3. **FALSE.** During our retirement years, the impact of inflation can actually be more severe than during our working years. This is true in two distinct ways.

   First of all, some retirement income sources (like defined benefit pensions or deferred compensation arrangements) do not include a cost-of-living adjustment (COLA), which means that inflation erodes the purchasing power of each successive payment. In addition, social security has a cap on annual adjustments, which could be lower than the rate of inflation in some years, eroding that purchasing power as well.

   Secondly, seniors often face a higher level of inflation than non-seniors because the items they spend the most money on tend to be subjected to price increases greater than simple inflation on groceries. For example, healthy retirees might spend on leisure and entertainment, less healthy retirees might spend on healthcare, and all retirees might be helping with education for grandchildren. Leisure, healthcare, and education all have historically higher price increases than basic inflation on most goods and services.

4. **FALSE.** Some assets are designed specifically to create income while others are not. Income can be created by most investable (working) assets in a portfolio or by ownership of rental real estate or other

business interests. However, most of the time a personal residence, which is one of the largest assets many retirees own, is not capable of creating retirement income. There may be ways to access equity but not to generate income, per se.

5. **TRUE.** Earning more than you spend is the first critical step to building wealth, followed by debt reduction, cash flow improvements, investment returns, and other cash flow positive strategic changes. If you are earning less than you spend, you will always be eroding your capital (or stunting the growth of your capital) and therefore it counteracts and works against wealth building.

EXTRA-CREDIT ASSIGNMENT

The extra-credit assignment for this course is to begin your financial inventory process by simply listing all of your assets on one column or sheet of paper and all of your liabilities on another column or sheet of paper.

Once you know your net worth, you will have the "You are here" sticker for your own financial journey map. This will allow you to begin taking the next steps toward reaching financial independence, including an examination of your cash flow and improvements to your personal budget, balance sheet, and income statement.

Sophomore Year:
Selecting a Major

FIRST SEMESTER

Arriving on campus for your second full year is a completely different experience than just one short year earlier. If you started at Retire U as a freshman, you now know the ropes and what is expected of you. You have found a group of friends, your activities, and the places where you feel a sense of belonging. If you are a transfer student coming to the Retire U campus as a sophomore, you're going to need to adjust to your new university and to break into groups of friends that are already established.

Sophomore year is not without its challenges. You're not yet an upperclassman and you're no longer the precocious freshman. It's also time to get serious about choosing a major and getting focused on your learning objectives and potential career path.

Since you're ambitiously looking to graduate into retirement, you're going to become a double major over the next few semesters. One major will be in financial independence and the other will be in retirement readiness.

The sophomore year in this course is going to cover financial issues most often associated with a person's early adulthood (ages 25–45 or so). In the first semester, we'll concentrate on some of the things to consider when getting married, buying a first home, and starting a family. The second semester will focus on the art and science of investing for growth, asset allocation, diversification, and portfolio management. Ideally, your college curriculum should build on itself as the semesters pass, and this course is designed to do the same thing.

Course Schedule for Sophomore Year—First Semester:

- Financial Planning 201: Home Is Where the Money Is
- Financial Planning 202: First Comes Love, Then Comes Marriage
- Financial Planning 203: I Believe that Children Are…Expensive!

Financial Planning 201:

HOME IS WHERE THE MONEY IS

For many families, their home is their largest asset and buying a first home can be a daunting process. Before buying a home, it's important to make sure that you're ready, financially and logistically, to do so.

For baby boomers and Gen-Xers, it was common to buy a first home shortly after accepting a first job. Millennials face a completely different set of challenges and have postponed home-buying decisions longer than previous generations. The reasons for doing so are twofold: 1) Millennials change jobs every three to five years, unlike their parents and grandparents, and 2) job changes are frequently accompanied by geographic changes. Since millennials are mobile, professionally and geographically, in lots of cases it makes no sense for them to buy homes.

Except for a few years in the early 2000s when home prices soared and eventually crashed in the real estate crisis that began in 2008, housing prices are historically stable and keep up with inflation. There are areas in the US where housing is still in an upward spiral due to heavy demand and low supply (see also: San Francisco, California), but for most clients, we use a 2 to 3 percent growth projection for residential real estate as a barometer.

Buying a home accomplishes two primary tasks—to put down roots in a community and to start building equity in an asset. Renting a home also has merits, especially if you are changing jobs and moving from place to place frequently. In general, you'll want to plan to spend at least seven years in a home before you try to sell it and move and ideally the time spent there would be longer than that.

Before we even address financial considerations, allow me to make a plea for you to hire a qualified Realtor to act as your buyer's agent throughout this process. Especially as a first-time buyer, you will have so many details to consider and questions to ask that I can't suggest to you strenuously enough that you hire an expert. He or she should get to know you and your preferences and should also know the geographic areas you are considering down to the specific neighborhoods and subdivisions.

When and if you are buying a subsequent home later in your life and you want to try to do it yourself, at least you will know more about what you're doing. As a first-time buyer, you don't even want to think of doing this yourself.

Assuming you are ready logistically—you have a stable career, have ties to a locality, are ready to commit to a long-term residence, and have hired a realtor—it is time to consider financial readiness. Unlike renting an apartment when your only financial considerations are the monthly rent and utilities, you have multiple financial considerations when buying a home, including the following:

1. Down payment
2. Closing costs
3. Mortgage payments
4. Improvements, alterations, and other considerations
5. Ongoing maintenance and management costs

Down payment

Buying a home requires some amount of down payment to secure the initial financing and to get you the keys. Sometimes it is possible to buy a home with as little as 3 percent down, although there are reasons to consider 10 percent or 20 percent deposits to obtain better mortgage terms.

Before you start looking at homes, you'll want to get prequalified for a mortgage to have a sense of what you can afford. We'll talk more about the mortgage process later in this course but for now let's use an example of a $250,000 home. For a first-time homebuyer, you might be able to put down as little as $7,500 (3 percent). Ideally, you'll want to build a down payment of $50,000 (20 percent) so that you can obtain a mortgage for $200,000 (80 percent) with the most favorable terms possible.

You can start saving for a down payment as soon as you get your first job out of college, but as we discussed earlier, make sure you're not saving for a house while suffering with heavy debt or negative cash flows. Once you're ready to save for a down payment, use a simple savings account or money market. Since this is short-term savings, you don't want to take investment risks on these funds.

Closing costs

In addition to the down payment, you'll have some other costs in the process of buying a home. You may be paying for an appraisal for the home you're considering, and you will certainly want to pay for a home inspection to make sure that the house's systems work and that the basement isn't full of water or termites.

You'll also have costs at the settlement table called closing costs, which include various charges to the local government, the title company, and other entities. We use 3 percent of the value of a home as the estimate for closing costs on a purchase so in our example we'll assume $7,500 in fees and expenses. The buyer's costs are much lower than the seller's costs, as the seller usually pays realtor's commissions in addition to transfer taxes and fees so we use 7 percent as the estimated cost of selling a home.

The costs to buy and sell a home are one of the reasons why it makes sense to plan for at least seven years in a house. If the house costs $7,500 to buy (3 percent of $250,000) and appreciates by 2 percent per year for seven years to about $287,000, when you're ready to sell it, the closing costs on the sale would be about $20,000 (7 percent of $287,000). So the house grew in value by $37,000 ($287,000 - $250,000) but cost $27,500 to buy and sell ($7,500 + $20,000), resulting in only a modest profit of $9,500, all things being equal. If you were to move after fewer than seven years, in many cases there would not be a profit and could be a loss, even if the home appreciated in value somewhat while you owned it.

It is possible to buy or sell a home without a Realtor, although I believe that especially as a first-time buyer a professional Realtor's advice can be extremely helpful. If either the buyer or seller chooses not to be represented by a Realtor, the seller's costs are reduced by the absence of one or both Realtors' compensation, and a savvy buyer can negotiate to share in those cost savings along with the seller.

Mortgage payments

You have built your down payment of $50,000 and have an additional $7,500 ready for closing costs to make your first purchase. Now it's time to secure financing for the remaining $200,000 in the form of a mortgage.

There are lots of different types of mortgages, and we'll address a few basic ones in this course. It is important to work with a qualified mortgage advisor who can assist you with the most favorable terms possible. It's also a good idea to request a Good Faith Estimate (GFE) from your lender and to have your financial advisor review it with objective eyes to make sure you're getting a fair deal with little or no surprises. You can shop for mortgages with multiple lenders, online, by phone, or in person, or you can use a trusted advisor if you know one.

Mortgage payments consist of four components, called PITI—principal, interest, taxes, and insurance. Principal and interest are the amount of the payment based on your total loan value. Taxes and insurance are amounts collected by your mortgage company (collectively called escrow payments). They are calculated to cover the real estate taxes imposed by your state and local municipalities and the homeowners insurance premiums charged by your insurer.

You have two basic types of mortgage options—fixed rate notes and adjustable rate notes. A fixed mortgage has the same interest rate for the duration of the loan, which can be 10, 15, 20, or 30 years. An adjustable mortgage has a stated rate for a set time (frequently one, three, five, or seven years) and then adjusts regularly thereafter based upon some metric. The metric is usually tied to the prime interest rate, which can be looked up on the *Wall Street Journal's* Market Data Center webpage at wsj.com/market-data.

Adjustable rate mortgages (or ARMs) normally have lower initial interest rates than fixed rate mortgages but their rates can increase over time to a specified limit. It is common to see an adjustable note allow for up to a 2 percent rate increase in a single year and up to a 5 percent maximum rate increase from the initial rate during the entire term of the loan.

As an example, let's use an adjustable rate note with a five-year initial stated interest rate with annual adjustments thereafter (called a 5/1 ARM due to the five initial years fixed and the adjustments in one-year increments). So if you were to borrow $200,000 at 4 percent in a 5/1 ARM, your interest rate would be 4 percent for the first five years, could adjust to as high as 6 percent in year six, 8 percent in year seven, and to a maximum rate of 9 percent in year eight and thereafter. Of course, ARMs can also experience downward rate adjustments if the measuring rate drops. As a result, ARMs should be more in demand when interest rates are projected to fall as opposed to when they are projected to rise.

An adjustable rate note can be a good option for homeowners with upwardly trending income and for homeowners who are planning to be in the home for a limited amount of time. If you are looking to buy seven years prior to exploring a move to a retirement community, for example, a 7/1 ARM might save you some interest. In general, however, fixed rate notes are safer options for the consumer because their costs are predictable.

Back to our example of the $250,000 house with a $50,000 down payment and a $200,000 mortgage loan. The amount of the payment will vary greatly based upon the length of the loan. In a 30-year fixed mortgage, the initial principal balance ($200,000) is amortized over the full 30 years, whereas in a 15-year fixed mortgage, the principal would have to be paid more rapidly. Since lenders are taking on less risk lending to consumers for shorter periods of time (they will be getting the loan paid back sooner), shorter-term notes have lower interest rates than longer-term notes.

In our example, let's assume that you can qualify for a 30-year fixed mortgage at 5 percent or a 15-year fixed mortgage at 4.5 percent. While the interest rate of the 15-year note is lower and the overall cost of borrowing will be lower over time, the payment will be higher each month. The interest rate, therefore, can't be the only factor to determine what is best for you.

Here are the payment breakdowns (excluding taxes and insurance):

- The principal and interest payment for the 30-year mortgage at 5 percent would be $1,084 per month.

- The principal and interest payment for the 15-year mortgage at 4.5 percent would be $1,552 per month.

Before committing to a shorter-term loan, you need to make as certain as possible that you can handle the higher payment on an ongoing basis. You can't switch from one mortgage to another without refinancing, which would create expenses to the bank and would be subject to whatever the prevailing interest rates are at the time of refinance. In a rising interest rate environment, you won't want to do a refinance to a new higher-rate loan, so make sure the payment you accept is affordable for you, now and in the foreseeable future.

We've discussed the P and I of the PITI payment, but what about the taxes and insurance costs? These costs are not impacted by the type of mortgage you select. In fact, these costs would need to be paid even if you had no mortgage at all and paid cash for the house.

Tax rates are stated by local governments as a percentage of the home's assessed value. The government sends tax assessments periodically—in our area they are sent every three years—and those assessments determine the taxes due. If you feel your assessment is incorrect (overly high, for example), you can dispute it with the government, although you may want to determine the benefits of doing so before you undertake that process.

For now, assume that the taxes on this home will cost about $2,400 per year (adding $200 per month to the escrow amount collected in your mortgage payment). This number will be much higher in certain areas of the US and potentially lower in others.

Homeowners insurance premiums vary based on lots of factors unique to both the property and the owner(s). For this example, assume that the insurance on this home will cost about $1,200 per year (adding $100 per month to the escrow amount collected in your mortgage payment).

Now that we've determined all the monthly costs, you need to decide which mortgage suits you best. Assuming you are going with a fixed mortgage option, you can choose between a 30-year note with $1,384 monthly payments ($1,084 for principal and interest, $200 for taxes, and $100 for insurance) or a 15-year note with $1,852 monthly payments ($1,552 for principal and interest, $200 for taxes, and $100 for insurance).

For first-time homebuyers, I usually prefer to see the longer-term mortgage with the lower payment, especially because younger buyers can have incomes that are less stable, student loans to repay, and rapidly changing life circumstances. It's better to have a smaller payment that you can easily afford than a larger payment that's a stretch for you.

Before we move on from the mortgage conversation, there is one additional detail that is important for homebuyers to understand, especially first-time homebuyers, called private mortgage insurance (or PMI). PMI is an insurance premium, that can be imposed by the lender, under which a borrower pays an additional amount every month to protect the lender from the borrower. It is usually applied when a down payment is modest (often less than 20 percent of the purchase price) and is, in all cases, a terrible deal for a buyer.

If you can take steps to avoid being subject to PMI, it is best to do so before you close on a loan. Once you close on a loan that includes PMI, it is very challenging to have the payment removed in the future. In essence, when buying a house and taking on a mortgage, do everything you can to avoid a PMI payment.

Improvements, alterations, and other considerations

You've saved your down payment and closing costs and you've been prequalified for a mortgage. Now it's time to start looking at properties and to consider some of the other factors and costs involved in a purchase.

Some of the factors are qualitative, like the type of home (single-family, townhome, condo), the neighborhood (rural or urban, older couples or young families), and the location (proximity to family members, jobs and hobbies, or favorite vacation spots). Other factors are quantitative, like homeowners association or condo fees, current condition of the property, age of the home, and costs of a job commute.

Some factors have both a qualitative and a quantitative component, such as the availability of quality public schools. For families considering children, this is critically important. You'll either pay more for a house in a neighborhood with optimal public schools or less for a house in a neighborhood with less optimal public schools, in which case your savings on housing costs might be offset by a decision to explore private or parochial schools instead of public schools.

When looking at a home to buy, you should consider your preferences for utility of space and for design and aesthetics. You should also be honest with yourself and your partner or spouse about your level of handiness. If you have a knack for carpentry and plumbing and want to make alterations or improvements to your own home, that is decidedly different than if you can barely change lightbulbs without risking injury and need to hire contractors to do most of those tasks for you.

Likewise, if you have a green thumb and want to handle gardening, landscaping, and lawn care, that will play a role in deciding to buy a house with a big yard. If you don't have that aptitude or interest (or the time to act upon it), consider the cost of landscaping and lawn care in your budget analysis.

I have seen estimates for decorating and furnishing a home for as high as 35 percent of the cost of a home itself. In our example, that means you might expect to spend as much as $87,500 on flooring, wall coverings, window treatments, furniture, and artwork for your new $250,000 home. You don't necessarily need to do all of that at once and ideally shouldn't try to do so. Live in the home for a while to see how you use the space and make whatever adjustments you'd like gradually over time. That said, plan on spending 10–15 percent of the purchase price on carpet, flooring, paint, and some of the basics when you first move in, especially if you are trading a one-bedroom apartment for a three-bedroom house.

Ongoing maintenance and management costs

Lastly, no discussion on buying a first home would be complete without a discussion on the maintenance and management of a home you own versus one you rent. When you rent an apartment and the dishwasher breaks, you call the landlord and a new dishwasher presumably arrives in a few days. When you own a home and that same dishwasher breaks, you are suddenly in a store or online shopping and paying for a new dishwasher to be delivered and installed. The same holds true on everything else about your home. A roof leak, a crack in your driveway, a rotting garage door, or something similar will test your ability to budget and remind you why an emergency fund is so important.

Every system in a house has a finite lifespan—your heating and air conditioning unit, your hot water heater, your washer and dryer, and every other appliance in your kitchen, bathroom, or elsewhere. When you buy a home, your home inspection should include the age and basic condition of all working systems. This won't prevent surprises but it might help you budget for routine and regular replacement.

If you know that you'll need to put a new roof on the house in the first five years of living there or that your heat pump is on its last legs, that might impact your desire to buy the home or the offer you make to the seller. In some cases, you might even be able to ask the seller to repair or replace certain things in the home as a condition of your purchase or to contribute funds toward your closing costs to offset the upcoming maintenance expenses.

THE BIG PAYOFF

The reason that most people buy a home is to have a place to live where they can welcome their friends or family as guests, raise their kids, and have the best-looking yard in the neighborhood. There is another reason that's next on the list.

With home prices increasing every year on average, as mentioned previously in this course, and with the principal portion of your mortgage payment building home equity, you are building an asset. That home equity could provide a sizable down payment on a larger home or the ability to buy a vacation home or rental property. Eventually, with enough home equity, if you choose to downsize your home in retirement, you may be able to do so without a mortgage and with excess cash on hand.

While buying a home should never be solely about asset growth, it can certainly be a meaningful contributor to your financial success and independence.

POST-COURSE EXERCISE QUESTIONS

1. **TRUE** or **FALSE**: You should always buy as much house as you can afford.

2. **TRUE** or **FALSE**: You'll need more than just your down payment amount to buy a home.

3. **TRUE** or **FALSE**: The interest rate on a 15-year fixed mortgage is usually higher than the interest rate on a 30-year fixed mortgage.

4. **TRUE** or **FALSE**: If you look to buy your first home and your estimated mortgage payment is less than your present rent payment, you can definitely afford to buy the house.

5. **TRUE** or **FALSE**: When your mortgage principal balance reaches $0.00, your entire mortgage payment ceases.

POST-COURSE EXERCISE ANSWERS

1. **FALSE.** A lender or mortgage broker might prequalify you for a mortgage of a certain amount but that does not mean that it is in your interest to stretch your housing budget to your absolute limit. Affordability matters when buying a home, but you don't want to be house poor by having such an expensive home that you lose the ability to do other things with any remaining disposable income.

2. **TRUE.** In addition to the down payment, you'll also need to cover closing costs and transfer taxes, as well as the cost of a move and potentially the costs of improvements or alterations to your new home. Saving the down payment is a great first step but it is only one of the financial requirements when you're ready to buy.

3. **FALSE.** In general, the longer term that a loan has to amortize, the higher the interest rate imposed. For that reason, a 15-year mortgage will usually have a lower rate than a 30-year mortgage. Essentially, a lender is charging greater interest in exchange for giving the buyer more time to pay the principal back. The length of a loan and the interest rate of a loan are two of the considerations when shopping for a mortgage for your home purchase.

4. **FALSE.** Unlike renting a home, which has predictable costs to maintain, buying a home has far more expenses to consider than just the mortgage payment. The costs of maintenance, repairs, improvements, taxes, and working systems add up substantially when you own a home so never assume that a prospective mortgage payment equal to your current rent payment makes buying a home affordable—it is only the beginning of the conversation to determine affordability.

5. **FALSE.** While you might no longer be making a mortgage payment once your principal has been paid in full, the escrow costs in your mortgage payment for real estate taxes and homeowners insurance will continue. The difference is that the tax bill and insurance premium will be billed to you directly for payment instead of being paid by the escrow account held by your mortgage company.

EXTRA-CREDIT ASSIGNMENT

If you are contemplating a first home, or even a move to a new home, your extra-credit assignment is to begin saving for the down payment and other initial costs to make the big move. Open a simple savings account or money market and start adding to the balance every month in an amount that is likely to be your increased cost after a potential move.

Completion of this assignment will serve two purposes. First, it will begin building your nest egg to allow for the down payment, closing costs, and moving expenses to be made from cash and not borrowed (hopefully, also eliminating the need to pay PMI). And second, by saving the additional amount each month in this way, you'll be able to practice your budgeting by living with the anticipated higher expenses so that you'll have a sense of how affordable life will be after you identify a new home and make the move.

Financial Planning 202:

FIRST COMES LOVE, THEN COMES MARRIAGE

You've met Mr. or Ms. Right and you're ready to settle down. You've gotten to know each other personally and to know one another's families and you're ready to start the next chapter of your lives together. Maybe you've lived together, maybe not. Maybe you've spent eight years together since being high school sweethearts or maybe you met nine months ago on a dating website.

What you've possibly not yet done is planned a life together—starting with a wedding, continuing with buying a home, merging families, and considering having one or more children. You may not have shared living expenses or made decisions about being a one-income or two-income household. And you've never filed joint income tax returns or considered the financial ramifications of a job loss, disability, or death of a spouse or partner.

This course is not designed to serve as premarriage counseling or explain the pros and cons of being married. Instead, the focus of this course is to discuss the financial ramifications of marriage.

Before getting married, I believe it is important to have candid discussions about money. Simply put, money is one of the things that couples fight about most and open communication can help prevent or minimize those disputes. Each of you needs to be financially transparent to one another. Do you have debt? Do you have family obligations or issues that could cost you money? Is there outstanding liability for legal matters? Are you a saver or a spender?

If you haven't ever worked with a financial advisor, entering a marriage is an optimal time to get started. If one of you presently works with an advisor, it's time to make an introduction and to add your future spouse to your financial plans. If each spouse has an existing financial advisor, it may make sense to choose one of the two; you may want to interview both together to decide how to handle that.

Once you are married, you'll want to re-title and/or consolidate certain banking accounts, change beneficiary assignments on insurance policies and retirement accounts, and explore both sets of employee benefit options (if both of you are employed and have benefits available). You'll also want to consolidate, change, or increase some of your other insurance coverages.

If one of you has decided to change your legal name, now is the time to do that as well—although you may want to wait until after your honeymoon if you're going to need your passport or driver's license to travel.

For banking, I normally suggest two checking accounts, both of which are titled jointly between spouses but one to be used primarily by each spouse. That way each of you has access to the funds, if needed, but you'll also have your own money for bills and gifts and access to cash.

We're going to talk about asset titling, estate planning, insurance, and beneficiary options later in your studies. For now, know that this is a perfect time to consolidate your financial affairs on to a single, shared balance sheet and a single, shared income statement.

Being married will change some of your limits for contributing to various accounts. For example, if you share a health insurance plan with an HSA, you'll now have a higher contribution limit. Conversely, your joint income might force you to reduce or eliminate certain contributions to IRA or Roth IRA accounts if your combined income exceeds various thresholds.

For these types of reasons, it is a good idea to hire a CPA or professional tax preparer to assist you and your financial advisor with your planning.

Just like the financial advisor conversation, if you each have your own CPA it will be time to pick one and move forward. If you've never used a CPA to file your taxes, now's the time.

Life is about to change in lots of profound ways but working together on the financial aspects of getting married will alleviate lots of potential problems down the road.

PRENUPTIAL AGREEMENTS

In some cases, we recommend prenuptial agreements before a couple gets married for various reasons. These agreements are much more important when one or both spouses have children from a prior marriage, own a business, or have some great disparity in wealth.

Prenuptial agreements can be written in a multitude of ways but generally are designed to provide a blueprint for the potential future dissolution of a marriage. They can allow for the title of all assets to govern distribution, can specify an amount of (or formula for) potential alimony or the waiver of alimony entirely, or can specifically include (or exclude) certain assets from being deemed marital property in the event of divorce.

If you are planning to get married and are thinking about a prenuptial agreement, we recommend that each future spouse has his or her own legal representation so that their interests can be explained and protected to whatever degree is possible.

Before you walk down the aisle, let's see what you've learned in our post-course exercise.

POST-COURSE EXERCISE QUESTIONS

1. **TRUE** or **FALSE**: Before getting married, it is important to have open communication with your future spouse about each of your present finances.

2. **TRUE** or **FALSE**: When getting married for the second or subsequent time, you should always have a prenuptial agreement.

3. **TRUE** or **FALSE**: Getting married can change each spouse's availability or eligibility for various savings and investment vehicles.

4. **TRUE** or **FALSE**: When you get married, both spouses always assume legal responsibility for one another's debts and obligations.

5. **TRUE** or **FALSE**: If you are legally married, you must file a joint income tax return.

POST-COURSE EXERCISE ANSWERS

1. **TRUE.** This is a critical time for complete transparency with and for one another. If you share openly at this time, you'll be able to work together to design a brighter financial future. If one or both of you don't share openly at this time, surprises could be unpleasant at a later date and could undermine the trust that is so important in a marriage.

2. **FALSE.** There is no specific mandate to have a prenuptial agreement for any marriage—your first or a later one. Prenuptial agreements are more common in second or subsequent marriages simply because financial lives tend to be more complicated once there have been children and/or divorces.

3. **TRUE.** Combining a household and therefore household incomes can have both positive and negative impacts on certain financial decisions. If one spouse has particularly strong employee benefits, for example, often both spouses can benefit from that access. On the other hand, being married can push a couple into a higher marginal income tax bracket or past income phaseouts to participate in certain types of savings and investment plans.

4. **FALSE.** Although there are many situations in which married couples will take on debts or obligations jointly, there is no absolute assumption of existing liabilities at the time of marriage. If couples choose to take on financial responsibilities together or to change the title on liabilities, joint responsibility is the likely outcome. When one spouse enters a marriage with excellent credit history and one spouse enters a marriage with suboptimal credit history, it may be wise to keep much of the credit separate to take advantage of the higher of the two credit scores. Maintaining good credit is also why we normally suggest that spouses maintain their own credit cards and use them both to maintain good standing in each of their credit profiles.

5. **FALSE.** This is a bit of a trick question. When you are legally married on December 31 of any year, the tax returns filed for that year must be marital returns. However, married couples' returns can be

filed as either Married Filing Jointly or Married Filing Separately. If you file jointly, all of your income, exemptions, and deductions are aggregated. If you file separately, you will generally each qualify for 50 percent of the exemptions and deductions allowable by law. In most cases, it is not beneficial to file separately, but your CPA or tax preparer can (and should) run both scenarios every spring to make sure you are filing optimally for your household.

EXTRA-CREDIT ASSIGNMENT

This course's extra-credit assignment will vary based upon your marital status.

If you are already married and have not already done so, consider hiring a financial advisor to walk you and your spouse through a combined financial planning process. This will open communication and allow for coordination of plans and the establishment of shared goals for the future.

If you are planning to propose or are already engaged, your assignment is to hold an open and honest discussion with your partner about your finances and possibly to engage a financial advisor together to assist.

If you are single and have no immediate plans to consider marriage, your assignment is simply to take care of your own financial affairs in such a way that when and if you meet the right person, you'll be very comfortable with full transparency and sharing with him or her.

Financial Planning 203:

I BELIEVE THAT CHILDREN ARE... EXPENSIVE!

Now you're an "old married couple" with a few years of wedded bliss behind you and you decide that you'd like to have a baby. Like our discussion on marriage, this course is not designed to discuss the pros and cons of having children or any of the psychological factors or decisions involved in parenting. But just like having children is a game-changer socially and psychologically, it also changes the landscape and scope of financial planning indefinitely.

Suddenly you have new expenses and new risks to consider. These expenses can be obvious, like the costs of diapers or day care, or less obvious, like the potentially decreased earning capacity of a household upon deciding to have one spouse work part time or not to work outside of the home at all. It is never a financial advisor's role to tell clients how to make these lifestyle decisions but we are asked to quantify them and to help make the decisions educated ones.

If one spouse decides to work part time or not at all outside of the home, indefinitely or for a few years, not only will there be a reduction in household income but there may also be a loss of various employee benefits, including insurance and retirement benefits. Lower income means fewer resources but may also mean lower taxes so there's a lot to consider in making this decision.

You also need to consider the cost of childcare in the event both spouses continue to work full time. If there is a grandparent or other family member able to help, this could be a very easy financial decision. On the other hand, if day care will cost $2,000 per month or the household income reduction would be $3,000 per month, there may be more debate as to what is optimal for your family beyond finances.

Having a child also increases lots of insurance costs. You'll likely be paying higher health insurance premiums under a family plan than under a spousal one. You'll also need a lot more life insurance knowing that one or more people are relying on your income even if you aren't around to earn it. We'll cover more of this next semester.

EDUCATION EXPENSES

The biggest cost in having children for lots of families is the cost of education. For some families, that might mean deciding to spend $30,000 per year for private school. Some families will also face the looming cost of a college education.

Saving for college is an important factor in choosing to be a parent but it cannot take the place of saving for your own retirement. The reason for that distinction is that it is possible (although not always wise) to borrow money to go to college but you cannot borrow for retirement. You must take care of your own financial responsibilities before trying to assist others with theirs.

When building a model to determine how much to save for college, you have several factors to consider. Are you interested in paying for two years of community college, four years at a public in-state university, or four years of private liberal arts college? Are there other family members who want to assist with tuition? Do you want your child to graduate without student loans or to have some of their own skin in the game? Lastly, are you also budgeting for private school along the way?

It is important to remember that all parents pay for school for their children in one way or another. If your kids attend private school, there is the obvious cost of tuition to consider. However, if your kids attend public school, in many communities the housing is more expensive in neighborhoods with excellent public schools than in neighborhoods with lousy public schools. So to send your child to a school where you believe he or she will thrive always costs money—either in the form of tuition or in the cost of a more expensive home (or sometimes both if moving near a private school escalates the cost of housing as well).

For clients who choose to pay for private school out of their annual income, we normally suggest saving for college in an amount that would pay for four years of an in-state public university. The reason is that the difference between a private college tuition and a public college tuition is likely equivalent to their son or daughter's 12th-grade tuition in private school. So, if they plan to save for public college and their child goes to a private one, they'll essentially keep their budget unchanged for so-called 13th–16th grades, in addition to using their college funds. If their child goes to a public in-state university, the funds will be ready to use and the parents get a "raise" by not having private school to fund anymore.

So how much should new parents save for college, assuming they have no adverse debt and have met their retirement savings target? To save for a four-year in-state public college education, assuming a reasonable rate of return and historical inflation of college costs, families would need to save $500 per month for their child from birth until age 18. For private college, it is $1,100 per month or so from birth until age 18.

My wife and I started a college savings fund for our daughter when she was born and have been funding it with $500 per month for over a decade. We're also paying private school tuition. It's amazing how the college fund has grown and how comfortable we are feeling about paying for college when the time comes, without a giant budget hit and hopefully without any loans.

One of the other considerations in saving for college is the potential availability of tax-favored savings through 529 College Savings Plans.[17] The

---

17 There is no guarantee that the plan will grow to cover college expenses. In addition, depending upon the laws of your home state or designated beneficiary, favorable state tax treatment or other benefits offered by such home state for investing in 529 College Savings Plans may be available only if you invest in the home state's 529 College Savings Plan. Any state-based benefit offered with respect to a particular 529 College Savings Plan should be one of many appropriately weighted factors to be considered in making an investment decision. You should consult with your financial, tax, or other advisor to learn more about how state-based benefits (including any limitations) would apply to your specific circumstances and also may wish to contact your home state or any other 529 College Savings Plan to learn more about the features, benefits and limitations of that state's 529 College Savings Plan. You may also go to www.collegesavings.org for more information.

529 plans were initially created to help families save money for higher education expenses for children, grandchildren, or others but have since been expanded to help parents also offset the cost of K–12 education up to a set annual limit.

The 529 College Savings Plans are named after Section 529 of the Internal Revenue Code (IRC), which created these types of accounts in 1996. While many people use these plans for that purpose, other considerations can make them fantastic vehicles for avoiding different types of taxes.

The 529 plans are individually owned by an adult person, meaning a person of majority age, but they can name a beneficiary who is a minor or an adult. Any adult may open a 529 plan for any named beneficiary—you do not have to be the parent or grandparent of the person named. When you fund a plan like this, there is no federal tax deduction. Some states have enacted tax parity, which allows limited deductions from state income taxes for contributions to *any* plan, while other states offer a state income tax deduction only for *specific* plans. Every state has unique rules and contribution limits, and you can review them at savingforcollege.com.

In addition to a possible full or partial state income tax deduction, 529 College Savings Plans offer other benefits as well:

Income tax-free growth and withdrawals

There are no capital gains or ordinary income taxes assessed on money in a 529 plan. When the money is withdrawn, if it is used for a *qualified purpose*, there are no taxes due whatsoever. After-tax money goes in and grows, and used properly, the account will never be taxed again.

A full list of qualifying expenses and eligible institutions can be found at savingforcollege.com. Generally, qualifying expenses include costs of attendance for undergraduate or post-graduate educations, with *no restrictions* as to the state in which a beneficiary lives or attends school. Note that as of tax reform in 2018, the plans have been amended to allow up to $10,000 per year per beneficiary to be used toward private school education.

Savings on estate taxes

Even though the federal estate tax rules have very strict guidelines requiring completed gifts to avoid taxation, the 529 plan is an exception to that rule. Balances are considered outside of the owner's taxable estate when he or she dies. For wealthy families, this provision can save estate and inheritance taxes for multiple generations.

Limited impact on financial aid

From a tax perspective, a 529 College Savings Plan is a panacea when it's used for its intended purpose. With the spiraling costs of education and so much attention being paid to financial aid and student loans, it is important to note that 529s do not adversely impact financial aid for the beneficiary in the same way that accounts in their own name would, which makes them even more attractive. For college funding, it is especially important to avoid UTMA or UGMA custodial accounts (which count against financial aid dollar for dollar) and to use 529 plans instead.

Revocable gifts: Unlike custodial accounts under the Uniform Gifts to Minors Act (UGMA) or the Uniform Transfers to Minors Act (UTMA), the account balance in a 529 plan does *not* belong to the beneficiary; it still belongs to the owner who opened it. The owner has a lot of flexibility in the event they need the money for other purposes or if the beneficiary gets a scholarship or elects not to attend school. It is also permissible to adjust the beneficiary assignment once per year, to maintain flexibility under changing circumstances. If the funds aren't needed for college by a specific generation, they can be held for the next generation with no gift or generation-skipping taxes due. Anyone can open a 529 for any beneficiary at any time, for as many beneficiaries as you'd like.

High contribution limits

Contribution limits for 529 plans are the same as the federally set annual gift tax exclusion, which is $15,000 per donor, per donee, per year as of 2020. This means a married couple can put up to $30,000 away each year for each child or grandchild without creating a taxable gift or requiring a gift tax return to be filed. In addition, parents, grandparents, or other adults may fund up to five years at once up front—so you could put $75,000 per adult, per beneficiary, into the accounts.

To maximize the benefits of income tax deferral, estate tax exclusion, and tax-free growth, for example, grandparents can move $150,000 out of their estate into accounts for each grandchild that will never be taxed again.

There is one downside to the plans. If the money is not used for qualified expenses, ordinary income taxes plus 10 percent penalties are due on any gains in the account. However, even with that restriction, if the idea of giving funds away creates any fear of running out of money during the donor's lifetime, remember that the gifts aren't irrevocable. The assets can be withdrawn by the donors, if necessary, with taxes and penalties due only on gains (but not on contributed funds).

With potential state income tax benefits, estate and inheritance tax benefits, tax-deferred growth, and tax-free withdrawals for qualified purposes, 529s are an incredible tool for tax avoidance and tax planning.

We've only scratched the surface in talking about the financial implications of parenthood, but hopefully you have a better sense of some of the planning involved related to your household income and employment, day care, and education expenses.

This concludes the first semester of your sophomore year. Before you start learning how to change diapers, let's see how much you learned in our post-course exercise.

POST-COURSE EXERCISE QUESTIONS

1. **TRUE** or **FALSE**: Funding a 529 College Savings Plan for your child may be deductible for federal income tax purposes.

2. **TRUE** or **FALSE**: The problem with 529 College Savings Plans is that the funds belong to the children when they turn 18.

3. **TRUE** or **FALSE**: Medical insurance premiums tend to be higher for families with children than for childless married couples or unmarried individuals.

4. **TRUE** or **FALSE**: When planning to have children, one consideration is the cost of day care or the possible reduction in income for one or both spouses.

5. **TRUE** or **FALSE**: Setting aside money for your children's education should always be a higher priority than savings for your own retirement because education costs are usually paid before retirement begins.

POST-COURSE EXERCISE ANSWERS

1. **FALSE.** Each state has different rules as to whether or not donors can deduct 529 plan contributions at the state level but there is no deduction at the federal level. Note that under current tax law, the federal tax code now limits deductibility of state and local income taxes, which means that paying fewer state income taxes may have some modest benefit at the federal level as a by-product of the 2018 federal tax law.

2. **FALSE.** Planned properly, contributions made to 529 College Savings Plans are completed gifts for estate tax purposes but they never belong to the named beneficiaries. There are two required steps to make sure this doesn't become an issue.

    First, it is important never to use even one dollar from custodial (UTMA or UGMA) money to fund a gift to a 529 plan. If even a single dollar of UTMA funds is deposited into a 529 plan, the donor loses the ability to change the beneficiary and the beneficiary becomes the owner when he or she reaches the age of majority.

    Second, when establishing a 529 plan account, make sure to list a successor owner on the plan who isn't the beneficiary. If mom opens a 529 for her daughter, for example, the successor owner can be dad or any other responsible adult but should never be the daughter. That way, if mom dies and still owns the account, it avoids becoming property of the beneficiary.

3. **TRUE.** Medical insurance premiums, whether in an employer-sponsored plan or an individual plan on a healthcare exchange, tend to be higher as more individuals are covered by the plan. In many cases with employer-sponsored plans, the employer may contribute to the employee's cost of health insurance but rarely if ever do employers cover the cost of dependents on the plan. So as an employee you should expect your premium costs per paycheck to rise substantially when you add a child to the plan.

4. **TRUE.** The cost of childcare is staggering, and whether one parent decides to leave the workforce or both parents stay fully employed and enroll their child in day care, the impact on household cash flow

will be very significant. Unless you have a retired grandparent nearby who wants to provide day care for their grandchild during the workday, you can expect childcare to be a major line item in your budget.

5. **FALSE**. Retirement (financial independence) should be the single top priority for saving and investments. There are lots of ways to pay for education—work study, grants, scholarships, student loans—but only one way to secure a dignified retirement. All parents need to fight the urge to sacrifice their own financial independence to educate their children or they will likely face a day when they aren't able to handle their own finances and will need their child's help in making ends meet. That outcome isn't good for the parents or the child and should be avoided if at all possible.

EXTRA-CREDIT ASSIGNMENT

Whether you already have children, or you're considering having children, spend time with your spouse talking about some of the financial matters described in this course. Make sure you are on the same page in terms of your own employment, childcare, public vs. private education, and college funding goals.

Becoming a parent is one of the most rewarding decisions people can make but also is one of the most challenging and expensive. Open communication in advance can help manage everyone's expectations and avoid some of the surprises that occur when you are suddenly a mom and dad.

SECOND SEMESTER

Your first three semesters on campus knocked out most of your general coursework at Retire U, so in the upcoming semester you'll start working toward one of your majors—financial independence.

Now that you have created your financial plan, gotten out of debt (or are on a strategic schedule to do so), and built the insurance components of your risk management plan, you need to start building wealth. This semester will introduce you to investing for growth, asset allocation, diversification, and portfolio management.

Course Schedule for Sophomore Year—Second Semester:
- Financial Independence 201: The Science of Investing
- Financial Independence 202: The Art of Portfolio Design

Financial Independence 201:

THE SCIENCE OF INVESTING

You've knocked out your basic requirements and you're ready to take a deep dive into investing. To many people, this is the fun part of the planning process, while to others it is the most frightening.

More often than not, when people call our office for a consultation, the first statement they make starts with something along the lines of "I [or We] have a portfolio that..." It seems that the desire to allocate, rebalance, or somehow optimize a portfolio is on the top of most people's minds.

Even before we talk about investment choices, asset classes, manager selection, etc., there are important decisions that each investor needs to make. In this course, we will discuss seven of the major components in investing that you should understand prior to opening your first account:

1. Risks Associated with Investing
2. Balancing the Risks and Rewards
3. Costs Inherent in Investing
4. Hiring Portfolio Managers vs. Doing It Yourself
5. Qualified vs. Non-Qualified Accounts
6. Active vs. Passive Portfolio Management
7. Strategic vs. Tactical Portfolio Management

Our course will attempt to cover each of these topics in the context of a rational fact base, along with the philosophical theories and emotional responses inherent in the investing experience.

Risks associated with investing

No conversation about investing can begin without first discussing the risks involved. Lawyers have written 200-plus page prospectuses on the subject in the name of consumer protection but I have yet to meet a client who has read one in its entirety. This course will aim to simplify the issues to get you thinking about them. It is not designed to replace the prospectus you receive (and allegedly read and understand) every time you make an investment.

During the data-gathering step in financial planning, you might be given an initial questionnaire that is dedicated to determining your risk tolerance as an investor. In my experience, these questionnaires are completely inadequate to assess fully the risk tolerance of a client and, in fact, can be problematic because the responses are often influenced by recent experiences.

WITH A GRAIN OF SALT

If a questionnaire is completed after a good year in the markets, responses are likely to be overly optimistic and reflect a more aggressive tolerance than may be accurate, whereas if a questionnaire is completed after a bad year in the markets, responses are likely to be overly pessimistic and reflect conservatism far exceeding an appropriate response level.

In addition to the challenges with self-reporting one's own risk tolerance, there is also the fact that couples and partners don't always agree on risk levels. One spouse may be more skittish, while the other is more of a daredevil. Care must be taken to make sure each spouse or partner is comfortable in a planning engagement by treating each account differently based upon its owner of record, stated purpose, and time horizon.

Lastly, when people think about investment risk, they usually focus only on the market risk—the possibility that an account value can go down. There are other risks we need to be concerned about, depending on the holdings in a portfolio. In addition to market risk, following are some of the other risks to consider.

Interest-rate risk

With certain securities or portfolios, one of the greatest risks is that interest rates will move in a direction adverse to the underlying holdings.

If, for example, a portfolio holds nothing but long-term bonds, then when interest rates rise the market value of those bonds could drop precipitously. In another example, if the account holds long-term certificates of deposit at 1.5 percent and interest rates rise to 6 percent, the account holder would either have to sell at an adverse price, pay a penalty for early withdrawal, or potentially miss out on the opportunity of earning a higher return on his or her funds.

The movements of interest rates can impact not only the value of a portfolio but can also expose you to opportunity costs incurred when missing out on more favorable interest rates.

Inflation and purchasing power risks

While market risk and interest risk are clear, the risks associated with inflation are subtle. Some have dubbed inflation a "stealth tax" because it can be sneaky at times and can hurt an investor's outcome. Inflation adjusts the value of a currency by creating a higher nominal cost for goods and services.

For an example of inflation, consider the postage stamp. As recently as the 1970s, the cost to mail a letter with the US Postal Service was $0.06. Some 40 years later, the cost to mail the same letter was $0.46. That means that the cost of a single stamp became *eight times* higher over those 40 years.

Inflation impacts all goods and services but does so unequally. That means the cost of housing, automobiles, education, groceries, leisure, and basically anything you can name will be more expensive in the future than today and by an uncertain amount. After graduating into retirement, you could enjoy 30 or 40 years in that stage of your life, so inflation could absolutely play a major role in determining the success of retirement-planning outcomes.

If a security or portfolio is providing a return greater than the rate of inflation, it is said to be providing a positive inflation-adjusted return. On the other hand, if the security or portfolio is providing a return that is negative, or that is positive but less than inflation, it is said to have a negative inflation-adjusted return.

Keeping ahead of inflation protects an investor's purchasing power. Failing to do so subsequently erodes purchasing power so that even an account balance that is higher from one year to the next might provide a lifestyle that is less adequate than in previous years.

Currency and exchange rate risks

A typical portfolio is likely to contain securities issued all over the world, not just in the United States. As a result, one of the risks in investing is the impact that constantly changing exchange rates between currencies play on a portfolio. If you have a portfolio denominated in the US dollar, but some of your securities are denominated in the Japanese yen, a movement of the number of yen equivalent to each dollar will impact your portfolio returns.

Note that we aren't just talking about the risk that a security's price is impacted by a currency exchange-rate adjustment due to its denomination but also the risk that the financial results (profit or loss) of the company issuing the underlying security is impacted by an exchange-rate adjustment. If you own shares of stock in a company domiciled in North Carolina that does significant business in Germany, for example, the returns could be impacted by the exchange rate between the dollar and the euro, even though it is a domestic (US) stock in your portfolio.

Political, legislative, and taxation risks

The risks created by politics, legislation, and taxation, both domestically and internationally, are distinct from one another but some may fall under the same unpredictable umbrella.

International relations can impact a portfolio in lots of ways—by impacting the exchange rate, seeing trade imbalances, tariffs imposed, or embargos applied. As we know all too well, politics in Washington can impact our portfolios, mostly because investors on a macro level prefer certainty to uncertainty and a steady stream of political uncertainty feels like the new norm.

From a legislative standpoint, much of the uncertainty overlaps into the realm of taxation. A simple change by Congress on the way that a dividend, interest payment, or capital gain will be taxed could send shockwaves through an equity or bond market, just like a change to deductibility of mortgage interest could impact real estate markets dramatically.

The tax reform in January 2018 was a major overhaul of the US tax system and impacted each American taxpayer in different ways. The changes are too numerous to review in this course but they impacted deductions, exemptions, exceptions, and limits in a myriad of ways that will likely keep all of us (and our CPAs) up at night trying to measure the impact and plan accordingly.

Liquidity and marketability risks

In addition to the macro-level risks discussed above, there is a risk on a more micro level to an investor holding securities that have limited liquidity or marketability. If a security cannot readily be sold, either due to a restriction or covenant or because there is simply not a willing buyer, it may impact the market price of that security adversely.

As an example, think of your home. In a so-called seller's market, there are more buyers than homes for sale so houses are readily marketable and prices go up. On the other hand, in a so-called buyer's market, there are more homes for sale than willing buyers so houses are difficult to sell (have limited marketability) and prices go down.

Some less marketable securities tout an illiquidity premium, which supposes that yields can be higher for investors when shares aren't salable. In some cases that may prove to be true but it isn't a given for every investment.

Behavioral risk

Beyond all the risks we've discussed, this may be the biggest of all. We all have a natural tendency to act on our emotions, causing us to do exactly the wrong thing at exactly the wrong time. Sometimes it is based on the knee-jerk reaction to sell near the bottom of a market cycle because you just can't take any more of a loss or to buy near the top of a market cycle because you don't want to miss out on such a great opportunity to make money.

Behavioral risk also brings out our own personal biases—on a variety of issues. For example, **proximity bias** is the tendency for investors to overweight their portfolios toward securities domiciled in their country of residence. In the US, that might mean holding 80 or 90 percent of a portfolio in American securities, even though the US equity markets make up only about 50 percent of the world's market capitalization.

There is also a **familiarity bias**, which can lead investors to choose only securities familiar to them. While household names can be a fine way to select certain services or products, it may not be the best way to pick stocks. In fact, in some cases, the household-name companies who put their names on the football or baseball stadium in your hometown may actually be illustrating a terrible habit of overspending instead of good fiscal management. Buying stock in companies simply because you've heard of them may not be the same for an amateur investor and a seasoned one. It may be better to rely on professional advice or research, as opposed to just brand recognition when making an investment.

There is an inherent **overconfidence bias**, which means that we all think we're above average—at everything. If you entered a room of 100 adults and asked people to raise their hands if they consider themselves to be an above-average driver, almost all (if not all) of the hands would go up. The same thing might happen if you asked for a show of hands from above-average investors. And that is simply impossible—some of the people in the room are simply average or below average at driving, at investing, and at everything else, and are overconfident.

There are impacts of how recently an event took place (the more distant, the less impact on us) and on loss aversion (losses impact us more negatively than gains impact us positively). Entire volumes have been written on the psychology of investing and have identified as many as 20 of these biases that impact investors.

We are our own worst enemies when it comes to our emotional reactions and personal biases, and that is why I suggest that even financial advisors use an objective and unrelated financial advisor themselves. I rely on a study group with seven other advisors in it and my relationship with them is invaluable to me personally, professionally, and financially.

It is important to use the contingency planning process to provide some relief from various types of financial risks and to control those risks that can be controlled. For those that can't be controlled, people need to rely on their advisors to help lead them through volatile times dispassionately and to avoid becoming victims of the behavioral tendencies and biases that can impact all of us.

If you're interested in learning much more about how psychology and behavior play a role in financial planning, my favorite books on the subject are *The Behavioral Investor* and *The Laws of Wealth: Psychology and the Secret to Investing Success* by Daniel Crosby, PhD, and *Behavioral Finance and Wealth Management* by Michael M. Pompian, CFA.

Balancing the risks and rewards

Before we move on from our conversation on risk in portfolios, we need to consider how the risks differ when we invest during different times in our lives. In the simplest of terms, there are only three kinds of investors—buyers, holders, and sellers. In some stages of our lives, we are only one type, but at other times, we may need to be two or three simultaneously.

When we are **buyers**, we are actively purchasing securities, often on a regular and automated basis via dollar-cost averaging. In this case, market volatility can actually benefit our portfolio because when market prices decline, our next automated purchase will be at a lower price than our prior purchase. For young investors—under age 50 or so—we tend to be exclusively buyers. That is, we are actively buying securities in our retirement and other accounts and aiming to accumulate wealth.

In 2008, when most equity markets lost more than a third of their total value, buyers who continued to buy regularly seized a potential generational opportunity to grow capital. Everything was on "sale" and buyers took advantage. Looking back more than a decade later, that market created enormous wealth for buyers of all ages.

As the name implies, when we are **holders**, we are neither buying nor selling securities in a given account. In this case, market volatility is not a good thing and, in fact, can create a delay in meeting various objectives.

Using 2008 as a prime example, for investors a few years from retirement who were neither contributing to nor withdrawing from their portfolios, the downturn caused a nearly five-year delay in recovery of asset values. These holders recovered, but very slowly, and many were forced to delay their retirement by some five to 10 years.

Investors who are actively drawing against their accounts to meet their lifestyles are **sellers**. Most sellers plan to withdraw from their portfolio at a set dollar amount or a set percentage every year. If you withdraw a set dollar amount and markets drop, you are forced to take a higher withdraw rate to sustain your lifestyle. If you withdraw a set percentage and markets drop, you experience a reduction in spendable income for a year or longer.

In 2008, those sellers without some form of defensive strategy in place made withdrawals against assets as their market value dropped. In essence, instead of picking fruit from their portfolio orchard, they started chopping branches off of their orchard trees to make ends meet. Fewer branches means less fruit—forever. And as a result, some of these sellers have never recovered and are unlikely to ever recover from the Great Recession.

Instead of being only a buyer, holder, or seller, it is often advantageous to segregate your assets into various tranches (or buckets, to use the nomenclature of the day) so that not all of your accounts are treated the same way. This is the combination approach.

For example, a gainfully employed 60-year-old worker might have multiple IRA accounts or retirement accounts from prior employers, in addition to a current 401(k) or other type of plan that is actively contributory. In this case, it may make sense to treat assets as follows:

- Treat the contributory (active) plan as if you are a buyer. That means being more aggressive in this plan than in other plans and it means contributing regularly regardless of market conditions. In this case, this account can take advantage of some volatility. The account will likely be exclusively in equities (stocks or stock mutual funds).

- Treat some of the other accounts as if you are a holder. These accounts would be in the five- to 10-year plan and could be fully invested but not as aggressively as the contributory account. Here you might hold value stocks or dividend-paying stocks, as well as alternative investments like private debt or real estate.

- Lastly, treat some of the other accounts as if you are a seller. The reason to do this is that if your life changes and you are suddenly unemployed—voluntarily or not—you'll want to have some resources that can begin creating income for you immediately in the absence of a paycheck. These accounts might hold cash, certificates of deposit, laddered short-term bonds or short-term bond funds, or other liquid and fairly conservative holdings that are unlikely to get hurt by adverse market conditions.

As you can see, it is possible to simultaneously be a buyer, a holder, and a seller. As a result, a thoughtful strategy must be deployed to segregate assets and accounts and to earmark them for specific purposes and time frames in your planning.

Costs inherent in investing

Like any product or service, investment management has various costs. Some of those costs are readily apparent on a statement (sometimes called fee transparency), while others are embedded in various products in the form of fees, commissions, or expense ratios.

If you elect the do-it-yourself (DIY) approach, the costs will be limited to your custodian(s) and your asset manager(s), both of which will be defined below. If you use advisors of some kind—a financial advisor, stockbroker, insurance agent, banker, etc.—you will also have a cost for their involvement.

Expense ratios are the underlying costs in a mutual fund[18] or exchange-traded fund.[19] These are not reflected on your statement but their impact cannot be ignored. That is because the returns you experience owning mutual funds are reported to you *net* of those underlying expenses. All funds have some cost to them. Some are very modest (a passively managed domestic equity fund might cost 0.05–0.25 percent per year), while some are very expensive (actively managed international equity funds can cost 2.25 percent per year or more).

---

18   Mutual funds are sold only by prospectus. Please consider the charges, risks, expenses, and investment objectives carefully before investing. A prospectus containing this and other information about the investment company can be obtained from your financial professional. Read it carefully before you invest or send money.

18   Investors should consider carefully information contained in the prospectus, including investment objectives, risks, charges, and expenses. Please read the prospectus carefully before investing. ETFs do not sell individual shares directly to investors and only issue their shares in large blocks. Exchange-traded funds are subject to risks similar to those of stocks. Investment returns will fluctuate and are subject to market volatility so that an investor's shares, when redeemed or sold, may be worth more or less than their original cost.

Your **custodian** is the holder of your actual accounts themselves and has custody of your cash, stocks, bonds, funds, or other holdings. Some large brokerage firms are self-clearing, which means that they are their own clearing firm. For independent advisors or those affiliated with small broker/dealers, registered investment advisors, banks, or insurance companies, there is usually a third-party custodian.

As we discussed earlier in your studies, the most common in the US are National Financial Services (NFS, LLC), Charles Schwab, and Pershing. You will find language on your statement to help you determine who your custodian is and any deposits made to an account are typically made payable to the custodian directly.

Custodians are paid in several ways—annual account fees, trading and transaction fees, alternative asset custody fees, and check-writing or debit card access fees, to name a few. Some also have fees imposed for account inactivity or for accounts below a certain market value. These fees are transparent on your statement. Your advisor does not share in these fees and, in fact, pays them also if he or she maintains personal accounts with the same custodian.

Broker/dealers (B/Ds) are those organizations that trade securities for their own accounts or on behalf of their account holders. They are usually paid a portion of the compensation in the form of an up-front or level commission. In a retail mutual fund, often called an "A," a "B," or a "C" share, your advisor and B/D are paid either a commission to buy the fund, a portion of the fund expense ratio, or both.

Investment Advisory Representatives (IARs) are licensed and authorized personnel who work for firms who advise high-net-worth individuals on investments, referred to as Registered Investment Advisors (RIAs). When you work with an RIA and own institutional or no-load funds, your IAR is not paid a commission or a portion of the expense ratio and instead will impose a portfolio services fee (usually a percentage of the assets in the account) transparently on your statement. They may also charge a retainer fee (usually a flat annual fee in lieu of or in addition to the portfolio services fee) by separate invoice for financial planning or other services unrelated to just the asset management.

Note that neither an IAR nor an RIA is a professional designation that is earned; they are merely acronyms for titles that indicate the roles they each play in an advisory relationship.

Your advisor may manage your accounts personally or may use an institutional third-party money manager to manage them. If a third party is used, the portfolio services fees tend to be higher, as there is another party in the mix.

The total costs paid by shareholders in managed accounts include the portfolio services fee to the IAR, the RIA, and the third-party asset manager, if one is utilized, as well as transaction costs, account-level custody costs, the expense ratios of underlying funds, and other potential fees.

As you learned in your freshman course, financial advisors have many different models on how to charge for their planning services. From an asset management standpoint, it is common to see advisory fees between 1 percent and 2.5 percent per year, depending on the firm you use, your level of assets being managed, and the level of service you need or want.

As a firm, we consider our value proposition to be based on financial planning and wealth management advice, client service, and other factors not strictly tied to asset management. I suspect that many independent financial advisors feel the same way. Our firm uses a model in which we charge a fee on assets (and/or a retainer fee for clients with less than our current account minimum under management), which covers our ongoing comprehensive financial planning services. The fee charged to the accounts is not solely for investment management but also covers the ongoing monitoring of our clients' financial plans.

As you might expect, costs may have an impact on investment performance. For example, to net a 6 percent return after expenses, an average return between 7 and 8 percent might be required by the fund managers. In a retail mutual fund share, returns are reported net of expenses but will vary due to the loads on a given share class. In an institutional, or no-load share, returns are reported net of expense ratios but a portfolio service fee may be applied after the return calculation.

In plain English, that means that account holders are paying for assets to be managed, whether those fees appear transparently on their statements or not. The key number to a client is always going to be the total return net of expenses and fees earned by the account.

For most investors looking to hire a financial advisor, one question they must consider is, "Can my financial advisor provide enough value, advice, and management of a client's behavioral biases or tendencies to cover his or her expenses?" Ultimately, it is up to the client to determine if there is *value* in the relationship, not only for investment management and for dealing with the behavioral risks facing each of us as humans but also in the form of time savings, family communication, and other intangibles.

The value is often derived when something goes wrong in a family's situation and the contingency plan must be activated. I think it has been said that any captain can navigate in calm seas; the captain you want with you is the one who can navigate in choppy seas.

Hiring portfolio managers vs. doing it yourself

With all of the research tools available online today and the easy access to accounts, there is no reason why you can't just do this yourself. However, the fact that Home Depot® will allow me to buy the supplies to build my own house does not qualify me as a homebuilder.

For individuals with the time, talent, and inclination to put together their own portfolios, a wealth of information is available to make that possible. I would argue, of course, that not everyone should attempt to do this on his or her own.

There are lots of rational reasons why this is so: people are too busy to be watching markets, there is so much information that it is hard to differentiate the nuggets of wisdom from the noise, and the investment options have continued to get more complicated and require an enormous amount of study just to stay abreast of them all.

As compelling as some of those reasons can be, allow me to suggest that the primary benefit to working with a financial advisor is not a rational one but an emotional one. Maintaining financial discipline is not unlike maintaining a personal fitness discipline. We can all buy a treadmill and put it in our basement but not all of us will use it regularly, if at all, and even those of us who use it may not use it *correctly*. By hiring a personal trainer, we can stay on track, motivated, and accountable, and I believe the results are generally better that way.

While people have been trained by our 24-hour financial media to "don't just sit there—do something" in the financial planning space, sometimes the best advice we can give to a client with a well-designed portfolio is to *do nothing and stay the course*. When markets are volatile and the media is signaling the end of the world as we know it, it may be prudent that you *do nothing*. When hot tech stocks are soaring and neighbors are bragging about getting rich quickly, maybe it is best for you to *do nothing*. When real estate speculators are flipping houses and making quick profits, you may benefit if you *do nothing*.

If this sounds a little boring, it can be. However, if you have set a course for financial independence, the emotional reaction to external events may just derail your plan. So just as an extra 10 minutes on the treadmill might sound tedious, doing it will produce results.

In early 2000, some people made a lot of money on tech stocks or flipping houses; others lost their entire nest eggs or are still stuck with real estate that they can't sell, even at a big loss. That isn't investing; it is gambling. If you find gambling entertaining, may I suggest that a trip to Las Vegas will be more fun than watching CNBC and picking stocks?

The only reason that your planning should change dramatically is because something major has happened in your life. That is when an advisor becomes a sounding board, a confidant, and a copilot. An advisor's ability to build portfolios might be better than yours or it might not. But their ability to help you maintain the discipline to stay the course in the face of challenging circumstances or external noise could be priceless.

For people who made dramatic portfolio changes in November 2008 believing that the world was, in fact, ending, they may never recover. For people who stopped paying themselves first and making regular contributions to their investment accounts, their recovery has been long and slow. But for those who kept paying themselves first and maintained their laser-like focus on their goals and not on the evening news' crisis du jour, they came out ahead.

It wasn't without some uncomfortable moments, however. As the personal training mantra would suggest, sometimes no pain means no gain. But the only thing we can control is our *behavior*, not the stimuli that make us think we have to *do something* all the time.

The benefit to solid objective advice is often related to your family, your life, and your emotions, more than to technical market metrics.

Just as it is true for those few people who have the discipline to get a workout every day and to do it properly enough that no personal trainer is needed, it is my fervent belief that only a small percentage of people should even attempt to do financial planning or asset management alone.

Qualified vs. non-qualified accounts

In the next course, we will be concentrating on types of asset classes often included in a portfolio. It is first important to discuss the various types of accounts that can be established (which are mutually exclusive from the actual underlying holdings). For the sake of simplicity, there are two primary types of accounts to consider for savings and investment: qualified and non-qualified accounts.

While many variations are somewhat beyond the scope of this book, for our purposes, we'll call any type of retirement plan or account a **qualified** account. This means that 401(k) plans, 403(b) tax-sheltered annuities, individual retirement accounts (IRAs), SEP IRAs, SIMPLE IRAs, and other retirement vehicles will be considered qualified for the sake of simplicity moving forward.

The definition of a **qualified retirement plan** has to do with the IRS determination that an employer-sponsored plan meets all the necessary criteria to receive favorable income tax treatment. Note that IRAs in their various forms are not qualified retirement plans by definition but will be grouped with qualified accounts for our purposes in this book.

The Roth IRA, which is a type of IRA, and the Roth 401(k), which is a type of employer-sponsored retirement plan, both have very distinct tax properties. They will also be considered qualified for our limited purposes here, since they have similar age restrictions to other types of IRAs and retirement plans.

Qualified accounts are designed for long-term retirement savings. With a few exceptions, they tend to have very significant penalties for withdrawals prior to age 59½ and should be considered long-term money that is unavailable for any purpose other than retirement. Sometimes an employer will fund these accounts for an employee, while other times the employee will make his or her own contributions. In a third scenario, there are lots of plans in which both the employer and the employee are making contributions for the employee's benefit.

If your employer is making contributions on your behalf, there is usually a vesting schedule that states that if your employment ends before a certain number of years have passed (often five to seven years), you will not be able to take all the funds the employer contributed on your behalf with you when you go. All contributions that you have made to a plan, however, will be 100 percent vested to you immediately and you'll be able to take those funds with you at any time you leave an employer.

Keep in mind that even when leaving an employer, any qualified accounts will still be subject to penalties and fees if you withdraw the funds prematurely. You can move funds from one plan to another (sometimes called a rollover and sometimes called a trustee-to-trustee transfer, depending on the type of account being closed and the specific type of account receiving the funds) without a fee, tax, or penalty under most circumstances.

The second general type of account to consider is a **non-qualified account**. For our purposes, this will include brokerage accounts, mutual fund accounts, deferred compensation plans, employee stock purchase plans, common stock dividend reinvestment programs, and for the remainder of this book, any account that is not defined as a qualified account.

Non-qualified accounts are very flexible and can usually have some liquidity feature should funds be needed earlier than originally anticipated. These accounts historically have received a more favorable capital gains tax treatment so long as assets are held more than one year. Also, they are easily accessible to you almost anytime. The reason for this distinction is that there is a vast difference in the way qualified and non-qualified accounts are treated, not only from a tax perspective but also from a liquidity perspective.

Once you have funded your cash emergency fund, it will be time to start funding qualified and/or non-qualified accounts as well. When you are first getting started with any of these types of vehicles, your major considerations include the following.

Your current tax bracket

The higher your tax bill, the more likely you are to benefit from making the maximum contributions possible to a qualified retirement plan on a tax-deductible basis. If your tax bracket is lower, either the Roth IRA or Roth 401(k) may provide a good mechanism for tax-deferred savings without the tax deduction up front.

Your likely tax bracket in retirement

Knowing that tax rates and rules change constantly and that none of us has a crystal ball, this can be tough. However, having a sense of your current income versus your future income and net worth will help determine which type of account to use.

If your future income is likely to be similar or higher than your present income, a Roth IRA or Roth 401(k) may be more favorable than traditional IRAs or qualified plans. If you are likely to have less income in your retirement years than you do today, the reverse is true. In that case, you will likely benefit more from the up-front tax deduction that a traditional IRA or retirement plan allows.

Your potential need for liquidity

If there is a possibility that some of your funds might be needed before age 59½, it is important to have them in non-qualified accounts where assets can generally be sold and the proceeds can be reached with minimal fees, penalties, or restrictions.

The availability of an employer contribution and whether it is contingent on you also contributing [i.e., a matching contribution on a 401(k) or 403(b)]

In a perfect world, you would be able to simultaneously make a maximum contribution to your qualified retirement plan, to receive a matching contribution or profit-sharing contribution of some kind from your employer, and to make meaningful contributions to a non-qualified account.

As most families do not reside in a perfect world, the place to start might be making enough of a contribution to an employer-sponsored retirement plan in order to maximize the matching contribution. In other words, if your employer's qualified plan will match $0.50 for every dollar that you contribute up to 6 percent of your salary, then if you put away 6 percent, they will put an additional 3 percent of your salary into the plan for you. That is like a tax-deferred raise, and assuming you stay with your employer long enough to vest in the matching contributions, it can make a big difference to your retirement income.

If your financial plan sets a minimum target for your savings rate at 15 percent and your employer is putting in 3 percent, you only need to come up with 12 percent of your gross income to hit the 15 percent target and stay on track. Using that same example, you are now putting away 6 percent to your qualified account and your employer is putting in another 6 percent so where does the rest of your monthly savings go?

If your income tax bracket is high, you may want to put more than 6 percent into the qualified plan until you reach your maximum allowable limit, after which funds can go into a non-qualified account. If not, you might benefit more by depositing your additional monthly savings into a non-qualified account after taking full advantage of your employer's maximum matching contribution.

This was an oversimplified conversation on qualified versus non-qualified accounts, but hopefully it highlighted a few of the thought processes required to make an important decision regarding what type of account(s) to fund once you start saving and investing.[20]

Active vs. passive portfolio management

The active versus passive debate is one that has raged for decades and is likely to continue for decades more. Let's review the two strategies a bit so you can understand the important differences between them.

Active management is a portfolio or fund manager's attempt to *beat* a market or index, aiming to use allegedly superior skills or research capabilities in selecting securities, timing market movements, and identifying

---

20   It is suggested that you consult your financial professional, attorney, or tax advisor with regard to your individual situation.

hidden opportunities or anomalies in the investing universe. With active management, trading will often be frequent, as the portfolio turns over holdings regularly, resulting in higher costs and taxes, but the premise is that the managers are skillful enough to offset costs and taxes with excess investment returns and therefore are worth the extra expense.

Passive management is the use of a portfolio that aims to participate in the returns of various indices or markets but makes no attempt to trade actively or to *beat* or *time* a market. Costs and taxes tend to be much lower and, in a nutshell, this strategy presumes that markets are efficient and cannot be timed or beaten with any degree of consistency and therefore it is better to own the market entirely. In a sense, it is an "if you can't beat them, join them" mentality.

With passive management, assets will be allocated in a fund or portfolio and left alone–a buy-and-hold approach. Sometimes passive managers will mirror their holdings to an index (appropriately called **index funds**), whereas sometimes they will employ a buy-and-hold approach without using a direct copy of the index.[21] That means that even with a passive manager, an investor may not have to accept a return equal to an index (on the upside or the downside of the market); there may still be opportunity for a manager to use a buy-and-hold strategy with an overlay of criteria to determine *which* securities to buy and hold.

Volumes have been written on this debate, opining on why one approach is somehow conclusively superior to the other. All of the arguments are lucid but I'd like to weigh in with my own philosophy on the subject.

First, I believe that equity markets are efficient—that is, they take all available information into consideration when securities are priced. As a result, few, if any, arbitrage opportunities or anomalies are available to investors and therefore it is very unlikely that a manager will uncover a security which is *mistakenly* underpriced.

Second, in my experience most active managers *trail* their benchmarks in any given year, which leads me to believe that active management in most cases is not worth the higher expenses. Betting on a small number of managers to select a finite number of securities, to buy just the right thing at

21 You cannot invest directly in an index.

just the right time and then to sell just the right thing at just the right time, feels like a more speculative approach than owning the markets entirely. It also can't be done with any regularity.

Remember that when one active manager is *buying* ABC stock, another one must be *selling* ABC stock. Therefore, one of them must be wrong about the immediate future of the stock price. And if you happen to own two active funds and one is buying ABC while the other is selling ABC, it isn't a breakeven for you. As a shareholder of each fund, you pay trading costs twice, taxes on any gains on the sale, and your effective "loss" is equal to two trading charges and any taxes due.

Third, in my opinion, passive management should not be constrained to link to a specific index. With apologies to the late John Bogle, the founder of Vanguard and arguably the father of passive investing, I am only partly in his camp. I do believe that costs matter and that taxes matter and that a passive strategy with the right diversification among asset classes makes more sense than trying to pick winners. *(Note: We will discuss diversification in the portfolio design course later in this semester.)*

That said, I do not like pure index funds very much, as they have a tragic flaw underneath the wrapper of low costs and market-matching returns. The problem with an index fund is that it is forced to buy securities or to sell securities without any flexibility at all.

Using the S&P 500® index[22] as an example, when Standard & Poor's announces that XYZ stock is joining the index, many investors buy up the shares of stock in anticipation of the company joining the index funds. This buying frenzy increases the stock price *before* an index fund can accumulate enough shares to keep its market index weighting. That means that an index fund often pays an artificially *high* price for securities it buys.

Likewise, when Standard & Poor's announces that XYZ stock is *leaving* the index, many investors sell the shares of stock in anticipation of the company leaving the index funds. This selling decreases the stock price *before* an index fund can divest itself of all of its shares. That means that an index fund often receives an artificially *low* price for securities it sells.

---

22 S&P 500 Index is an unmanaged group of securities considered to be representative of the stock market in general. You cannot directly invest in the index.

Lastly, while passive management (without purely indexing) makes more sense to me as a core strategy than active management, it is not a panacea. I do believe that, as a satellite strategy, it is fine to use some active management in a portfolio, especially in the fixed income securities markets where arbitrage opportunities can be more plentiful.

Strategic vs. tactical portfolio management

Just as we discussed the debate on active vs. passive investment management, we can have a similar discussion on the merits of strategic vs. tactical management.

Strategic money management is based on a study called "Determinants of Portfolio Performance" by Gary P. Brinson, Randolph Hood, and Gilbert Beebower in 1986, which asserted that 93.6 percent of all investment returns is related to asset allocation and that only a small impact is attributable to security selection and market timing.[23]

If strategic management sounds a lot like passive management, it is because they have a lot in common. The difference is that we define passive management to refer to the treatment of holdings in a specific *fund* within a portfolio, whereas we define strategic management to refer to the construction of the *portfolio* itself.

If you or your advisor should employ strategic management, it means that you will be selecting funds or managers and in the absence of compelling rationale, you will be leaving them alone for the long term. It does not mean that you won't want to rebalance your portfolio periodically to keep the asset allocation close to the desired one—in fact, you will absolutely want to do that to maintain the integrity of the chosen portfolio.[24]

However, it does mean that once you select an appropriate allocation among various asset classes (discussed in greater depth in the next course), you will not deviate from that allocation until and unless something chang-

---

23   Gary P. Brinson, L. Randolph Hood, and Gilbert L. Beebower, Abstract from "Determinants of Portfolio Performance," *Financial Analysts Journal* 42 no. 4, (1986): 39–44, https://doi.org/10.2469/faj.v42.n4.39.

24   Rebalancing assets can have tax consequences. If you sell assets in a taxable account, you may have to pay tax on any gain resulting from the sale. Please consult your tax advisor.

es in your *life* to justify an alteration.[25]

Tactical money management, on the other hand, is a timing strategy that will have an investor moving in and out of asset classes, sectors, securities of a specific country, or similar factors on a regular basis. In that way, tactical money management means the possibility of changing direction, focus, and even risk characteristics of a portfolio constantly.

In some ways, tactical management is touted as a defensive mechanism. The idea is that a tactical manager can go to cash just before a market downturn or that the manager can get out of Greece and into Brazil *just in time*, for example, and is supposedly going to protect investor interests in avoiding big losses. While that may be true sometimes, it is equally possible to be untrue in other instances.

To me, tactical management proliferated in the wake of the 2008 market downturn in an attempt by managers (and even some advisors) to demonstrate that they are *doing something*. In essence, the tactical managers are on the rooftops shouting that, "Buy-and-hold is dead." I am not so sure that is true.

I am also not suggesting that there is no merit to the strategy—and would not attempt to discount the value of quantitative research or the value of allowing a manager to get your assets out of harm's way when a threat is perceived. But while tactical managers may have the ability to exit a market to protect against downside risk, they also tend to be slow to reenter the market, thus also missing potential recovery. In general, I see tactical management as a useful tool only as a satellite position within some portfolios, as opposed to a core investment strategy.

In this course, we have discussed some of the major decisions facing investors prior to even broaching the topic of portfolio construction. Hopefully, you now have a sense of what type of investing appeals to you and what types of accounts are appropriate for you, and you are ready to start looking at asset allocation and portfolio design.

---

25   Using asset allocation as part of your investment strategy neither assumes nor guarantees better performance and cannot protect against loss of principal due to changing market conditions. Using diversification as part of your investment strategy neither assumes nor guarantees better performance and cannot protect against loss of principal due to changing market conditions.

POST-COURSE EXERCISE QUESTIONS

1. **TRUE** or **FALSE**: Market fluctuation is the only risk to consider when investing.

2. **TRUE** or **FALSE**: One challenge with funding qualified plans and IRA accounts is not knowing what capital gains tax rates will be in the future.

3. **TRUE** or **FALSE**: Active portfolio management usually has higher costs than passive portfolio management.

4. **TRUE** or **FALSE**: One benefit of working with a financial advisor is assistance in managing the behavioral risks inherent in investing.

5. **TRUE** or **FALSE**: The benefit of strategic asset allocation is taking advantage of market timing strategies.

POST-COURSE EXERCISE ANSWERS

1. **FALSE.** While market risk is a consideration in investing, there are lots of other risks to consider, including interest—rate risk, inflation risk, liquidity risk, and the most important of all—behavioral risk.

2. **FALSE.** Qualified plans and IRA accounts are not subject to capital gains taxes. Only non-qualified accounts create capital gains or losses when securities are sold in an account. Qualified plans and IRAs are highly impacted by what your *ordinary income tax* rates will be in the future.

3. **TRUE.** There is a lot of debate as to the merits of both types of portfolio management, but active management is typically more costly than passive management and sometimes much more so.

4. **TRUE.** Managing behavioral risk is sometimes the single biggest benefit of working with an objective financial advisor. Serving as a sounding board and anchor in rough market conditions is an invaluable role that a financial advisor should play.

5. **FALSE.** The purpose of strategic asset allocation is to avoid attempts at timing markets. Tactical asset allocation purports to take advantage of market timing strategies.

EXTRA-CREDIT ASSIGNMENT

This course contains so much dense material that choosing a single extra-credit assignment isn't easy. Instead of a single assignment, this course has three different options and I encourage you to choose one.

If you were to take only one action as a result of completing this course, it would be to consider one of three next steps:

- If you have never used a financial advisor, consider meeting with one and asking for some feedback on your existing portfolio allocation. You can still be a DIY investor but getting another set of eyes on your statements once in a while might prove to be invaluable.

- If you currently use an advisor, particularly one who espouses market timing, stock picking, or potentially expensive active management, consider getting a second opinion. Much like the DIY investor, you don't have to change advisors but you might benefit from another perspective on your portfolio, just as you might benefit from a second opinion if facing a medical decision.

- Consider reading one or more of the recommended books on behavioral risks and investing listed earlier in the course. You may find them enlightening and might even identify some of your own behaviors that, if corrected or adjusted, might benefit your investment plan.

Financial Independence 202:

THE ART OF PORTFOLIO DESIGN

In this course, we'll dig deeper into the asset classes that make up your investment portfolio or the collection of investable assets that you own in your various accounts. Every investor is different so not all of the asset classes discussed in this course will be appropriate for you. Your portfolio should ideally hold a balance of the asset classes in a way that is uniquely suited to your goals and objectives.

Please seek advice from a financial, tax, or legal professional before acting upon information in this course, as it is being presented in a general way and may not be suitable for you or your family's specific situation.

PRIMARY ASSET CLASSES

In this course, we will cover the four primary asset classes, each of which has many subclasses. Those four main asset classes are as follows:

1. Cash and Cash Equivalents
2. Fixed Income Securities
3. Equities
4. Alternative Investments

This is not to suggest that all portfolios need to have access to all these asset classes (or the various subclasses). It is to give you a broad 30,000-foot view of the investment universe to get you thinking about your portfolio on a macro level, rather than as just a collection of holdings.

We'll start with the three traditional asset classes and then we will talk about the alternative asset classes that are used for various reasons in portfolio construction.

Cash and cash equivalents[26]

During your freshman year, we talked about establishing an emergency fund. This is the first place where money will go when you begin to save, and with some exceptions, it may be the only place you should be putting money away until you reach the emergency or opportunity fund target.

The emergency fund will be in liquid cash or in what is frequently called a **cash equivalent** vehicle. A cash equivalent account is one that has cash-like risk characteristics and can be converted to liquid cash basically in an instant and usually without fees or penalties.

Cash can be held in bank savings accounts, money market accounts, certificates of deposit, savings bonds, and floating rate funds (made up of ultra-short-term senior bank debt instruments). For most families, a basic savings account or money market account at a bank or credit union is adequate. This is not a place to get fancy; it's a place to maintain liquidity and access to capital.

If you are going to hold assets in the bank, make sure the funds are covered by FDIC insurance so that in the event of a bank failure, your accounts (up to a high limit, currently $250,000) are backed by the full faith and credit of the US Treasury. With some custodians, multiple banking institutions can be utilized in the same account to increase the FDIC insurance on cash for account holders who want to maintain very large cash positions.

---

26 Bank accounts and certificates of deposit are FDIC insured up to applicable limits, but other cash equivalents discussed may not be FDIC insured. Consult your financial professional for more information.

Fixed income securities[27]

Fixed income securities can take many forms—bonds, bills, notes, commercial paper—and can be differentiated by type, by time horizon (maturity), by credit quality, by issuer, by currency, and by other factors. In other words, fixed income as a category is very broad.

Conventional wisdom suggests that bonds and other fixed income securities (used interchangeably throughout this course) are less volatile than stocks.

Bonds are used in portfolios for two primary reasons: To dampen volatility in the overall portfolio and for income purposes. In that sense, fixed income securities can be purchased for total return—meaning both capital appreciation and income potential. Most fixed income instruments pay a stated coupon rate for a stated time until maturity, when the face amount is returned to the investor.

Buying a bond is *loaning* money to a corporation or local, state, or federal government in exchange for interest payments. Bonds can be bought when they are issued at maturity value or they can be bought in the open market at any time prior to maturity—possibly at a premium over maturity value or possibly at a discount to maturity value, depending on which direction interest rates have moved since the bonds were issued, investor sentiment, credit quality changes, and so forth.

The market value of a bond tends to move in the opposite direction from trending interest rates. That is, if you own a bond paying 4 percent interest and current interest rates allow bonds to be issued at 6 percent, you would expect to receive less than the maturity value for your bond if you tried to sell it in the open market prior to maturity. The same is also true in reverse. If you are getting 6 percent on a bond and current interest rates are at 4 percent, someone would be willing to pay you more than the maturity value for your bond in the open market to get a higher-than-market interest payment.

---

27   The value of debt securities may fall when interest rates rise. Debt securities with longer maturities tend to be more sensitive to changes in interest rates, usually making them more volatile than debt securities with shorter maturities. For all bonds there is a risk that the issuer will default. High-yield bonds generally are more vulnerable to the risk of default than higher rated bonds.

Some fixed income securities have specific tax advantages. For example, municipal bonds issued by local governments tend to provide income that is not taxed at the federal level and often at the *state* level for residents of the issuing state.[28] Of course, if a bond is tax free, the interest payment will tend to be lower, so whether taxable or tax-free bonds make sense for you will depend on your income tax bracket and the prevailing interest rates at the time. You will want to avoid owning tax-free bonds of any kind in a qualified retirement account or IRA, since those accounts offer tax deferral already and you generally won't get any additional benefit from the tax-favored nature of the bonds.

Another factor in determining the volatility and income and growth potential of fixed income is the credit quality. Highly rated bonds (those rated AA and AAA, by Standard & Poor's) pay the lowest interest rates because they carry the least amount of default risk (defined as the issuers' inability to continue making interest payments or to return the principal at maturity). On the other hand, so-called junk bonds are high yield instruments because their risk of default is much higher, and therefore the interest payment and overall anticipated return must be greater to induce investors to buy them.

Think of it in the same light as two potential car buyers walking into a dealership. If you walk in with a high credit score, your risk of default is low and you'll get a much better interest rate on a car loan than if your credit score is low and you have a history of defaults. With a low credit score, you will pay a higher interest rate for the same car loan *if* you can qualify for the loan at all.

Generally, the longer the term a bond carries, the higher the rate of interest will be on the bond. This is not always true but it is common. That is because to induce investors to tie up their principal for a longer time, they need to be offered a higher rate of interest. It is not much different than a five-year CD at the bank paying more than a six-month CD.[29] Same premise. In addition, the longer the term that a bond has remaining until

---

28 A substantial portion of income will be exempt from federal income tax, but income may be subject to local or state income taxes and the federal alternative minimum tax (AMT). Capital gains, if any, will be taxable.

29 Bank certificates of deposit are FDIC insured up to applicable limits and offer a fixed rate of return.

its maturity date, generally the more volatile the market price will be in the secondary bond market.

Some bonds are issued by US corporations or governments and some are issued by foreign corporations or governments. While international bonds carry additional potential risks due to currency fluctuation against the dollar or potentially less predictable political or legislative climates, they can also create a nice currency hedge and an excellent diversifier for a portfolio. Bonds issued in developed world countries will behave differently than emerging market debt and one or both might be worth considering when constructing your portfolio.

When interest rates are very low, investors tend to favor short-term fixed income instruments over long-term ones. This is because you don't want to lock in a low rate of income for a long period of time. So rational investors choose to give up some yield in the short term to avoid giving up potentially more significant yield in the long term.

Note that buying individual bonds and buying bond mutual funds or exchange-traded funds are not the same and they should be treated differently.[30] In a large bond portfolio (say $500,000 or more), it may make sense to use individual bonds so that some control can be maintained in terms of credit quality, issuer and industry diversification, and length of time to maturity. You can use individual bonds to match up your income needs with the yield of each bond (or the portfolio as a whole). If you plan to hold bonds until they mature, you may not care as much about the market value of each bond.

On the other hand, with bond funds, you are allowing a manager to allocate into a diverse portfolio. You lose the ability to match up your income and time horizon directly to the holdings in the fund, and at some point, taking income may mean selling shares of the fund. As a result, the market price of the fund itself can become very important to you.

---

30   Mutual funds are sold only by prospectus. Please consider the charges, risks, expenses, and investment objectives carefully before investing. A prospectus containing this and other information about the investment company can be obtained from your financial professional. Read it carefully before you invest or send money.

In a rising interest rate environment, I tend to shy away from traditional bond funds, simply because the fund managers will be forced to sell underlying bonds at an adverse time if investors choose to sell the fund emotionally during a price decline. To try to protect ourselves and our clients from the behavioral risk of *other* investors, we favor exchange-traded bond funds with finite lifespans and set maturity dates. We can hold them until maturity before reinvesting and can gain liquidity annually by using a ladder of funds with staggered maturities. We also avoid suffering portfolio damage due to the stampede of the masses at exactly the wrong time because these funds cannot be held in most 401(k) plans due to their finite lifespans.

Whether you should be holding 0 percent of your portfolio in fixed income or 100 percent (or more than likely, somewhere in between) is beyond the scope of this book and starts to get into specific advice. However, you can utilize your financial advisor or various online resources to turn your risk tolerance profile into a suitable portfolio for your family.

Equities

When someone asks you in passing, "What did the market do today?" in the US, they typically mean the stock market. Oddly enough, the market index most closely followed by the news media and the public is the Dow Jones Industrial Average (DJIA), which comprises only 30 stocks.[31] In a world with some 15,000-plus public companies, to American investors "the market" is only 30 of them!

In fairness, the Dow is designed to be a placeholder of sorts for the overall US equity markets, but there are plenty of days when the S&P 500, the NASDAQ, the Wilshire, the Russell, and/or other indices move in different directions than the DJIA.[32] Also, their volatility and index movements can vary widely from day to day.

A typical mutual fund portfolio may have thousands of underlying securities built in it, including shares of stock in public companies, fixed

---

31 The Dow Jones Industrial Average is a popular indicator of the stock market based on the average closing prices of 30 active US stocks representative of the overall economy. You cannot directly invest in the index.

32 NASDAQ Composite Index measures all NASDAQ domestic and international based common type stocks listed on the NASDAQ Stock Market. Today, the NASDAQ Composite includes approximately 5,000 stocks, more than any other stock market indices. Because it is so broad-based, the Composite is one of the most widely followed and quoted major market indices.

income securities, cash, and alternative investments. So while the DJIA's closing level every afternoon makes for interesting trivia, it does not represent the overall outcome of a typical portfolio. The only portfolio the DJIA would mirror is the portfolio that owned only those 30 stocks and nothing else. In other words, it is interesting but not terribly important except as it relates to the American investors' psyche.

As in the universe of fixed income securities, there are lots of different kinds of equity investments and they can be sorted in many ways as well. The most common ways to sort them are as follows:

- By size of company (from smallest to largest: nanocap, microcap, small-cap, midcap, large-cap, and megacap)
- By investment style (growth stocks vs. value stocks)
- By country of domicile
- By sector or industry (technology, healthcare, financial services, etc.)

As believers in passive management not tied to an index, our firm tends to advocate for holding funds of various types that approximate the sum of the global markets in equities. Up to 50 percent of our equity holdings may be in non-US companies—including holdings in developed nations and emerging markets.

In 1992, Nobel laureates Eugene Fama and Kenneth French developed the Fama-French three-factor model to describe stock returns. The model added risk factors related to size and value to market risk factors and determined evidence of outperformance.

Specifically, Fama-French suggests that over time, small companies will tend to outperform larger ones. This makes some sense because smaller companies have more *room* to grow. However, since small company stocks carry more risk than more stable large company stocks, it is also important to make sure we own *lots* of them for diversification purposes. We may not get rich like the early investors in Microsoft, Google, or Apple but our portfolio also may not implode if we overweight the likes of WorldCom, Enron, or Lehman Brothers.

Fama-French also suggests that over time, value stocks will outperform growth stocks. This is logical because, by definition, a value stock is one that is presently trading below its intrinsic value. In other words, it is *on sale*. The stock market is a funny anomaly in the human condition, as it is one of the only places where people are afraid to buy something that is inexpensive.

Every November on Black Friday when Nordstrom has a sale, there could be a line around the building at four in the morning but when stocks are on sale, people instinctively think something is *wrong* with them. This isn't the damaged and defective clearance aisle; it is an opportunity to find quality companies trading at below-market values.

The bias toward small companies and value stocks is not a magic button or a "get rich quick" plan. It is simply a methodology informing our money managers what to overweight when buying and holding for the long term. Note that there are always time frames, even recently, when one or more factors fail to hold true.

Before we move on from the three traditional asset classes, I'd like to share some thoughts on portfolio rebalancing. Much ado is made over the ideal time and frequency to rebalance a portfolio. Some advisors suggest annual rebalancing, some quarterly, and some as often as necessary when style drift has occurred.

Rebalancing a portfolio means selling securities that have become over-weighted in favor of buying securities that have become underweighted in a portfolio.[33] In plain English, that means selling some of the winners and buying more of the losers in the portfolio. This is counterintuitive but also very important.

If you do not rebalance a portfolio during a bull market, your exposure to equities may become higher than your risk tolerance would support. Likewise, if you do not rebalance a portfolio during a bear market, your exposure to equities may become lower than your risk tolerance suggests and could impair your portfolio's ability to recover from a downturn.

There are several reasons to avoid rebalancing too frequently. First, every time you rebalance, additional trading costs can impact your portfolio adverse-ly. Second, in a non-qualified account, rebalancing before a full calendar year

---

33   Rebalancing assets can have tax consequences. If you sell assets in a taxable account, you may have to pay tax on any gain resulting from the sale. Please consult your tax advisor.

has passed can create short-term capital gains, which are taxed as ordinary income. Last, rebalancing too frequently can reduce the possibility of profiting from sustained momentum amongst the so-called winners in the portfolio.

I believe that in the absence of a major event (see also: September 2008), rebalancing every 13 months or so manages costs, reduces the possibility of adverse short-term capital gains taxes, and allows for some momentum throughout the year. Of course, there are other possible reasons to rebalance, including at the time of a large deposit into or withdrawal out of an account, in anticipation of changing capital gain tax rates legislatively, or to harvest losses (or in some cases, gains) prior to year-end for the timing of taxes due.

This section only scratches the surface on the traditional asset classes, but I hope it provides both a framework to get you started and a list of things to consider when building your portfolio.

To restate this simply, the three traditional asset classes are stocks, bonds, and cash. In a bundled investment solution or a fund of funds, which holds underlying mutual funds in a single fund wrapper, the portfolios are sometimes labeled to reflect the percentage exposure to equities versus the percentage exposure to fixed income and cash. For example, if you own a 60/40 portfolio, typically that means that you have 60 percent of your portfolio in stocks and 40 percent in bonds and cash.

Alternative investments[34]

As the name suggests, alternative investments are those investments *not included* in the category of traditional investments above. Alternative investments carry very different kinds of risk and return parameters than stocks, bonds, and cash and should only be used with complete understanding of the upside and downside of doing so.

---

34 Alternative investments, including hedge funds, real estate, and managed futures, involve a high degree of risk, often engage in leveraging and other speculative investment practices that may increase the risk of investment loss, can be highly illiquid, are not required to provide periodic pricing or valuation information to investors, may involve complex tax structures and delays in distributing important tax information, are not subject to the same regulatory requirements as mutual funds, often charge high fees which may offset any trading profits, and in many cases the underlying investments are not transparent and are known only to the investment manager. The performance of alternative investments, including hedge funds and managed futures, can be volatile. An investor could lose all or a substantial amount of his or her investment. These types of investments may not be suitable for all investors. Please consult with a financial or legal professional before investing in alternative investments.

Endowments at major universities and ultrahigh net-worth families ($25,000,000-plus) have been using alternative investments as a substantial portion of their portfolios for many years. However, only in the last 15 years or so have these investments become readily available to retail investors.

There are many types of alternative investments. Most investors will hold no more than a few of them at any given time. Some of the primary types are:

- Real Estate
- Private Debt/Business Development Companies
- Managed Futures Contracts
- Hedge Funds/Funds of Hedge Funds
- Oil and Gas Partnerships
- Private Equity/Venture Capital

Each of these categories contains details that vary widely from issuer to issuer, so I strongly encourage you to talk to your advisor about them and to read the prospectuses and other legal disclosures before adding any of these assets to your portfolio.

Real estate

For most investors, real estate investing is their first foray into the alternative investment world. This does not mean buying a townhouse, apartment building, or office building to rent and manage on your own. Unless you intend to start a real estate enterprise, including buying, selling, leasing, and managing the properties, owning just one or two rental properties is a good way to become underdiversified immediately.

Investing in real estate is typically done through a real estate investment trust (REIT)—which can be traded on an exchange or non-traded and owned privately—or through a mutual fund, exchange-traded fund, or interval fund that owns traded REITs.[35] These investments allow retail investors to participate in the commercial real estate market with a modest initial investment ($10,000 or so) instead of the high capital required in buying a building directly.

---

35 Investing in real estate entails certain risks, including changes in the economy, supply and demand, laws, tenant turnover, interest rates (including periods of high interest rates), availability of mortgage funds, operating expenses, and cost of insurance. Some real estate investments offer limited liquidity options.

To me, real estate is not something to own in any significant way in a mutual fund. The reason is that with a mutual fund, the redemption of shares must be on demand at the close of the market every day. Imagine a situation in which many shareholders decide to sell at the same time. Real estate holdings aren't like stocks that can be sold on an open market; we're talking about buildings that can take months or longer to sell.

To avoid having to sell properties in a hurry to accommodate fund redemptions that could be devastating in the real estate market, real estate funds often own liquid assets. As a result, traded real estate correlates very closely to equity indices so it may limit some of the diversification being sought by owning the fund in the first place.

Historically, in lieu of a liquid mutual fund, retail investors could choose to own non-traded REITs, which were bought directly from sponsors and held for seven to 10 years with limited or no liquidity. The ideal scenario was to receive dividends based on earnings in the trust (which were either reinvested, often at a discounted price, or taken in cash) and then to hold the shares until a liquidating event. That liquidating event was designed to be the sale of the whole trust or parts of it, the sale of underlying assets in the trust, or the initial public offering or listing on an exchange that made the trust liquid, at which time we would generally explore selling the shares for the reasons described above.

Naturally, some of the non-traded REITs performed well and had successful liquidity events, while others did not. This created a quandary for the investing community and for retail investors. Today, real estate is more often packaged in **interval funds**, which allow for limited liquidity at various intervals.[36] They aren't fully liquid like a mutual fund so they avoid some of the redemption issues discussed previously, but they also aren't fully illiquid like traditional non-traded REITs so they help investors balance income needs with liquidity needs. In most cases, they are also able to be held in managed investment accounts so they

---

36   Investors should carefully consider the investment objectives, risks, charges, and expenses of an interval fund. This and other important information about the fund is contained in a prospectus, which can be obtained by contacting your financial advisor. A prospectus should be read carefully before investing.

aren't subject to the inflexible commissionable structure of traditional non-traded REITs.

Interval funds typically limit the amount of liquidity in a given quarter to 5 percent or so of the outstanding shares. The good news is that this prevents a mass exodus, which could damage the fund's performance for remaining shareholders. The bad news is that in the event a shareholder requests a full redemption at the same time as lots of other shareholders, the amount able to be liquidated might be limited to less than the number of shares they wish to sell.

Real estate investments in any form can be broad in nature or sector specific. A core commercial real estate trust may hold office buildings, in-dustrial warehousing space, hotels, apartment complexes, retail space, and/or other types of commercial properties; whereas a sector-specific real es-tate trust might hold only healthcare buildings, hotels, office buildings, or some other limited category of properties.

One of the reasons that commercial real estate can be a good first en-try into alternative investments is familiarity—investors understand the underlying assets. In terms of desirability, much can be gleaned from the example of Enron. When Enron failed in the early 2000s, the once-rag-ing stock became worthless and the bonds defaulted. However, they kept paying their rent to the bitter end. The landlord got paid, even when some employees didn't.

That is the power of real estate—if a company doesn't pay its rent, the real estate property is collateral and can potentially be re-let or sold by the owner. For as long as a company is trying to avoid bankruptcy or to exit from a bankruptcy already declared, real estate payments are often one of the last things to default because most companies would literally cease to exist without their physical space if it was mission crit-ical, whether that space is a storefront, a warehouse, or a manufacturing plant.

As you might expect from our conversation on equities and fixed income, at our firm we generally suggest maintaining some real estate holdings in the US and some internationally, although we tend to stick to developed nations and to avoid emerging markets in this investment space, due in large part to political and legislative uncertainty.

Private debt/business development companies

Another alternative asset class that has largely adopted an interval fund model is private debt funds in the form of Business Development Companies (BDCs).[37]

While buying corporate bonds is lending money to a public company, BDCs loan funds to small or midsize privately owned companies in the US that are not traded on any exchange. The funds are regulated by the Investment Company Act of 1940 and usually get 1099 income-tax treatment, making them more like a REIT than a limited partnership or other more complex structure.

Bonds normally have fixed coupons attached to them. The buyer agrees to lend money to a public company for a stated interest rate for a set number of years. Held to maturity, that can be a fine income strategy. However, in a rising interest rate environment, as we discussed above, bond prices tend to fall as interest rates rise. With a BDC, the loans are made at variable rates, designed to participate in rising interest rates rather than being hurt by them.

When we talked about mortgages during your freshman year, we espoused the virtues of *borrowing* at fixed rates when rates are rising. With a BDC, you take advantage of *lending* at variable rates when rates are rising.

Like real estate interval funds, most BDCs have low minimums for initial investment and offer simplified income tax treatment, making them viable alternative holdings for appropriate investors. In my opinion, BDCs can offer additional diversification and portfolio upside for those investors willing to accept some limited liquidity, particularly in a flat or rising interest rate environment.

---

37 As is the case with any investment type, investors considering investing in a Business Development Company should understand how they work and if their unique qualities align with their investment objectives and tolerance for risk.

Managed futures contracts[38]

Futures contracts are, by themselves, one of the most aggressive asset classes considered for most portfolios. That is because they are literal contracts to accept delivery or to make delivery of physical commodities (natural resources, precious metals, financial contracts, or agricultural crops, for example) or they bet on the future movement of various indices, equity markets, or interest rates.

The technical reason that we would consider such an aggressive asset class for a portfolio is that the correlation coefficient is small or slightly negative for most other asset classes we hold. In plain English, that means that returns on managed futures contracts do not behave like any other asset class and therefore can create less volatility in a portfolio, even though, by itself, it is a volatile asset. It is not uncommon to see large swings in managed futures valuations from one month to another, so it is important if you own them that you can tolerate those price movements and they are a small enough portion of the portfolio that a terrible quarter or year in this asset class may not damage the overall portfolio returns too severely.

In 2008, managed futures were a saving grace for many portfolios, posting positive returns when nearly every other asset class was dropping precipitously.[39] However, they have also had long stretches of time when they held down the overall portfolio returns with subpar results. As our firm does not try to time markets, we do not flit in and out of this or any asset class and we take the good with the bad. As such, we do maintain this asset class in some portfolios as a small position.

---

38   Trading security futures contracts involves risk and may result in potentially unlimited losses that are greater than the amount you deposited with your broker. Because of the leverage involved and the nature of security futures contract transactions, you may feel the effects of your losses immediately. Under certain market conditions, it may be difficult or impossible to liquidate a position. Under certain market conditions, it may also be difficult or impossible to manage your risk from open security futures positions by entering into an equivalent but opposite position in another contract month, on another market, or in the underlying security. You may be required to settle certain security futures contracts with physical delivery of the underlying security. All security futures contracts involve risk, and there is no trading strategy that can eliminate it. You should thoroughly read and understand the customer account agreement with your brokerage firm before entering into any transactions in security futures contracts.

39   One widely known index used to track returns on managed futures contracts is the Barclay CTA (Commodity Trading Advisor) Index. The Barclay CTA posted a 14.09% gain in 2008. You cannot invest directly in an index.

Managed futures can be owned as mutual funds or as direct investments with asset managers. Most of these funds have daily or monthly liquidity so the risk of being stuck in a long-term investment without access to capital in these positions is limited.

Hedge funds/funds of hedge funds[40]

Very few investment vehicles cause as much public outcry as hedge funds. Compared to most investment vehicles, they are loosely regulated and afforded some very favorable tax treatment, much to the chagrin of the public.

In some ways, **hedge funds** are black boxes. Some lack transparency and reporting; therefore, their results may vary wildly from time to time and from fund to fund. They are also very expensive, with fund managers charging up to 2 percent per year as a base asset management fee *plus* up to 20 percent of the fund's annual gains in many cases.

Technically, hedge funds are not an asset class but are an *access* class, providing access to alternative investment exposure. As the hedge can be broadly defined, each of these investment instruments is somewhat unique and carries some risks unique to the fund and its holdings. The risk is extremely high and these investments are not appropriate for everyone; they are for savvy investors looking for additional potential upside and willing to take on the risk of complete default, as single-manager hedge funds do blow up from time to time.

40 Alternative investments, including hedged funds and managed futures, involve a high degree of risk, often engage in leveraging and other speculative investment practices that may increase the risk of investment loss, can be highly illiquid, are not required to provide periodic pricing or valuation information to investors, may involve complex tax structures and delays in distributing important tax information, are not subject to the same regulatory requirements as mutual funds, often charge high fees which may offset any trading profits, and in many cases the underlying investments are not transparent and are known only to the investment manager. The performance of alternative investments, including hedge funds and managed futures, can be volatile. An investor could lose all or a substantial amount of his or her investment. Often, hedge fund or managed futures account managers have total trading authority over their funds or accounts; the use of a single advisor applying generally similar trading programs could mean lack of diversification and consequently higher risk. There is often no secondary market for an investor's interest in alternative investments, including hedge funds and managed futures, and none is expected to develop. There may be restrictions on transferring interests in any alternative investment. Alternative investment products, including hedge funds and managed futures, often execute a substantial portion of their trades on non-US exchanges. Investing in foreign markets may entail risks that differ from those associated with investments in US markets. Additionally, alternative investments, including hedge funds and managed futures, often entail commodity trading, which involves substantial risk of loss.

For those reasons, some investors prefer to use **funds of hedge funds**, which allow access to up to 30 or 40 hedge funds within a single investment vehicle. In other words, rather than sending $100,000 to a single hedge fund manager, you can use a pooled investment for that same $100,000 and can send what amounts to $2,500 to each of 40 hedge fund managers.

These funds of funds give an investor the potential upside without the need for precision in terms of selecting which hedge fund will outperform the pack. It also allows investors to weather the storm if one or more of the underlying hedge funds blow up entirely.

In most cases, due to the cost, complexity, and lack of transparency in these investments, we do not recommend that our clients hold them, unless a compelling case for a specific investor can be made.

Oil and gas partnerships

There are very few asset classes that I simply am too uncomfortable to own and an oil and gas partnership is one of them. These partnerships aim to profit either from working interests in oil or natural gas or from exploration to try to find new sources of oil or natural gas.

These partnerships qualify for some of the most favorable tax treatment of any investment vehicle. However, the problem I have with these partnerships isn't the income stream, the process of drilling, the politics, or any of the mechanics of the operation; the problem is the extreme liability assumed by each shareholder.

To be a shareholder and to get what is a very sizable income tax deduction up front, each investor must be willing to be a *general* partner for some time prior to becoming a *limited* partner. While limited partners have liability only to the extent of their investment of capital, general partners have *unlimited liability* in the event of a lawsuit.

For example, if the fracking process for natural gas or the drilling process for oil goes wrong and creates contamination of an area, impacting people or wildlife, the lawsuit that follows can name each general partner. Further, each one can lose *everything they own* if the suit is settled or resolved in favor of the plaintiffs over the partnership's liability insurance coverage.

I looked at several of these partnerships as a financial advisor and as a possible personal investor—who wouldn't want a big tax break? However, after my personal due diligence, I couldn't get comfortable enough to own these partnership interests, which means I'm not comfortable enough to encourage my clients to own these partnership interests, unless a compelling case for a specific investor can be made.

I perceive the downside risk of principal loss and the legal risk as a general partner to be too great and will continue to avoid it and to advise our firm's clients to do the same. If you elect to participate, do so with extreme caution.

Private equity/venture capital[41]

The last of the alternative investments is perhaps the most exciting but access to some of the programs can be limited in some cases to only the wealthiest potential buyers. Private equity and venture capital funds are designed to help start-up and privately-owned companies grow, and while the downside of starting new ventures is significant, the upside for investors who help fund growth in private companies can be huge.

The upside generally includes deal sweeteners like warrants (derivative securities that provide an investor the right to purchase securities from the issuer at a specific price within a certain time frame) or an outright equity stake in the private companies such that when one of them makes it big, the investors do extremely well.

Private equity funds are very illiquid and can require a significant contribution of capital. A minimum initial investment is often at least $50,000 and can be as high as $1,000,000 or more. Also, many of these funds only allow investors who meet certain financial criteria to participate, which often include a very high liquid net worth, a very high income, or some combination of both.

For the right families, these investments can create significant windfalls if the risk is properly offset by the fund managers' selection of investment opportunities but private equity and venture capital funds are certainly not for everyone.

---

41   Investing in private equity entails certain risks, including, but not limited to, market, economic, or industry conditions; bankruptcy of underlying companies; higher fees which may offset trading profits; and lack of liquidity. An investor could lose all or a substantial amount of his or her investment. It is important for investors to assess the risks and returns specific to the investment strategy.

Summarizing alternative investments

I have a few final thoughts on alternative investments in general. While an endowment is designed to be perpetual, a household is not, so only modest use of alternatives is indicated for most families. Many alternative investments are illiquid and cannot be readily sold, which means they must be used sparingly enough to avoid a situation where an investor gets into a cash crunch and can't get capital from his or her portfolio. In your specific situation, you will need to analyze and understand the various risks and uses for alternatives and to make sure you have a clear understanding of what you are buying before you do so.

To close this course on portfolio construction, if you are just getting started with investing, you will likely be investing in some pooled investment vehicle like a mutual fund or exchange-traded fund (ETF).[42] These vehicles offer significant diversification with reasonable expenses. In other words, it would be tough to buy lots of individual stocks or bonds each year with a few thousand dollars, but in a mutual fund or ETF, a few thousand dollars a year could buy you very small positions in a very large number of different stocks, bonds, or other assets.

When investing, you always need to consider your risk tolerance, your objectives, various expenses involved, and the types of asset classes appropriate for you. You may want to utilize a financial or tax advisor (or both) to assist in your selection and monitoring of your portfolio.

Congratulations on completing your sophomore year. I believe that the sophomore year is the toughest year, not only of college but of this curriculum as well. You're still knocking out some of the basics, which requires heavy lifting and dense information. You'll continue to gain focus in your junior year.

---

42 Investors should consider carefully information contained in the prospectus, including investment objectives, risks, charges, and expenses. Please read the prospectus carefully before investing. ETFs do not sell individual shares directly to investors and only issue their shares in large blocks. Exchanged-traded funds are subject to risks similar to those of stocks. Investment returns will fluctuate and are subject to market volatility so that an investor's shares, when redeemed or sold, may be worth more or less than the original cost.

POST-COURSE EXERCISE QUESTIONS

1. **TRUE** or **FALSE**: The four primary asset classes to consider in a portfolio are stocks, real estate, cash, and hedge funds.

2. **TRUE** or **FALSE**: The Standard & Poor's 500 Index (S&P 500) comprises the 500 largest companies in the world.

3. **TRUE** or **FALSE**: Bond prices tend to increase when interest rates rise.

4. **TRUE** or **FALSE**: Not all available asset classes are appropriate for every investor.

5. **TRUE** or **FALSE**: It is important to rebalance a well-managed portfolio at least quarterly.

POST-COURSE EXERCISE ANSWERS

1. **FALSE.** The four main asset classes to consider in a portfolio are stocks, bonds, cash, and alternative investments. Real estate and hedge funds are types of alternative investments but are not primary asset classes to consider.

2. **FALSE.** The S&P 500 is an unmanaged index of 500 widely held stocks that is generally considered representative of the US stock market. There are no international stocks in the index.

3. **FALSE.** In general, bond prices have an inverse relationship to interest rates. When interest rates rise, existing bonds tend to see their values fall, and when interest rates fall, existing bonds tend to see their values rise.

4. **TRUE.** All investors are different in terms of goals, ages, time frames, risk tolerances, and so many factors unique to each situation. Some asset classes can be appropriate for one investor but not for another, which is why it is so important for your financial advisor to understand the intricacies of your financial picture.

5. **FALSE.** While rebalancing is an important step in maintaining a well-managed and balanced portfolio, in general, annual rebalancing is sufficient. Rebalancing more frequently than once a year can have adverse consequences, including higher transaction expenses, the possibility of incurring short-term capital gains and paying higher taxes, and the loss of any potential momentum being enjoyed by one or more asset classes in the portfolio.

EXTRA-CREDIT ASSIGNMENT

Your final extra-credit assignment for your sophomore year is to analyze your existing portfolio holdings. Of the asset classes described in this course, determine which ones you own presently and what percentage of your portfolio is in each asset class. Once you have taken this portfolio inventory, consider meeting with a financial advisor to determine if your current allocation is appropriate for you or if you could benefit from adding or eliminating asset classes or holding a different allocation.

Junior Year:
Gaining Influence & Acumen

FIRST SEMESTER

In your junior year of college, it's time to hit your stride—knocking out courses toward your double major and gaining confidence as you move closer to graduation. You have found your academic passions, identified and become fully engaged in your extracurricular activities, and found your group of lifelong friends. Ideally, you have started to build a compelling résumé and lined up a professional internship to get some job experience.

In planning to graduate into retirement, these are the years between ages 45–55 or so. For many professionals, these are the highest earning years and the highest income tax years.

For many families, they are also some of the most expensive, as we reach the "sandwich" years. We are often paying bills for or otherwise assisting our children as they prepare for college as well as our parents who are getting older and may not have the financial resources they need or the physical ability to care for themselves.

In general, life expectancy is growing and the population of the US is aging, with more and more people celebrating their 100th birthdays every year. That leads to more pressure on retirement assets and the possibility of more intrafamily support—financially and otherwise—than ever before.

Your world has never been busier personally or professionally than it is during this phase of your life. Let's get you ready for the decisions that need to be made.

Course Schedule for Junior Year—First Semester:

- Financial Independence 301: Maximizing Your Peak Earning Years
- Risk Management & Protection 201: Defense against the Dark Arts (of Aging)

Financial Independence 301:

MAXIMIZING YOUR PEAK EARNING YEARS

During the junior year of your financial life, you will be able to afford to save and invest more than ever before—and will want to take advantage of every tax deduction you can find. At this stage, you should be free of adverse debt. Your student loans are gone, your credit cards are paid in full, and your only loan payments should be for mortgages on your primary home and possibly on a vacation home if you have decided to take that leap.

Your retirement illustration can now give you a clearer picture of how close to your pre-retirement income you can get once you leave the full-time workplace at some point. Your plan can also calculate an **ideal** target to be able to replace 100 percent of your pre-retirement income (net of savings but before taxes) at some future date. That target becomes your **number** to reach financial independence—that coveted moment when work is forever optional.

Retirement plans and IRAs

Now is the time for both spouses in a household to be making maximum contributions to tax-deductible retirement accounts. In the year in which you celebrate your 50th birthday, you'll have the ability to make **catch-up**

contributions to qualified retirement plans and IRA accounts. It seems that this tax provision gained the name "catch-up" under the presumption that those reaching age 50 are somehow *behind* on reaching their retirement targets. Hopefully, that won't be your situation. You'll want to use the catch-up for additional tax deferral from your highest income tax years to some lower tax years in the future.

If you are employed and have access to a 401(k), a 403(b), or other types of qualified retirement plans, your contribution limit jumps from $19,500 (the limit for everyone as of 2020) to $26,000 (due to the $6,500 catch-up provision at age 50). You'll need to be specific with your HR department, benefits coordinator, plan administrator, or on the plan's website that you want to take advantage of the catch-up; it won't happen automatically.

In addition to your contributions to an employer-sponsored retirement plan, many plans also provide for employer contributions on behalf of employees and these take different forms. In some cases, an employer may agree to make a **matching contribution**. A matching contribution is made on behalf of employees if, and only if, they make contributions of their own money via payroll deduction. An employer match can be made dollar for dollar or on a percentage basis and is usually capped at a set level.

One common example of an employer's matching plan would be that the employer contributes $0.50 for every dollar that an employee contributes, up to 6 percent of an employee's salary. In this case, if the employee contributes 6 percent of salary, his or her employer will contribute 3 percent on the employee's behalf. Therefore, if your employer offers a match and you have to contribute a certain amount of your salary to receive it, do it! This is essentially a tax-deferred raise and as close to "free money" as exists.

Another less common way for employers to contribute to employee retirement accounts is in the form of a profit-sharing contribution. In this case, the **profit-sharing contribution** is unrelated to any company profits and is seldom guaranteed. However, if the employer wants to contribute for *any* employees, there are actuarial tests and guidelines that force that employer to make contributions to *all* employees to a certain level.

You'll find all of the rules of your employer's retirement plan in a document called the summary plan description (SPD), which outlines the rules for contributions, withdrawals, and, importantly, the vesting schedule. Many plans have vesting schedules under which an employee may forfeit some or all of an employer's contributions on their behalf if they do not stay employed at the company for some period of years.

There are many variations of matches, vesting schedules, profit-sharing contributions, and other details that are beyond the scope of this course. If you want to know more about your plan, check the SPD.

In the scenario described previously, a married couple over 50 with two employer plans could save $52,000 on a tax-deductible basis each year—not including any matching or profit-sharing contributions made by the employer. At a hypothetical combined federal and state income tax rate of 35 percent, that means reducing your income tax bill by $18,200 each year.

If one spouse is not employed outside the home or one or both spouses work for a company without an employer-sponsored retirement plan, you may be able to contribute to an IRA, possibly on a tax-deductible basis, depending on your combined income. The rules are complicated but your financial advisor and CPA should be able to help you navigate them. As of 2020, the IRA contribution limit is $6,000 per individual, with an additional catch-up amount of $1,000 for people who have reached age 50.

Retirement accounts for self-employed individuals and small business owners

Retirement and tax planning strategies are abundant for small business owners and self-employed individuals, especially those with no employees. The IRS allows business owners of any age to contribute up to 25 percent of their earned income to a Simplified Employee Pension (referred to as a SEP IRA), with a total limit of $57,000 as of 2020. There is no catch-up provision at any age on these plans. The caveat for business owners with employees is that whatever percentage of income is contributed for the employer must also be contributed for all eligible employees, which makes these plans less attractive and effective depending on the number of employees and total payroll.

Instead of a SEP IRA, small business owners can also establish various types of qualified retirement plans. These plans are complicated and well beyond the scope of this course. However, if you are a highly compensated business owner, it will be worth checking with your financial advisor and a third-party administrator (TPA) to determine which type of plan would allow you to make the largest tax-deductible contributions to your own account.

Qualified plans require IRS approval and annual non-discrimination and payroll testing, and the business owner must file tax returns and various plan documents so the costs to establish and maintain them can be high. But structured properly, the tax advantages can outweigh the costs and lots of creativity in plan design is allowable by law.

The plans range from profit-sharing plans to defined benefit plans, which can be especially attractive to older business owners with either no employees or a small number of employees who are significantly younger.

We're going to leave this topic after barely scratching the surface but as you move toward your graduation into retirement, if your "second act" might be consulting or business ownership, lots of planning opportunities may exist for you to consider.

Roth IRAs

We have already discussed the tax planning around 529 College Savings Plans, HSAs, traditional IRAs, qualified retirement plans, and whole life insurance at length. In these years, if you are eligible to do so, you may also want to be funding backdoor Roth IRAs in addition to your tax-deductible retirement account contributions, just to stash away additional money beyond the reach of the tax collectors legally.

As you will recall, contributions to traditional IRAs and qualified retirement plans are usually tax deductible when they are made and withdrawals are taxed as ordinary income in the year received. Roth IRAs have just the opposite income tax treatment; contributions made are not tax deductible, but the account can grow tax free and there is no tax collected when it is withdrawn so long as the plan rules are followed.

Roth IRAs are ideal for people whose tax rate is likely to be higher at retirement than it is currently, especially young workers or those who are earning less. They're also great for people who want to reduce their taxes in retirement or want to leave some money to their heirs tax free. The main advantages involve flexibility, income tax planning, savings during retirement, and the backdoor Roth IRA.

Flexibility

In general, you can make withdrawals at any time, although to avoid taxes or penalties you need to hold the money in the Roth IRA for at least five years and be age 59½ or older before you take a withdrawal. As you might expect, there are several other exceptions so talk with your financial or tax advisor or check the IRS' website at irs.gov/retirement-plans/roth-iras.

Income tax planning

Unlike traditional IRAs and qualified retirement plans (under most circumstances), which have required minimum distributions (RMDs) commencing in the year after the account holder turns age 72, Roth IRAs do not have RMDs or require any withdrawals during the account holder's lifetime. The Roth IRA balance can continue to grow for an unlimited length of time during the account holder's lifetime. This makes the Roth IRA especially useful because it can be inherited without any income taxes accruing to the heirs. With a few minor exceptions, as a result of the SECURE Act that passed in 2020, non-spousal beneficiaries are now required to distribute their entire inherited IRA or Roth IRA within 10 years of the original account holder's death.

Savings during retirement

Unlike traditional IRA contributions, which are not allowable after age 72, Roth IRA contributions are allowable at any age for working people (within certain income limits). Contributions to a Roth IRA are made from W-2 income so if you continue to work in some capacity beyond age 72, they make a great savings vehicle for later life.

Both spouses in a marriage can contribute to a Roth IRA in the same year. As of 2020, the annual contribution limit is $6,000 for people under age 50 and $7,000 for people in the year of their 50th birthday and beyond. You can put money away and never pay taxes on it again during your lifetime if you do it right.

With these tax advantages, everyone should just open a Roth IRA, right? Unfortunately, it's not quite that easy. There are phaseouts and income limitations on who can contribute, which may make you ineligible. But there is a way around that for some higher earning taxpayers.

The backdoor Roth IRA

While you may not qualify to make a direct contribution to a Roth IRA, it is possible to convert a traditional IRA to a Roth IRA at any age.[43] And in most cases, people with earned income or spouses with earned income are also allowed to make **non-deductible** contributions to traditional IRA accounts, providing a way around the income limitation. This means that you can contribute to a traditional IRA but forego the usual immediate tax deduction.

Distributions from a Roth IRA are not treated the same as distributions of non-deductible contributions from traditional IRAs. In a traditional IRA, non-deductible contributions create basis in the IRA, which must be declared on Form 8606 when filing federal income tax returns in the year of the contribution and thereafter so long as basis exists in the account. That basis can be withdrawn income tax free from the IRA at retirement, but the **earnings** on the non-deductible contributions are **not** withdrawn income tax free.

The non-deductible contribution made to a traditional IRA account can be returned free of tax but the contributions grow tax deferred, not tax free. In addition, withdrawals from IRAs are made pro-rata so that if the basis in a traditional IRA represents 2 percent of the account value, all withdrawals will be 98 percent taxable and 2 percent tax free at retirement (you cannot identify and withdraw the tax-free money only).

Enter the backdoor Roth IRA. The way to use this backdoor is to make the non-deductible contribution to a traditional IRA, then immediately convert that to a Roth IRA, such that the full value of the contribution **and any growth** is nontaxable upon withdrawal. When you make this conversion, you declare it on the same Form 8606 with the IRS so you don't face double income taxation.

This backdoor Roth IRA can be an incredibly powerful tool but to take full advantage of the strategy, it requires account holders to have little or no

---

43 Converting a traditional IRA to a Roth IRA is a taxable event and could result in additional impacts to your personal tax situation, including the taxation of current social security benefit payments. Be sure to consult with a qualified tax advisor before making any decisions regarding your IRA. It is generally preferable that funds are available to pay the taxes due upon conversion from funds outside of your IRA. If you elect to take a distribution from your IRA to pay the conversion taxes, please keep in mind the potential consequences, such as an assessment of product surrender charges or additional Internal Revenue Service penalties for premature distributions.

money in traditional IRAs when the strategy is deployed. That is because when the IRA is converted, taxes would be due on all but the account's basis.

If you have a small traditional IRA, you'll pay income taxes on the taxable portion when you convert but the full non-deductible basis will enter the Roth tax free. If you have a larger traditional IRA, you can still take advantage of the backdoor Roth IRA if you are part of a 401(k) or 403(b) plan, which will accept rollover contributions. To do this, you can roll the money from your traditional IRA into your 401(k) or 403(b). That will mean you no longer have a traditional IRA and you may then qualify for the backdoor Roth IRA.

These rules are very complicated, and you may want to check with your financial and tax advisors to ensure you make contributions, rollovers, and conversions properly to reduce future taxes and avoid current ones.

The good news is that the IRS is aware of this loophole for creating backdoor Roth IRAs and has affirmed that they are an acceptable form of retirement and tax planning. It was initially an unintended consequence of legislation but the loophole doesn't appear to be under any type of IRS scrutiny or challenge.

A bit more on Roth IRA history: In 2010, the federal government wanted to raise revenue. It thus allowed traditional IRAs to be converted into Roth IRAs with the taxable income being split equally between the 2010 and 2011 income tax returns. My wife and I elected to convert our entire traditional IRAs to Roth IRAs in 2010 and we paid significant taxes in 2010 and 2011 to do so. However, since that time, our accounts have grown without taxes, the future withdrawals will be fully income tax free, and we've been able to take advantage of the backdoor Roth IRA strategy.

While you can no longer split the income taxes of a conversion over two tax years, you can do partial conversions rather than full ones to time the recognition of taxable income. If you have an abnormally low income one year—either due to a job loss, pay reduction, or a large ordinary tax loss of some kind—you may want to consider partial or full Roth IRA conversions at that time to pay income taxes at the lowest possible bracket and to allow future growth to be untaxed.

Specifically, if you leave full-time work prior to age 72, it may make sense to do partial Roth IRA conversions in each year prior to the commencement of the RMD requirements, especially if you also elect to delay receipt of your social security retirement income.

In this way, your highest earning years may actually be followed by a short time period that includes your lowest earning years and is an ideal time to pay taxes on some of your traditional IRA funds. In other words, take the tax deduction when you're in a high tax bracket, grow the funds tax deferred, and then pay the taxes due on the funds when you're in a lower tax bracket. That is tax arbitrage at its finest and is perfectly legal.

Before we leave the subject of Roth IRAs, your qualified retirement plan might allow for Roth 401(k) contributions with after-tax dollars. This is generally only a good idea in your very early working years when you're in a low income-tax bracket and have many years to grow the funds before taking withdrawals in retirement.

As an employee participant in the plan, you can choose to put 100 percent of your contribution to the 401(k) or 100 percent of your contribution into the Roth 401(k). You can also split your contributions into some of each type of account, equally or unequally, if it makes reasonable tax sense for you to do so.

Employer matching or profit-sharing contributions can never be made into a Roth 401(k). If you contribute to a Roth 401(k), however, your employer's contribution would still be made into a traditional 401(k) on your behalf and you would have both types of accounts simultaneously.

POST-COURSE EXERCISE QUESTIONS

1. **TRUE** or **FALSE**: Qualified retirement plan contribution limits are increased for investors who have reached the age of 50.

2. **TRUE** or **FALSE**: It is impossible to fund a qualified retirement plan and a Roth IRA in the same tax year.

3. **TRUE** or **FALSE**: It is possible to fund a 401(k) and a Roth 401(k) in the same tax year.

4. **TRUE** or **FALSE**: Contributions to a Roth IRA are always tax deductible because they are made with pre-tax dollars.

5. **TRUE** or **FALSE**: For self-employed individuals, some retirement plan options offer even larger contribution limits than an employer's 401(k) plan.

POST-COURSE EXERCISE ANSWERS

1. **TRUE.** There are so-called catch-up provisions in the tax code that allow people to make larger contributions to various plans or accounts when they reach specific ages. One such catch-up example is that qualified retirement plan contribution limits increase in the year in which a participant turns age 50.

2. **FALSE.** There are several situations in which a taxpayer can fund a qualified retirement plan and a Roth IRA in the same tax year, including the use of the backdoor Roth IRA strategy.

3. **TRUE.** If a plan's Summary Plan Description allows for a Roth 401(k) provision, employee contributions can be made to the pre-tax traditional 401(k) or the post-tax Roth 401(k), or they can be split and an employee can contribute funds to both. In addition, all employer contributions to employee plans are made to the traditional 401(k), even if the employee is only contributing to the Roth 401(k).

4. **FALSE.** Contributions to Roth IRAs are always made with after-tax dollars, which do not create tax deductions.

5. **TRUE.** SEP IRAs allow self-employed individuals to make much larger contributions than employees in employer-sponsored plans. The SEP IRA contribution limit is $57,000 in 2020.

EXTRA-CREDIT ASSIGNMENT

If you are enrolled in your employer's qualified retirement plan, or you are eligible for but not yet enrolled in the plan, request a copy of the Summary Plan Description (SPD) and read it. If you have questions, ask your HR department or plan administrator to answer them or review the SPD with your financial advisor.

You may not be taking full advantage of your employer's plan provisions and may be leaving a potential tax-deferred raise on the table by doing so. Once you know the plan's rules, you can arrange to utilize the plan in an optimal way that helps you reach financial independence.

Risk Management & Protection 201:

DEFENSE AGAINST THE DARK ARTS (OF AGING)

It has been said that getting old is not for the faint of heart and I believe that to be 100 percent true. None of us can imagine ourselves in frail condition—even if we've watched our parents or grandparents struggle with age-related impairments—but what the future holds for any of us as we age is clearly unknown.

In this course, we'll expand on our discussion of risk management and prepare for some of life's contingencies related to getting older. We've already covered emergency funds and various types of insurance but we have not yet addressed planning for long-term care.

If you asked members of the public at random about these topics, you might get blank stares and you'd almost certainly get feedback that these topics are for very old people. Quite the contrary is true, which is why these courses are in the curriculum for the junior year. Some of these topics need to be addressed even earlier but for almost all adults, now is the absolute latest time you'd want to start on this planning.

Long-term care planning
It is hard to imagine what our lives might be like if we were unable to take

care of ourselves, either in our advanced years or due to an accident or illness. Long-term care is the least appealing of the risk management topics we're going to discuss.

One thing we need to get clear right away is that people often confuse long-term care planning with long-term care insurance (LTCI). While LTCI is one tool available for long-term care planning, it is not the only tool and isn't right for everyone.

We can pay for long-term care for ourselves or our loved ones in basically four ways:

1. Self-Insure
2. Traditional LTCI
3. Life Insurance-LTCI Hybrid
4. Annuity-LTCI Hybrid

Self-insuring for long-term care

There are two kinds of people who do not need LTCI: those who are so wealthy that a claim would be irrelevant to their financial security and those who are nearly Medicaid qualified and basically bankrupt.

To self-insure is quite simply to make the decision not to use an insurance option to offset or plan for long-term care. That decision is made by families who can't afford the care, refuse to buy it, or have enough resources not to need it financially. Sometimes that decision is made by an insurance company that refuses to offer coverage after completing underwriting on an individual or couple.

If you are wealthy enough that you could handle a $120,000 or so annual addition to your expenses (adjusting for the impact of inflation over time) without missing a beat, you do not *need* long-term care insurance. You might *want* to have LTCI as a wealth-preservation hedging strategy but you don't *need* it to preserve your financial wherewithal.

If you or a loved one is nearly penniless, the only option might be to rely on the government's safety net of last resort, Medicaid.

Don't confuse Medicaid with Medicare. Medicare is federal health insurance for individuals over age 65, and all working Americans pay premiums for Medicare throughout their earning years. Medicaid is for those senior citizens who have no financial resources in their later years. The facilities available and level of care provided by that type of program may not be what you would select for yourself or a loved one under ideal circumstances.

For the rest of the population, LTCI can be a defense against the financial nightmare of outliving our money and a key component to our risk management. There are several ways to place coverage in force.

Long-term care insurance

Most people mistakenly think of long-term care insurance as "elder care" insurance or "nursing home" coverage. You do not have to be elderly to have a claim nor do you have to be confined to a nursing home under most policies.

LTCI is *not* only for the elderly. A perfect example of that is Christopher Reeve, who played the lead role in the *Superman* movies in the 1970s and 1980s and, as an otherwise healthy adult, was paralyzed in an accident that caused him to spend his final years incapacitated.

LTCI is designed to cover some of the enormous costs involved in caring for an individual who is unable to perform activities of daily living, or ADLs. Generally, claims fall into two categories. One is cognitive (for someone who develops Alzheimer's disease or other impairment) and the other is physical (for someone frail or incapacitated).

To have a claim, usually an insured individual must be unable to perform two of the six ADLs as defined by the contract. These are typically listed as bathing, dressing, eating, transferring (from bed to chair or chair to bed), toileting, and continence.

LTCI is more affordable if you are young and healthy and gets much more expensive if you wait until you are older or less healthy to obtain it. However, in policies with premiums that are not guaranteed and can increase, there is also risk in obtaining the coverage at too young an age. With healthcare costs escalating, the premiums can become exorbitant unless the policy has some provision to be fully paid up at some specified future date.

The primary reasons why people do not buy LTCI (other than cost, if it is prohibitive) are that they believe their children will care for them, their health insurance or Medicare will cover them, or that they are going to die quickly and naturally and never need it. It is important to understand that medical insurance *does not* cover long-term care expenses and Medicare only provides a small benefit for up to 100 days and only for certain types of care.

Even with supportive children, people are not thinking about the realities of caring for a disabled person. It is one thing to have your kids stop by to bring you lunch or to help you pay your bills and another thing entirely to have them come to the house to give you a bath or to help you use the toilet. None of us wants to be in that condition but if we are, we certainly don't want to burden our children with our care. Besides, adult children generally have jobs and families of their own and they often live out of town.

Traditional long-term care insurance[44]

The least expensive form of LTCI is a traditional policy. The reason for the lower cost is two-fold: 1) The policies usually provide "use-it-or-lose-it" benefits and pay nothing to the insured or heirs if the coverage isn't exhausted, and 2) the premiums are not guaranteed and can be increased over time by the insurer.

The closest comparison to traditional LTCI in the insurance world is auto insurance. You don't buy auto insurance *hoping* to have an accident; you buy auto insurance *in case* you have one and the insurance company doesn't give your money back if you don't.

Traditional LTCI is designed to provide a daily or monthly benefit for a set period of years in the event of a claim. While it is too complex to go into all the details in this limited space, there are a few things to consider when exploring a traditional LTCI policy. Your financial advisor or insurance agent can help you decide what makes the most sense for you.

Monthly or daily benefits

Monthly benefits are preferable to daily ones when you file a claim because your use of medical services can vary widely day to day. Depend-

---

44 Long-term care insurance benefits may be subject to limitations, waiting periods, and other restrictions.

ing on where you live, a typical recommended monthly benefit may be $6,000 per month or more. The LTCI benefits do not need to insure against the entire cost of care in your area; they just need to provide enough of an offset to preserve your assets and quality of life, especially if you are married and don't want your cost of care to bankrupt your healthy spouse.

Other provisions

You will want to ask the following questions to better understand your policy.

Indemnity or reimbursement contracts

If the claims paid are less than the monthly benefit amount, what happens to the excess? An indemnity contract will pay you the full amount and a reimbursement contract will hold the excess and extend the benefit period of the policy.[45]

Joint policy discounts

Can a policy cover more than one individual? Discounts are available when two people apply for coverage together and share benefits.

Inflation protection

Does the benefit keep pace with rising healthcare costs? Inflation protection is crucial to this product, especially for people under 70–75 years old who obtain it.

Premiums *not* guaranteed

Will my premium go up in the future? Traditional LTCI premiums are usually *not* guaranteed. Some hybrid options (discussed next) offer premium certainty if structured properly.

Riders and endorsements

What options should I add to my coverage? Some of these policies offer lots of available bells and whistles and they are often a waste of money. Buy insurance only to pass risk you cannot bear and don't add extra cost unless there is some unique compelling reason to do so.

---

45   In a reimbursement contract, the monthly amount reimbursed is the cost of covered long-term care expenses actually incurred, which may be less than the monthly maximum benefit. The monthly maximum benefit may be pro-rated based on the actual number of days that the insured is chronically ill or confined to a facility.

Life insurance-LTCI hybrid[46]

One of the biggest aversions that people express about traditional LTCI is that the premium dollars are gone if the coverage isn't used (and most people believe they'll never use it). If you want to ensure that there is some benefit paid under a contract regardless of your future health or longevity, you can combine the benefits of a life insurance policy with the benefits of a long-term care insurance policy.

There are several differences between this type of hybrid and a traditional policy and other details you need to understand before you commit to paying premiums:

Cost of coverage

Because the insurance company is responsible for long-term care claims, a death benefit, or in some cases a combination of both, the cost of a life insurance-LTCI hybrid is substantially higher than a traditional LTCI policy.

Premium guarantees

Unlike the traditional LTCI policies, some (but not all) life insurance-LTCI hybrids have guaranteed premiums.

Paid-up policies

One of the primary benefits to these hybrid policies is that premiums can be paid in a single lump sum or over a finite time frame and then the policies are fully paid up.

For high income earners in their 40s or 50s, it can be cost effective and wise to use one of these contracts and to have all the premiums paid prior to the year of planned retirement.

Policy types

We have utilized two types of these policies for clients' families—one for married couples and one for unmarried people or widows.

For married couples, a survivorship whole life policy with an LTCI rider allows for relatively modest costs. The reason is that the life insurance policy pays nothing until the death of the *second* insured and only pays a death

---

46   Policy benefits may be reduced by any policy loans, withdrawals, terminal illness benefit, or long-term care benefits paid under the policy. Death proceeds and return of premium benefits will be reduced when long-term care benefits are taken. Values assume no prior distributions of any kind taken. Certain benefits may not be available until a specific age is attained. An elimination period may apply before long-term care benefits are available. See your policy for details.

benefit if the benefit amount wasn't exhausted by the combined long-term care claims of both insureds.

For unmarried individuals (or individuals whose spouse cannot qualify medically for coverage), a universal life insurance policy with a secondary no-lapse guarantee may make more sense. The policy can be paid over a finite period and has guaranteed premiums and a guaranteed death benefit to a specified age. The insured can use some portion of his or her own death benefit every month (usually 2 or 4 percent) for long-term care claims. While these policies do not allow for inflation protection, the death benefit can be structured to be large enough to handle claims even after the costs of care have risen.

Annuity-LTCI hybrid

The final way to insure for some long-term care benefits is with an annuity-LTCI hybrid contract. As with the life insurance-LTCI hybrids, there are lots of variations available. In general, however, these annuity-LTCI hybrid contracts are best suited for individuals or couples who *cannot* obtain traditional LTCI or a life insurance-LTCI hybrid due to medical underwriting or advanced age.

While we have barely scratched the surface on long-term care planning, the bottom line is that it is a huge financial risk. The cost of caring for a disabled person can quickly bankrupt a healthy spouse, partner, or other family members without the right plan. There are other strategies for asset protection that can be utilized, including the use of trusts or the retitling of assets, and your financial and legal advisor can review them with you.

WHAT YOU SHOULD DO NOW

- If you are over age 55 and have not explored the four possible strategies to pay for long-term care insurance, now is the time.

- If you are between 45 and 55 and have the wherewithal, this might be a good time to explore options that can be fully funded before your target retirement age.

- If you are under age 45 or if you are any age and have living parents or grandparents, you may want to engage in a family discussion about long-term care expectations and solutions. The cost of care impacts more than just the individual receiving it and caring for a family member takes a toll on loved ones financially and personally.

This concludes the first semester of your junior year, and you are three short semesters away from graduating into retirement. Next semester we will focus on the legal and estate planning portion of the financial plan.

POST-COURSE EXERCISE QUESTIONS

1. **TRUE** or **FALSE**: People should wait until they are ready to retire to explore long-term care insurance.

2. **TRUE** or **FALSE**: The only solution for long-term care planning is to buy long-term care insurance.

3. **TRUE** or **FALSE**: Long-term care insurance can be combined with life insurance or other financial products to create additional benefit combinations.

4. **TRUE** or **FALSE**: Medicare typically covers about 50 percent of the cost of long-term care but only for up to three years.

5. **TRUE** or **FALSE**: Structured properly, long-term care insurance can provide benefits for skilled nursing care in your own home.

POST-COURSE EXERCISE ANSWERS

1. **FALSE**. There are many types of LTCI available, some of which are ideally purchased many years before retirement and some of which are available for purchase many years into retirement. Retirement is not a deadline or ideal time to buy LTCI but it is a date useful in determining the types of LTCI to consider and the optimal way to structure premium payments.

2. **FALSE**. Long-Term Care Insurance (LTCI) is one of the potential tools available in long-term care planning but is not the only solution and is not right for everyone.

3. **TRUE**. LTCI can be combined with individual universal or whole life insurance, survivorship life insurance, and various types of annuity contracts to create customized benefit solutions.

4. **FALSE**. Medicare pays for a very small percentage of long-term care expenses and only for up to 100 days.

5. **TRUE**. Long-term care insurance can be issued to cover care in nursing homes, assisted living facilities, continuing care retirement communities, or in an insured's own home.

EXTRA-CREDIT ASSIGNMENT

The extra-credit assignment for this course is to have a family discussion about long-term care plans for all adults over age 45.

If you are uncomfortable leading a family discussion like this one, ask your financial advisor to help you. If it is geographically possible, try to have everyone together in the same room. These are hard conversations and the phone isn't the best means to handle them, especially if some of your relatives are already advanced in age.

The cost of care is so extreme that it can impact several generations of a family and the stress on family caregivers is intense, especially when a family member has Alzheimer's or another form of cognitive impairment. The right strategy can make a big difference to everyone in the family.

SECOND SEMESTER

By the time you're in your second semester of junior year, you should ideally start thinking about what your plans might be post-graduation. It's not time to be making decisions on any details but having the big picture in your mind will allow you to start a glide path for a smoother landing.

On the path to graduating into retirement, this means having some sense of how your personal plans might change when you're empty-nested or what to consider as your next professional challenge. You're going to spend most of senior year thinking in detail about life after graduation; that is, what you plan to do if or when you end your primary career—whether or not you have reached the point of financial independence.

We have covered almost all the basic elements of your financial plan in your curriculum but have not yet completed the risk management strategies. This semester, we'll focus on the estate planning, asset titling, and beneficiary designations that serve as critical components and decision points in your plan.

Course Schedule for Junior Year—Semester Two:

- Risk Management & Protection 202: Estate Planning Isn't Only for the Rich
- Risk Management & Protection 203: Who's on First—And What Comes Next

Risk Management & Protection 202:

ESTATE PLANNING ISN'T ONLY FOR THE RICH

When people hear the term "estate planning," they generally conjure up images of very wealthy families. However, each of us has an estate made up of the property we own, however modest, and there is more to estate planning than property.

Most individuals should have four legal documents, regardless of their level of wealth or the complexity of their financial or family situation:

1. Last will and testament
2. Durable financial power of attorney
3. Living will
4. Advanced healthcare directive

In addition, there are various types of trusts that can be set up for asset protection, creditor protection, tax reduction or avoidance, and/or asset disposition. We'll address a small number of these trusts later in the course, and you'll absolutely want the advice and counsel of a qualified estate planning attorney to assist you in this process.

This course will give you some basic understanding and familiarity with the documents so you can feel more confident approaching an attorney to advise you. It won't make you an estate planning expert or ready to tell an attorney what documents are right for you.

Before we begin with the details of each document, it is important for you to know that all four of these documents are revocable—you can destroy or modify them at any time during your lifetime so long as you are competent to do so. Note also that I am writing this as a financial professional and not as an attorney, and you should consult legal counsel before creating or executing any of these or other legal documents.

Last will and testament

The will is the one of the four basic documents with which most people are at least somewhat familiar. We've all seen Hollywood renditions of a will reading and people anxiously sitting around a table waiting to find out their share of their family's fortune.

However, a will is much more than a document to distribute property; it will also name all the people you want to leave responsible for your affairs when you die. While there are lots of reasons to have a will, one of the benefits of executing a will is to convey your property according to your wishes. In the absence of a will, the courts in your home state will decide where property goes based on default statutes (called intestate laws), with no regard to your relationships or preferences.

Your will can list specific items to go to named people (called bequests), like "my diamond engagement ring to my daughter, Sally." It can also just split property among a few beneficiaries evenly (or unevenly if you prefer).

In most cases, you may want to reference a memorandum in your will, rather than listing specific bequests of tangible personal property, for two reasons. First, it is easier to change your mind and doesn't require all new documents (or a codicil or amendment) to do so. Second, it can reduce the likelihood that the specific property listed will require an expensive and time-consuming appraisal during the probate process for estate tax purposes.

For example, the will can simply ask the personal representative to take any attached memorandum into consideration when distributing property to heirs and a sheet of paper can say, "I'd like my daughter, Sally, to have my engagement ring." If the will doesn't require the personal representative to give your daughter the ring and instead asks him or her to consider giving the ring to her, then you can generally avoid an appraisal for estate tax purposes. As always, ask your attorney for specific legal advice.

When property or cash is left to minors, a trustee will need to be named (or appointed) to handle their funds for them. Personally, I have yet to meet an 18- or 21-year-old mature enough to handle sudden wealth. As a result, I often suggest that documents be drafted to provide trusts for children or grandchildren until they are much older than just the age of majority in their state of residence.

Instead of paying a lump sum to young adults who might not be ready for the responsibility, I often see assets held for an heir's benefit, with the principal paid out in three lump sums—at ages 25, 30, and 35. That way, they can learn how to handle larger sums of money at 25 and will be better prepared at 30 and 35 to preserve some of the inheritance. At least if they make a mistake with some of the funds at 25, they may be less likely to repeat it when the remaining funds are paid to them.

For cases involving heirs who are not good with money or who have issues with substance abuse or gambling, funds can be held in trust for life. It is also possible to skip children and leave funds directly to grandchildren, although depending on your level of wealth, this can trigger an additional federal tax—the generation-skipping transfer tax (or GSTT)—for which you will need to plan carefully to avoid or minimize.

Just as importantly as dividing your property, you will use your will to name responsible parties to handle your affairs as you leave them behind, as follows:

Personal representative

This person handles the payment of your estate's debts and the collection and distribution of your property when you die. It is usually a job that lasts about nine months. It requires someone good with details and preferably someone local to you so that they can handle courthouse visits or other details in person.

Unless your world is very complicated or you do not have a responsible family member local to you, it may be best to name a family member rather than your attorney. Your attorney would generate significant fees to handle this role for your estate, while your family member will usually waive any fees that could be paid to them by the estate.

You will want to name a first choice (generally your surviving spouse, if you are married) and a second choice in this role, in the event you outlive your spouse or he or she is unable or unwilling to perform these tasks when called upon.

Guardian

This person (or people) will be asked to accept the responsibility to raise your minor children upon your death and will usually be family members. I suggest naming a single person rather than a couple, even if you are naming a sibling and his or her spouse because in the event of a divorce between them, this can become very awkward and may require a court to render a decision before guardianship can begin.

You will ideally want to name someone who has a relationship with your children already and may prefer someone who has children of his or her own. You'll want to name a first choice and a second choice in this role, which is naturally irrelevant until both parents of the minor children are deceased.

Trustee

Depending on the complexity of your estate, you may have one or many trusts created under your will (called testamentary trusts). The trustee will be asked to accept the responsibility to handle the financial affairs for your children or other heirs and can be an advisor, a bank's trust department, or one or more individuals, including family members.

The trustee you name does not have to be the same person listed as the guardian for the kids. Some people are adept with money but have no experience with kids, while others are great with kids but can't balance a checkbook. If you are fortunate enough to have a close family member who has a good relationship with your children and can manage money, he or she can absolutely play both roles under your will.

You'll want a first choice and a second choice in this role, and in most cases no trustee is needed until both parents of the minor children are deceased.

Durable financial power of attorney

While the provisions in your will do not take effect until your death, the other three legal documents will be effective only during your lifetime.

The durable financial power of attorney names the person (called your attorney-in-fact) who can step into your shoes to make financial decisions for you if you cannot make them yourself. It could be that you are in a coma and someone needs to pay your bills or it could be that you broke both your wrists in a car accident and cannot sign your name.

If you are married, this person is almost always your spouse, although you can name anyone you choose. Every adult should have one of these documents. For parents, it is important to have financial powers of attorney executed for your children as soon as they reach the age of majority (18 or 21 in most states) because parental rights end when kids reach that age and you won't be able to step into their shoes for financial matters unless they give you permission in one of these documents to do so.

Understand that this is a very powerful document and you must have complete trust in the person you name. If you'd prefer, you can have your attorney or financial advisor hold the original document instead of giving it to the person named as attorney-in-fact so that it can't be used until the need arises.

These documents can go into effect immediately upon being signed or can be springing documents, which are not useful until and unless multiple physicians attest that you are unable to make financial decisions for yourself. I strongly suggest the immediately effective documents (especially if you are married and naming your spouse) to avoid the need for a lengthy delay under duress waiting for various physicians to deem you incompetent.

As with the various roles under the wills, you'll want to name a first choice and a second choice under this document. In my experience, it is best to name a single person to act alone, rather than a group of people to act collectively so that affairs can be handled as efficiently as possible. Depending on the language in the document, if you name all three of your children to serve, for example, they may all need to sign every document when account activity is required and they may also have to agree on every action being taken. Kids often can't agree on what movie to see, much less on how to handle each of their parents' assets or accounts.

Living will and advanced healthcare directive

I am going to lump the last two documents together because many attorneys do the same thing. It is not uncommon for the living will and advanced healthcare directive to be in a single document as Part A and Part B.

Living wills are documents in which you name the person who can speak freely with physicians or hospital staff to act on your behalf. Advanced healthcare directives (interchangeably called advanced medical directives) are the documents in which you are providing the medical community with your wishes regarding your care in the event you cannot make your own medical decisions.

The subjects covered in these documents are very morbid but it is easier to make these decisions while you are healthy than it could be if you are later sick or incapacitated. You'll make decisions about your care regarding pain medication, feeding, life support, and organ donation, if you were to become in a persistent vegetative state.

You can avoid adding major family drama to the traumatic experience of your illness or accident by having these documents drafted and giving them to the appropriate family members. Naming a responsible party for your advanced medical directive is nearly identical to naming an attorney-in-fact under your durable financial power of attorney. If you are married, the logical choice is to name your spouse and you'll want to name a backup.

Also, similarly to the financial power of attorney, I encourage people to name one person instead of multiple people so the physicians know with whom to consult when treatment is being recommended. If you name multiple people, they would not only all have to be consulted but they'd also all have to agree to make this a smooth process and important life-and-death decisions can be required very quickly at times.

If you have multiple children and want to minimize the likelihood of conflict between them, you can take these three actions. Name one child as your responsible party, discuss it with your kids in advance to avoid surprises or hurt feelings, and request (but do not require) the child you name to consult with his or her siblings, if logistically possible, prior to making major decisions.

Common types of trusts

There are dozens of legal documents that can be drafted and executed to convey your wishes and some of them have very specific and infrequent applications. An estate planning attorney will be familiar with all of them.

Some trusts I see regularly as a financial advisor, and I'm going to name a few, in the simplest of terms, here. This list is by no means exhaustive or comprehensive.

Revocable living trust

As the name implies, a revocable living trust is created by a grantor (the person transferring assets into a trust) during his or her lifetime and can be revoked at any time while he or she is alive. There are no tax benefits or creditor protections provided by this type of trust, as it is a **pass-through entity**.

The biggest benefit of this type of trust is that assets in the trust can be distributed upon the death of the grantor without a time-consuming or expensive probate process. The probate process is one in which the state courts require an inventory of all a decedent's assets, a review of the will, and the paying of the decedent's bills or expenses prior to distribution of the assets to heirs. In some states, Delaware for example, probate costs can be very high and are worth trying to avoid with simple trust planning.

Irrevocable life insurance trust (ILIT)

Estate taxes are imposed by the federal government and some states have estate taxes, inheritance taxes, or both. Death benefits paid under life insurance policies owned by the decedent are includable in the tax calculation. As a result, wealthy families can seek to avoid the taxation of those death benefits by having life insurance policies applied for, owned by, and payable to irrevocable trusts.

These types of trusts were very common prior to the tax reform in January 2018, which raised the limits for estate tax exemptions dramatically. As of 2020, the federal estate tax exemption per individual is $11,580,000.

During my career in the financial planning industry, I can remember when individuals could only pass $600,000 to heirs without a federal tax bite. For people who already have these trusts in place, I usually recommend that they keep them. But fewer families will need to create these trusts in the near term, except for residents of those states with especially low limits or high tax rates.

As the name implies, these trusts cannot be modified after creation, although they normally hold only life insurance policies with little or no cash value and the trust could sell the policy to a different trust if modifications were needed to the trust language.

These trusts can still be useful planning tools for wealthy families, especially those with large, illiquid assets like farmland or direct business ownership.

Charitable trusts

There are lots of ways to combine charitable giving and income or estate tax planning. For families with highly appreciated assets who want to increase their income and avoid capital gains taxes, sometimes charitable trusts can provide creative solutions by making gifts of "split-interest."

In most cases, that means allowing a charity to benefit from an asset's income or use during the grantor's lifetime while keeping the asset for heirs or allowing family to enjoy the income from an asset until death or a specified future date and to leave the asset to charity at that time.

Other trusts

Other trusts are designed for special needs planning, generation skipping, wealth replacement, tax minimization, and so many other uses that it is impossible to list them in a brief course on basic estate planning. Just know that you can accomplish almost anything you'd like with the right attorney and the right estate planning tools at his or her disposal.

This concludes the basic course on estate planning documents, but there is more to discuss on risk management and estate planning in the next course.

POST-COURSE EXERCISE QUESTIONS

1. **TRUE** or **FALSE**: The only purpose of executing a will is to determine who receives your property when you die.

2. **TRUE** or **FALSE**: Once you execute your estate planning documents, you'll want to review them periodically, especially after times of major life changes.

3. **TRUE** or **FALSE**: Your advanced healthcare directive will help determine how your family will pay for your end-of-life medical expenses.

4. **TRUE** or **FALSE**: Your financial power of attorney can only be relied upon during your lifetime and is not useful after you die.

5. **TRUE** or **FALSE**: Your estate planning documents should ideally be drafted and executed in your state of residence and only by an attorney licensed to practice in that state.

POST-COURSE EXERCISE ANSWERS

1. **FALSE.** While the will does serve that purpose, it also has other functions, which include naming responsible parties to handle your affairs, including guardians for your children, trustees, and personal representatives for your estate.

2. **TRUE.** When your life circumstances change or when new legislation or tax rules are adopted, you will want to review your estate planning documents. In addition, I recommend making sure your financial powers of attorney and advanced medical directives are no more than five years old so that financial institutions and medical facilities are more likely to honor them.

3. **FALSE.** Your advanced healthcare directive will allow you to express your wishes for care during your incapacitation or end of life but has nothing to do with how those wishes will be addressed financially.

4. **TRUE.** Your durable financial power of attorney allows your attorney-in-fact to act in your stead for financial matters during your lifetime but is not effective once you die. At that time, the will and any trusts are the only documents still in effect.

5. **TRUE.** Every state has unique rules and regulations around inheritance and estate laws, including the possible levying of taxes. When you move to another state, it is advisable to seek counsel licensed in that state to review your existing documents and to determine if modifications are needed that may be state-specific.

EXTRA-CREDIT ASSIGNMENT

For this course, the extra-credit assignment will depend if you currently have executed estate planning documents or not.

If you do not yet have these documents, the assignment is to meet with an attorney in your home state to draft and execute the documents described in the course that are appropriate for you.

If you already have executed estate planning documents, review them in light of the material in this course and consider meeting with your existing attorney or an alternate one in your home state if any of the following scenarios applies to you:

- Your documents are more than five years old.
- You have changed your state of residence since the execution of your current documents.
- One or more of your named responsible parties has died or has become less optimal due to geography, illness, or any other reason.
- You have gotten married or divorced or had children born since the execution of your current documents.
- One or more of your grown children has gotten married or divorced or had children born since the execution of your current documents.
- **Any other material life changes have occurred, including dramatic change in your personal wealth or health or a change in your personal wishes or family dynamics.**

Risk Management & Protection 203:

WHO'S ON FIRST—AND WHAT COMES NEXT

It may sound simple but some of the biggest mistakes that families make result from the way they title their assets and how they name (or don't name!) their beneficiaries. This course is designed to help simplify and clarify these decisions and hopefully to ensure they get made thoughtfully and accurately.

ASSET TITLING (OR WHAT'S MINE IS YOURS AND WHAT'S YOURS IS MINE...RIGHT?)

In many cases, assets are titled jointly between spouses as a matter of convenience. However, for federal or state estate tax considerations or other dispositive reasons, it can be important to have assets in each spouse's name individually.

In addition to tax and dispositive planning, there are also liability issues in titling of assets. In some states, it is important, for example, not to title an automobile in joint name because it could subject both parties (and their joint assets) to a lawsuit in the event of an accident involving either spouse behind the wheel. It is better to title an automobile to the primary driver alone, if possible, to protect some types of property from a lawsuit.

All joint accounts are not created equal. There are different ways to title property between two or more people and the elections you make are critical in the planning process:

Joint tenants with right of survivorship (JTWROS)

This is the most common way to title property between two or more people. It means that each owner holds an indivisible share of the property and that upon the death of one owner, the remaining owners will automatically acquire the deceased owner's share, usually equally.

The challenges with JTWROS are that it doesn't allow for use of certain tax credits to protect against estate taxation, it doesn't allow property to pass under a will or to be used by the personal representative to pay the estate's liabilities, and it doesn't protect the various owners from lawsuits against the other owners.

Joint tenants in entireties (TEN ENT)

This type of property ownership is only allowed between married spouses and is only recognized in certain states. Functionally, it is identical to JTWROS, with the exception that it provides some liability protection in the event that one spouse or the other is sued. This is often the best choice for titling a personal residence shared by a married couple.

Joint tenants in common (TEN COM)

This type of registration allows each partial owner to maintain their own personal divisible share of the property. The benefit is that it allows for multiple owners, even with varying percentages of ownership, and it allows each owner to leave their share of the property under their will to whomever they'd like.

It also allows for use of credits for estate tax purposes, especially if two spouses opt for this registration. However, it does not offer the liability protection and it can put owners in a difficult position if one owner dies, leaving his or her share evenly between four children, all of whom become owners of a single piece of property.

If the property is liquid (i.e., a mutual fund portfolio), that isn't a big deal since shares can be identified and sold. However, if the property is a house at the beach and a few owners want to keep it while a few owners want to sell it, conflict can occur.

Beyond joint property, there are several ways to title property, either in a temporary way (for example, allowing ownership for life but not allowing control of its disposition at death) or in trust as described in the last course.

If you wish to bypass the language in the will to transfer non-qualified assets directly to one or more beneficiaries, you can title an individual account as Payable on Death or Transfer on Death, sometimes referred to as **POD** or **TOD** accounts. This will not avoid inclusion in an estate tax calculation, but it will allow accounts to be re-titled to a beneficiary more quickly upon your death. Note that there are sometimes valid reasons to *want* property to pass under the will so it is rarely advisable to title *all* your individual accounts as TOD.

Some states abide by community property laws, which means that all property acquired by either spouse during the time they were married is marital property (usually excepting inheritance by one spouse or the other so long as the inherited property is never re-titled jointly or comingled with community property).

Before moving on, let's discuss the impact of titling property to minors. Every state maintains their own age of majority (usually 18 or 21) and has different rules about custodial accounts. Some follow the Uniform Gifts to Minors Act (UGMA), while others follow the slightly different Uniform Transfers to Minors Act (UTMA).

If an account is titled to a minor (or if a minor inherits property), it requires an adult or corporate custodian or trustee to safeguard that property for the benefit of the minor. These accounts are *irrevocable*; that is, once an account is titled to a minor, it belongs to the minor and cannot be used for other purposes.

The problems with naming minors as account owners are numerous, but the two biggest are: 1) Minors are seldom ready to handle large sums of money at a young age, and 2) funds in a minor's name will typically reduce the amount of financial aid available for college dollar for dollar. Titling assets directly in a minor's name is rarely, if ever, advisable.

It is better to set up trusts for minors, either under your will or by gifting to an account owned under a trust agreement. These require an attorney to draft but they can be set up to hold funds for a young person's use until they are much older than the age of majority (or even forever) and won't impact financial aid as adversely.

As we discussed earlier, some college planning accounts allow minors to be named as *beneficiaries* as opposed to owners. That can have multiple benefits, including a better financial aid outcome and the ability for parents or grandparents to direct the funds to a college (or even to change the beneficiary on an account) while keeping it outside of the parents' or grandparents' estates for tax purposes.

The titling of assets is critical and complicated enough that I recommend getting assistance from your financial advisor and attorney as a part of your overall planning. It can be a cumbersome process to re-title property but it is rarely expensive and is much easier to accomplish while everyone is alive and competent, as opposed to after someone dies or becomes incapacitated.

BENEFICIARY DESIGNATIONS [OR TO THE WIDOW(ER) GOES THE SPOILS...RIGHT?]

When completing your contingency planning, in addition to titling your assets properly, you will also want to name beneficiaries on various accounts and insurance policies very carefully. That is because the beneficiary designation on an account or insurance policy supersedes anything listed in the will.

For example, if your will says that you want your three children to share equally in your assets but your IRA names only your oldest child, your former spouse, or anyone else, only the person or people named on the beneficiary designation can inherit that property *no matter what your will states*.

You'll have lots of considerations when making beneficiary elections, some of which are state specific, so this course can only provide a cursory review of those decisions. You'll want to talk with your attorney, financial advisor, and insurance agent to make sure the elections you make are appropriate in your situation.

If you intend your will to have trust provisions to hold assets for your children until specific ages, you need to make sure that property passes under the will to fund that trust. We often see life insurance proceeds designated that way. The primary beneficiary may be your spouse and the contingent beneficiary may read, "Trustee(s) under the Last Will and Testament of the Insured." This makes sure that the trust is funded and it has other potential estate planning benefits including the utilization of various tax credits and liquidity for the estate.

Special rules apply when a spouse is the named beneficiary of a qualified retirement plan or IRA account. In that case, the surviving spouse can deposit those assets directly into his or her own IRA account and can generally use them with the same rules as their own IRA assets. There are lots of exceptions to this rule when dealing with one spouse over age 72 and one under that age and spouses with significant age differences between them. You'll want to consult your tax advisor or CPA prior to making elections under these plans.

IRA accounts and qualified retirement plans are eligible for a different type of special tax treatment if they are paid directly to named beneficiaries (or to trusts with very specific language relating to the accounts) who are not surviving spouses. These provisions are called **stretch** provisions.

For beneficiaries other than spouses on qualified retirement plan accounts or IRAs, the stretch provisions have historically allowed a beneficiary to fund a beneficiary distribution account, called an IRA-BDA, and to take distributions annually, based on their current and corresponding IRS life expectancy tables.

As of January 2020, the benefits of stretch IRAs and Roth IRAs for non-spousal beneficiaries have been greatly reduced by the SECURE[47] Act. This act now requires non-spousal beneficiaries of IRAs and Roth IRAs (and qualified retirement plans) to withdraw the entire account balance within 10 years of the original accountholder's death. In the case of traditional IRAs, that could be an enormous income tax bill for the heirs and in the case of Roth IRAs, it means that the tax-free nature of the Roth IRA becomes a temporary one rather than a lifetime one.

---

[47] The SECURE Act is formally the Setting Every Community Up for Retirement Enhancement Act of 2019, which was passed by the U.S. House of Representatives in July 2019 and approved by the US Senate on December 19, 2019.

For example, that means that a 25-year-old beneficiary is forced to make a full distribution (or series of distributions) within 10 years of the original accountholder's death. What would have created a very positive long-term impact by protecting the account balance subject to tax-deferral for his or her lifetime is now a form of tax trap. Heirs will want to use these BDAs wisely and opportunistically, with the help of their financial and tax advisors.

The process of naming beneficiaries can be more involved than just listing their names or their titles (i.e., "children of the account holder"). You can designate beneficiaries to receive a percentage of an account either *per capita* ("by head") or *per stirpes* ("by root") and the difference is very significant.

Let's say you have three children and each of your children has two children of his or her own. If you name your children as your beneficiaries equally on an account and they are all living when you die, they will each get one-third of the account balance. However, if one of your children predeceases you, those two Latin words become very important.

In a *per capita* arrangement, distribution is split evenly only among your living beneficiaries. So your assets would be split 50-50 only between your two children living at the time. This would disinherit two of your grandchildren accidentally.

If instead you name your kids under a *per stirpes* arrangement, your two living children in this example would still get one-third each and your two grandchildren who are the children of your deceased child would split the remaining one-third share equally. In this scenario, your family would share "by root" rather than "by head" so no one would accidentally be disinherited.

FINAL ESTATE PLANNING ITEMS

Before we leave the topic of estate planning, there are a few more items that you may want to consider in your planning. First, I recommend that you prepare a letter of instruction or similar document to be left behind with detailed information about whom your heirs should call and where certain documents are in the event of an emergency or death. In addition to contact information for your financial advisor and estate attorney, this might include other named responsible parties, clergy, or other members of your extended personal network.

Your heirs also need to know if you have documents on file with your county's Register of Wills or at your attorney's office or if you maintain physical documents or property in a safe deposit box or elsewhere.

I also suggest that you store a list of online passwords where your family members or other named responsible parties can access them. You'll want a secure place, as it shouldn't be left on your desk at work. One of the great difficulties for a surviving spouse, children, or advisors is getting access to accounts and information if passwords are not available.

This concludes the second semester of your junior year, and you have just one year left before graduating into retirement. Most of the basics have been covered, and now we need to shift our focus to strategies during the various life transitions ahead—financial and otherwise.

POST-COURSE EXERCISE QUESTIONS

1. **TRUE** or **FALSE**: If an asset or account is titled jointly between two people when one dies, the other always takes possession of 100 percent of the asset or account.

2. **TRUE** or **FALSE**: Beneficiary designations on qualified retirement plans and IRAs can dramatically impact the options available to heirs when they inherit the accounts.

3. **TRUE** or **FALSE**: The beneficiaries you name on your life insurance policies will receive death benefits when you die, even if your will directs otherwise.

4. **TRUE** or **FALSE**: There are different rules regarding options for spousal beneficiaries versus non-spousal beneficiaries on qualified retirement plan and IRA accounts.

5. **TRUE** or **FALSE**: It is convenient and effective to name one or more charities as beneficiaries of a portion of your qualified retirement plan or IRA accounts.

POST-COURSE EXERCISE ANSWERS

1. **FALSE.** That is accurate for accounts titled as joint tenants with rights of survivorship or tenants by the entireties but is not accurate for accounts titled as tenants in common.

2. **TRUE.** Naming individuals outright as beneficiaries on qualified retirement plans and IRAs can allow them to take advantage of inherited IRA rules (or stretch IRA provisions), which can make a huge difference for your heirs. Note that some trust language can provide similar ability but you'll need a capable attorney to draft that language to avoid any expensive tax mistakes.

3. **TRUE.** The beneficiary designations on life insurance (as well as TOD and retirement accounts) will take precedence over any language to the contrary in the will. The will is only impactful for property that is passing in the absence of some other titling or beneficiary arrangement.

4. **TRUE.** When spouses are widowed and inherit the IRA or qualified retirement plan assets from their deceased spouse, they can generally just transfer the assets from the spouse's accounts into their own IRA and treat the assets accordingly. This can help alleviate immediate minimum distributions that would be required for any non-spousal beneficiaries. Note that there are a number of exceptions to these rules, and you'll want to consult your attorney and financial advisor to manage these decisions properly when the time comes.

5. **FALSE.** While it may seem convenient, it is very ineffective and can be damaging to your non-spousal beneficiaries if a charity is named as one of the beneficiaries because it eliminates the ability for your individual heirs to use the stretch IRA provisions and subjects their entire inherited portion of the IRA account to income taxation in the year they receive it. That can be an extremely expensive mistake for your loved ones.

   Naming charities as beneficiaries on IRA accounts can be highly effective as long as the charities are the *only* beneficiaries on the account. If you want to leave some of your IRA money to charity, create one IRA account to name only charities and one IRA account to name only individuals.

EXTRA-CREDIT ASSIGNMENT

Your assignment for this course is to take a complete inventory of your beneficiary designations for all of your family's accounts. Note that you'll want to know not only the primary beneficiaries but also the contingent beneficiaries (in the event your primary beneficiaries pre-decease you).

The types of accounts that often have beneficiaries you'll want to verify include:

- Qualified retirement plans
- IRA accounts, including Roth IRAs, SEP IRAs, and SIMPLE IRAs
- Life insurance policies
- Transfer on Death (TOD) accounts
- Employee benefits—not only life insurance but also deferred compensation or profit-sharing plans

Once you have completed the extra credit from this course and the last course, you'll be able to verify that both your will and your beneficiaries are set up properly to avoid all types of challenging problems when you die.

Senior Year:
Making Your Mark & Presenting Your Thesis

FIRST SEMESTER

You have a few realities to ponder as you enter the senior year of your financial life:

- Life is going to be more expensive than you expect.
- You are going to live longer than you imagine.
- You will need to make sure you have resources that you cannot outlive.

In college as you enter your senior year, you are now at the top of your game. You can focus on your major, on your job search, and on determining the big decisions that will come upon graduation.

Preparing to graduate into retirement is no different. You are likely past the peak earning years of your life, but depending on your chosen profession, your income may remain strong and predictable through your last day on the job. Assuming your kids' education expenses are behind you and they didn't boomerang back into your basement, these will also be some of the least expensive years of your life. The combination of high income and low expenses is an ideal recipe to play catch-up and to build upon the foundation for financial independence that you began in your junior year.

There will be milestones to celebrate, personally and professionally, and psychologically you may experience a shift from focusing your energy and attention on activities that are "musts" to activities that are "wants." You may be developing the proverbial bucket list of things you want to do, see, and experience before you draw your last breath, but you're still busy driving financial growth to reach the day you don your cap and gown.

In the first semester of your senior year, we'll be concentrating on preparing your assets to shift from an accumulation mode to an income creation and preservation mindset. This may involve asset segregation or other strategies that fit properly with your financial wherewithal and your income needs. We'll also be looking at income strategies and preparing for what could be your last paycheck in the coming five to 10 years.

Course Schedule for Senior Year—First Semester:

- Financial Independence 401: Being "Wealthy"
- Retirement Readiness 401: Preparing Assets to Create Income

Financial Independence 401:

BEING "WEALTHY"

We've defined retirement as the lack of needing to work, not the absence of work itself, and we've covered concepts that build wealth. But what does it mean to be *wealthy*?

Being wealthy is a feeling more than a condition, and there are lots of ways to be wealthy, not just financial ones. When someone is described as having a "wealth of knowledge" on a subject, it suggests an abundance that can be shared with others. Post-graduation we will be reviewing lots of ways to leave a legacy and will include a discussion on philanthropy. For now, let's define being wealthy as having an abundance of resources that allows for financial independence.

At this stage of your life, you may be able to leverage your wealth of experience and knowledge to add to your financial wealth. You may choose to enhance your own skills to stay sharp in anticipation of your next career move or entrepreneurial venture. You may also start consulting, coaching, or mentoring younger professionals in your field or other companies in your industry and can create a significant additional income (and future career path) in doing so. A few financial forks in the road may begin to appear at this stage of your career and many of them can be lucrative and rewarding.

There are a few universal suggestions or best practices to consider as you reach the five- to 10-year window to your graduation. Not all will apply to you, of course, but in general, these are some of the most common decision points at this stage of your financial life:

Eliminate or dramatically reduce debt

The happiest and most successful retirees I have known have three things in common: 1) They are virtually or completely debt-free, 2) they have good personal health habits, and 3) they have something exciting or enriching to do when they wake up in the morning.

The time to eliminate debt is now. You don't have to be mortgage-free in retirement, but if you do have a mortgage, it should likely be the only debt on your personal balance sheet and it needs to be manageable. If you co-signed for student loans for your children, now is the time to pay them down and off. You don't want to be retired and making payments for debt service.

Increase personal savings rate

As your expenses related to childcare, education, and major purchases wane at this time, you can somewhat painlessly redirect those resources into your personal savings and investments. During your early career, a 15 percent savings rate would have been considered successful but now you'll want it closer to 25–30 percent of your income.

This is true for two reasons. First, the more you save and invest at this time in your life, the sooner you'll reach the asset level that triggers your financial independence and leads to graduation day. Second, if you can live on 70–75 percent of your income while you're working, it will set a much more realistic and attainable target for your replacement income after retirement. If you're still living on 100 percent of what you earn, you'll need to replace 100 percent of your pre-retirement income to live comfortably after graduating and that can be difficult (if not impossible) to achieve.

Reduce unnecessary expenses

No one likes a budget. Suggesting that you skip the daily four-dollar latte is simply not going to move your financial needle very much. However, some expenses that can add up may not be as important as they once seemed. Maybe these are habitual—social clubs or memberships you don't use as much anymore, subscriptions that auto-renew but you don't need, or services for cable TV or other entertainment that you may barely watch. Maybe they include acquiring stuff that you simply don't need. Maybe these expenses mean lavish dining or travel that can be scaled back without ruining the experience.

Whatever your situation, consider that a reduction of $1,000 a month in unnecessary expenses means $12,000 per year that you don't need to replace after graduation and a whopping $300,000 less wealth that you need to grow prior to retirement, using just a 4 percent withdrawal rate for income.

Begin to declutter your home

For adults who have lived in their homes for a long time, stuff accumulates. Not only are houses often overflowing with "stuff we might use someday" but lots of adults also maintain storage units for their possessions—or their kids'—that they may not actually need. If you haven't used it in several years, you may not want to keep it and certainly don't want to pay someone to hold onto it for you.

Some retirees will stay in their pre-retirement homes for life, others will consider downsizing for various reasons. Whether you plan to move or not, decluttering during your lifetime is a great way to remain flexible and to ensure that your property goes to the people you'd like to have it. You may also get to see them enjoying it.

Decluttering can also create meaningful tax benefits should you choose to donate some of your unwanted property and may reduce your costs of storage or property insurance as well.

In my lifetime, I have watched personal family members as well as clients clean out the property of their deceased parents or other loved ones. It is a daunting task, often under duress, and rarely goes the way their relatives might have intended. Start to declutter during your later working years or early retirement years rather than waiting until there is an urgency to move for health reasons or a tragedy that necessitates a daunting project for others.

Start thinking about where you may want to live in retirement

Once your full-time employment has ended, your need to remain in a specific geographic area may also subside. We will be talking about this topic in-depth in your second semester of senior year, but for now at least open your mind to the possibility of relocation at some point during your retirement years.

**Start thinking about your adventures in retirement,
personally and professionally**

It's time to build (or refine) the **bucket list**. We will be covering this topic in great length in the graduation day chapter. Start to think about the things you want to do or achieve, the places you want to go, and the experiences you want to have and with whom you want to share them—and do it now.

Ultimately, one of the great determinants of a successful retirement is one that contains enrichment, excitement, fun, and meaning. This is the first true step to designing what that might entail for you.

Hopefully, this course helped create some direction for your sail as you set a course toward the next phase of your life. There is much to do—and you're too busy to do most of it without a nudge. So consider yourself nudged and use these suggestions to make your path to graduation day more attainable financially.

POST-COURSE EXERCISE QUESTIONS

1. **TRUE** or **FALSE**: Once you have finished educating your children, you may have the wherewithal to save significantly more money toward your own financial independence and to maximize your personal wealth.

2. **TRUE** or **FALSE**: The three things that the most successful retirees have in common are being debt-free, enjoying good health, and having no responsibilities whatsoever so they can enjoy their leisure.

3. **TRUE** or **FALSE**: When thinking about graduating into retirement, reducing unnecessary expenses can be an important step to reaching financial independence.

4. **TRUE** or **FALSE**: Since one of the strategies to enjoy financial independence might include downsizing your residence, now is the time to start thinking about where you want to live and decluttering your present home to be prepared.

5. **TRUE** or **FALSE**: Having a bucket list can be helpful in designing the retirement lifestyle that suits you best.

POST-COURSE EXERCISE ANSWERS

1. **TRUE.** The years during which children are being educated—especially their college years—can be the most expensive years for any family. Once that expense has been eliminated (or at least been replaced by a more manageable student loan payment), the funds that had been directed toward education can be repurposed and can allow for much larger contributions to retirement plans, personal savings, or debt reduction. The path to financial independence may be forged over 40–50 years but the final five to 10 are often the most critical determinants of success.

2. **FALSE.** While good health and being debt-free are two of the three things that most successful retirees have in common, the third element is that they have something exciting on the horizon. Far too many people retire without a plan to stay engaged and enriched in their lives. If you lack a good reason to get out of bed every morning, you are far more likely to sleep in and simply to putter around the house or watch mindless television. That isn't living; it's waiting to die.

3. **TRUE.** Some expenses during our working years seem irrelevant simply because of our personal earnings. However, if non-critical expenses can be reduced prior to retirement, it will have a positive impact on the income you require from your portfolio and personal savings to maintain your independence. We'll be discussing this in greater depth in the next course.

4. **TRUE.** Some retirees stay in their homes and others elect to move. There are expense and tax reasons, logistical and geographic reasons, and personal and family reasons to explore both options. Even if you don't plan to downsize, using the years when you have greater vitality and can tackle the decisions about personal property personally will make a difference for your family. Try not to leave your heirs with a houseful of stuff. Instead, have a plan to determine what to gift to family, what to gift to charity, and what to recycle or take to the community dump.

5. **TRUE.** The concept of a bucket list is one that is often discussed tongue in cheek but having a variety of goals, plans, experiences, and adventures for the chapter of your life after graduating into retirement is actually a very healthy and productive idea. This list can contain anything that brings enthusiasm and vigor to your life.

EXTRA-CREDIT ASSIGNMENT

This course's extra-credit assignment should be fun. Regardless of your present age, take a piece of paper and write down five to 10 things that you'd like to make sure to do during your lifetime.

These can be places to visit (think Bora Bora), adventures to try (sky-diving, anyone?), or friendships or other relationships you want to cultivate or restore. If you reduce these things to writing, you are far more likely to make them happen.

Remember also that this list is not made in stone. It can change as your life changes. It might even be something worth revisiting and updating every year or two to make sure it remains relevant and that you're starting to check off the items you've completed to make room for new ones.

Retirement Readiness 401:

PREPARING ASSETS TO CREATE INCOME

$$FVAD = A (1+ r)^1 + A (1 + r)^2 \ldots + A (1 + r)^n$$

As you can see from the formula, building a portfolio of assets to accumulate wealth is a "basic" exercise in time value of money. You put A dollars into an account every year and grow it at r percent for n years and voilà! The output reveals how much money you'll have at that time.

In the real world, you may be able to control the A variable and the n variable but the r variable will never be steady. Not only will returns vary over time but the impact of inflation and the sequence and series of returns will have a dramatic impact on the outcome.

Still, it is possible to accumulate capital using this simple formula so long as you adjust the trajectory over time for actual results.

AFTER A, N, AND R...MORE LETTERS?

Planning for income is an entirely different matter—and one that is much more complicated and difficult. This is because additional variables are added, including the taxation of withdrawals, the predictability and duration of income, the impact of longevity and spending adjustments, and the timing of those variables in conjunction with changing market conditions.

These variables are why two things are true:

1. There is no reliable rule of thumb for a sustainable withdrawal rate in retirement.
2. Very few people should try to undertake this exercise without professional guidance.

Multiple strategies exist for income planning in retirement, and the biggest determinant for which prevailing strategy is right for you is your required withdrawal rate.

Your withdrawal rate is calculated by first determining the amount of your working assets (those assets from which income can be derived) and the amount of income you need to live your life (your annual spending) that does not come from some other income source. So if you are collecting social security, pension income, a lifetime annuity payment, or other passive income, those payments reduce the withdrawal rate required from your working assets.

The three basic strategies we'll explore in this course are:

1. Total return
2. Asset segregation
3. Annuitization

In some cases, a retiree will utilize one of these strategies exclusively, while in other cases some combination will make more sense. But let's look at each of these strategies individually first, using the same basic assumptions for each scenario:

Assumptions: You have a retirement income need of $10,000 per month. Social security is paying you $2,000 per month but you have no pension or other income stream available. So you have an $8,000-per-month shortfall, which needs to come from your working assets.

Total return

The total return strategy is best suited for people with very small required withdrawal rates (generally 2.5 percent or less). The strategy is simple: all your working assets are in one combined portfolio and the withdrawal each year is made from the overall portfolio in conjunction with an annual rebalancing such that all asset classes remain in their intended percentages of the portfolio over time.

The benefits of this strategy include ease of monitoring and rebalancing. The drawbacks are that there are no provisions for market downturns or adverse economic conditions.

If in our example, the income need is $8,000 per month, or $96,000 per year, the working assets are $7,200,000 and the required withdrawal rate is 1.5 percent. This portfolio may be able to continue to generate $96,000 per year (adjusted for annual inflation) indefinitely, simply due to the size of the principal and the low rate of withdrawal.

In that case, let's assume that the portfolio suffers a 33 percent loss in one year and drops to $4,800,000. The required withdrawal rate would only increase from 1.5 percent to 2 percent, which continues to be very sustainable and doesn't create a meaningful threat of running out of money.

In the case of a very modest withdrawal rate, the total return strategy can work well and can be designed with the goal of outpacing inflation and growing the principal over time. In this scenario, this retiree may have more money in 10 years than he or she does presently.

Asset segregation

Most retirees do not have the luxury of a large nest egg described in our first scenario. The asset segregation strategy is used for retirees with a required withdrawal rate of 2.5–4.5 percent or so.

Let's say the working assets using our fact set are $2,400,000. Now the required withdrawal rate to create $96,000 per year is 4 percent. In this case, a total return strategy might work if markets and portfolios only went up, which we all know is not possible.

To demonstrate that reality, if we applied the same 33 percent reduction in the portfolio value, the principal drops to $1,600,000 and the withdrawal rate jumps to 6 percent. That would be a recipe for running out of money quickly because the portfolio likely couldn't keep up with the withdrawals, much less the withdrawals plus a rate of inflation.

Unless a retiree can withstand a 33 percent reduction in withdrawals (in this case using $64,000 instead of $96,000 the following year), the total return strategy cannot be used in this case and generally cannot be used in conjunction with a required withdrawal rate higher than 2.5 percent or so.

A different kind of bucket list

With the asset segregation strategy, various assets are assigned to accounts for specific purposes and time frames. Sometimes these time frames are called tranches or buckets, so if you've heard of the **bucket strategy**, it might indicate some form of asset segregation.

In the simplest terms, this means that some assets are set aside as **short-term assets** for the next five years of withdrawals (years zero through four of an income plan), some are set aside as **intermediate-term assets** for the following five years of withdrawals (years five through nine of an income plan), and some are designated as **long-term assets** meant not to be used until a period of 10 years or more has elapsed.

Short-term bucket

The short-term bucket can be further segregated by the year of use. So, for example, perhaps 12 months of planned withdrawals will be held in cash and the remaining 48 months of planned withdrawals would be allocated to certificates of deposit, bonds, or bond funds with set maturity dates in one, two, three, and four years to make sure that cash is available when it is needed throughout the 60 months. The elements of paramount importance in this short-term bucket are availability of capital, liquidity, and minimal risk of principal loss.

Intermediate-term bucket

The intermediate-term bucket is a great spot for income-producing securities, such as real estate funds, private debt or credit funds, dividend-paying blue-chip stocks, annuities, or longer-term fixed income securities. Here liquidity is less important than in the short-term bucket but it is still helpful to know that income can be generated and/or principal can be raised once the five- to nine-year time frame begins.

Long-term bucket

The long-term bucket is designed for growth of principal. It may contain various stocks or equity funds, including private equity. Liquidity is not terribly important, as these assets will not be utilized for 10-plus years. The risk of principal fluctuation will be present in this bucket, as market movements will impact valuation of the securities in this bucket significantly.

From a return standpoint, it is reasonable to estimate an annual rate of return of about 2 percent for the short-term bucket, 5 percent for the intermediate-term bucket, and 7 percent for the long-term bucket. The plan is to preserve purchasing power by keeping up with the impact of inflation over time, while providing current income.

Let's assume in our fact set that the retiree in question is 75 years old, has a $2,400,000 portfolio, and needs the $96,000 per year to live comfortably (a 4 percent withdrawal rate).

In this case, assuming an inflation rate of 3.5 percent with withdrawals adjusted every five years and the rates of return indicated above (2 percent/5 percent/7 percent), the allocation of the $2,400,000 portfolio would look like this:

$435,000 – Short-Term Bucket (18%)
$447,000 – Intermediate-Term Bucket (19%)
$1,518,000 – Long-Term Bucket (63%)

Over the first five years, $96,000 per year would be withdrawn from the short-term bucket. With no other changes (and assuming the rates of return above), the following would be true in five years at age 80:

$0 – Short-Term Bucket
$570,000 – Intermediate-Term Bucket
$2,219,000 – Long-Term Bucket

The overall portfolio would have grown to $2,699,000. However, adjusted for inflation, the required withdrawal would now be $114,000 per year (or 4.22 percent of the working assets).

In theory, this math works. However, in practice, if this were implemented exactly as illustrated, this 80-year-old retiree would now hold an 82 percent allocation to stocks in his or her portfolio. As a result, the goal is to take advantage of good years in equity markets to make withdrawals of excess gains from the long-term bucket to replenish the short- and intermediate-term buckets and to restart the 10-year clock or lengthen the remaining time prior to using the long-term assets.

If equity markets are strong in year one, selling stocks at high valuations to replenish the conservative portions of the portfolio will restart the 10-year allocation. If equity markets aren't strong or the long-term bucket loses value in year one, this retiree can avoid selling stocks at low valuations because he or she still has nine years remaining before needing to rely on those assets for income production.

This is a process that ideally adjusts at least annually. Instead of a simple rebalancing used in the total return strategy, this is a process of transferring funds between accounts from one bucket to another or to proactively elect not to do so, based on market conditions and returns.

This strategy works between the 2.5 percent and the 4.5 percent withdrawal rates, assuming inflation isn't rampant. In our example, after five years the withdrawal rate is 4.22 percent, which remains below the 4.5 percent threshold so it can be maintained for another five years. When and if the withdrawal rate increases above 4.5 percent or so, it is time to use the third strategy, in full or in part, to maintain income and a dignified retirement.

Annuitization

To **annuitize** is to trade a principal sum irrevocably for an income stream. Almost any principal amount can be annuitized, and because income calculations are made based on life expectancy, if annuitization is explored as a strategy, it is generally better for older retirees than for younger ones.

Annuitization does offer some benefits, the most notable of which is that payments can be guaranteed for life. Also, using annuitization as one of the bucket components in the asset segregation strategy can help preserve the other buckets by reducing required withdrawals from liquid or volatile assets.

The biggest drawbacks to annuitization are that the decision to annuitize is irrevocable and the principal is no longer available during the annuitant's lifetime or potentially even for their heirs upon the annuitant's death.

There are financial tools that can be used when annuitizing to provide some income or wealth replacement to heirs if that is a priority for a retiree. Be sure to discuss these strategies with your financial, tax, and legal advisors before making decisions—especially irrevocable ones.

This concludes the first semester of your senior year, and you have but one semester left until you graduate into retirement. In the next semester, we'll focus on some of the biggest pre-retirement (and at-retirement) decisions, including housing, pensions, insurance, and social security.

POST-COURSE EXERCISE QUESTIONS

1. **TRUE** or **FALSE**: You can withdraw 4 percent of your assets each year without facing the risk of running out of money.

2. **TRUE** or **FALSE**: The government has recognized the potential need for playing catch-up as retirement approaches and has legislated ways to help people do so.

3. **TRUE** or **FALSE**: Some assets are better utilized for growth, while others are better utilized for income.

4. **TRUE** or **FALSE**: Your taxes will always be lower in retirement than during your working years.

5. **TRUE** or **FALSE**: Planning to be retired means having only conservative investments in your portfolio.

POST-COURSE EXERCISE ANSWERS

1. **FALSE**. This question is a perfect example of how one size never fits all and "rules of thumb" can be dangerous to your wealth. Some retirees can withdraw 4 percent a year from their working assets without running out of money but others cannot. There are too many factors and variables to list but some include longevity, interest rates, market conditions, marital status, physical health, and prevailing tax laws. While 4 percent can be used as a barometer, it should never be considered gospel.

2. **TRUE**. The government recognizes the benefits of people supporting themselves financially in retirement and have set out rules and conditions to allow for extra savings and tax benefits beyond certain ages. Some include catch-up provisions on qualified retirement accounts and IRAs, similar provisions on HSAs, and tax benefits for long-term care premiums and medical costs, which often escalate with age.

3. **TRUE**. The characteristics of different asset classes lend themselves to different highest and best uses. For example, cash equivalents, fixed income instruments, investment real estate, dividend-paying stocks, and annuities may best be used to generate income, while growth stocks and private equity may be best used to stimulate or maintain portfolio growth.

4. **FALSE**. While tax rates are often progressive and dependent on income levels, planning to be in a lower tax bracket in retirement may be the same as planning to fail to grow wealth. If you reach financial independence and live on an income comparable to the one you enjoyed during your working years, your income tax bracket may not be lower. In fact, growing wealth coupled with government deficits and escalating national debt service may potentially lead to higher taxes in retirement. That is the main reason why **tax diversification** is as important as asset allocation and portfolio diversification.

5. **FALSE**. While your overall risk tolerance may change when you retire, holding only conservative investments in your portfolio can be a recipe for running out of money quickly. Not only will that

allocation cause a greater dependence on using principal instead of income to live, but net of your withdrawals, it will almost surely trail inflation and your purchasing power (and therefore lifestyle) will suffer. It is important to continue to have some element of growth in your portfolio, even after retiring from full-time employment.

EXTRA-CREDIT ASSIGNMENT

For this course's extra-credit assignment, go back to the balance sheet and income statement that you created several semesters ago and determine the withdrawal rate you would need if you wanted to retire immediately.

As a reminder, the calculation looks like this:

- Take your total gross income, including any employer-paid contributions or matches.
- Subtract the amount you are saving or investing annually (again, including the employer-paid amount).
- Subtract the amount of any costs that could be eliminated immediately. This could be your kids' tuitions (if they are about to graduate), your mortgage payment (if you plan to pay it off, downsize, or use a reverse mortgage), or any other costs that you could eliminate today if you retired immediately.
- Take the remaining figure (gross income minus savings minus excess expenses) and divide it by your total available working assets. This will yield a percentage.
- Note whether the percentage would allow you to retire today under the total return method, the asset segregation method, the annuitization method, or not at all.
- If you aren't ready to retire or this percentage isn't optimal for you, use it as a measuring rod and challenge yourself to reduce this percentage every year during your remaining accumulation years until you're ready to claim financial independence and to graduate.

SECOND SEMESTER

"Senioritis" is an affliction that commonly impacts second-semester seniors at high schools and colleges around the country. The symptoms of senioritis begin to manifest themselves around the time that the final semester begins and become more severe once the next step of life's journey has been determined.

For seniors in high school, senioritis begins once college acceptances have been received, and for seniors in college, senioritis begins once a job offer has been accepted.

Unlike in high school or college when senioritis is mostly innocuous, in preparing to graduate into retirement it can be problematic and should be avoided.

Planning for the final years of full-time work has received lots of attention in the media and in marketing messages by financial services companies. Every company slinging financial products and services seems to have nicknames for the final five years or so leading up to a formal retirement and for good reason. As in football, moving the ball to the two-yard line is good but unless you can cross the goal line, there is no touchdown.

This semester involves two capstone courses—one relating to housing decisions in retirement and one detailing some of the biggest financial decisions of your life, many of which need to be made simultaneously. Think of that matrix of decisions as your senior thesis or dissertation; you have all semester to work on it but only one moment to present it.

Course Schedule for Senior Year—Second Semester:

- Retirement Readiness 402: To Move or Not to Move... That Is the Question
- Retirement Readiness 403: These Are the Days...of Big Decisions

Retirement Readiness 402:

TO MOVE OR NOT TO MOVE...
THAT IS THE QUESTION

Of the series of major decisions impacting retirement, one of the largest and most challenging—financially and emotionally—is deciding where to live during different phases of our retirement years. As a financial professional, when I ask pre-retirees where they plan to live when they retire from full-time employment, I often get blank stares.

HOW DO YOU THINK OF YOUR HOME?

As we dig deeper into the conversation, questions inevitably surface about logistics, aging in-place, healthcare, proximity to family, friends, and activities, and other qualitative concerns, in addition to the quantitative questions relating to affordability of housing options.

The concept of "downsizing" is one which often carries the negative connotations associated with corporate reductions-in-force and layoffs. However, "downsizing in retirement" is a process by which couples or individuals begin to reduce the size of their homes, the complexity of their lives, and often monthly expenses as well. Planned properly, downsizing can be a rewarding and productive process. Like many decisions we face when our lives are changing, downsizing under duress due to medical or financial issues can be stressful and disheartening.

The purpose of this course is to describe some of the DOs and DON'Ts of the process of downsizing in retirement and to encourage productive conversations around this important topic with family members and various advisors, ideally in advance of any necessity caused by adverse triggering events.

The DOs and DON'Ts of downsizing in retirement

While it would be possible to provide a laundry list of to-do items when planning to downsize, I've tried to capture what you need to know into **five DOs** and **three DON'Ts** to assist you. We'll first focus on the five primary steps to make this process as effective as possible:

1. Planning well in advance
2. Exploring various types of housing arrangements that suit you physically
3. Understanding your financial resources and implications
4. Determining desired geographic areas
5. Building a team of specialists to assist you along the way

Then we'll talk about the three primary pitfalls to avoid:

1. Underestimating the impacts of aging, physically and otherwise
2. Taking on more ongoing financial responsibility than your resources allow
3. Keeping your intentions and desires unknown to your loved ones

FIVE DOS OF DOWNSIZING IN RETIREMENT

1) DO start planning three to five years in advance

The process of moving is never an easy one and the experience is different for everyone. Some people move multiple times to various states or countries throughout their lives, while others spend their entire lives in the same zip code and may spend several decades in the same home.

For most families, moving to a new home is a process of moving *toward something* like a new job, school, or marriage and it is usually to a larger or more expensive home than the last. But for those planning to retire, the experience can feel like a move *away from something*, which makes the whole process uniquely challenging.

During the years that precede the planned move, there are several questions you'll want to ask and have answered. It's always better if you can take your time and be thoughtful instead of being rushed as you gather this information.

What will my retirement years look like?

This is a loaded question and one which leads to more questions than answers, at least initially. If you're used to working 50–60 hours a week, what do you plan to do with your newfound time? Does your retirement involve consulting or working part time such that you will need proximity to an airport or a home office? Will you need a home with guest bedrooms for visiting friends and family? Can you age in-place in your current home with a few modifications? What will your retirement income look like and how might that impact your lifestyle? Do you want to be close to family members, friends, hobbies, or volunteer organizations? Do you have loved ones who can assist you as you get older? Do you have provisions made for retiree healthcare or long-term care?

It is unlikely that you know all the answers to these types of questions presently. But before you begin the process of modifying, refinancing, or selling your home, take the time to work through as many of the details and logistics as you're able.

What am I planning to do with all of this stuff?

As we discussed in an earlier semester, families generally acquire possessions over the years and then make sure they can accommodate that volume of stuff when they move from one house to the next—and the larger the home, the more stuff a family is likely to amass. Whether you've been in your present home for 10 years or 50, downsizing usually means reducing the amount of possessions, which creates the somewhat daunting task of deciding what to keep and what simply won't fit in a smaller home.

In addition to being lots of work, the process of shedding possessions is an emotional one, especially if you're downsizing due to the death of a loved one. The families who have the most success with this process start early and communicate openly with one another. Find out if one or more siblings, children, or grandchildren want some of the possessions you plan to eliminate and make the process a transparent one and as fair as possible.

Once you determine which possessions to keep and which to give to family members, you'll want to sort the remaining items based on their value and usefulness. In other words, determine what can be sold or donated to charity and what needs to be hauled to the dump. There are services available to remove unwanted stuff from your home, and some are expensive solutions, so if you're fortunate to have able-bodied family members who can help, it may save you some money in the process.

Keep good receipts for the donations; they may provide tax deductions for you in the year the gifts are made. Talk to your tax advisor to make sure you can take a tax deduction for your gifts, if that is an important factor in deciding what to donate and to whom.

The remaining DOs and DON'Ts in this course will also take time to implement so give yourself a long enough time frame to work on these items gradually. I find that three to five years is the right length of time to plan this process, in an ideal world.

2) DO explore various types of housing arrangements that suit you physically

The options for housing in retirement are as diverse as the needs of the retiree population.

The first consideration is whether you can age in-place physically over the long term. If you have a home with several flights of stairs and a master bedroom on the top floor, there may come a time when it is either impossible or uncomfortable to navigate the staircase. Knees and hips can be replaced but stairs are often exceedingly challenging as we age nonetheless. Some homes can be modified with chairlifts or other equipment but that depends on your ability to afford those modifications and your comfort in doing so.

If your home is a single story or at least has a master bedroom on the first floor, aging in-place could be a legitimate strategy. However, you also need to consider the upkeep of the property and how much work is involved on your part in keeping your home livable.

If you cannot age in-place in your present home and you need to plan a move, you have lots of available options to consider.

You could move to a smaller house with no stairs or to a condominium. If you're used to a big yard and garden, a condo might seem unappealing but even a ranch-style house could allow you to navigate it well into your retirement years. For some, a condo community is the best of all worlds, especially if it has proximity to grocery stores, restaurants, and various conveniences. It also has modest maintenance requirements and offers fully independent living.

On the other hand, if you like a truly maintenance-free existence, you could consider renting a home or apartment. There are pros and cons to renting, but the absence of a down payment and the flexibility to move again anytime might outweigh any financial or tax benefits to ownership.

The size of the baby boomer population has led to a proliferation of over-55 communities across the US. These communities offer proximity to neighbors of similar ages and interests and may include clubhouses, swimming pools, restaurants, golf courses, and other amenities, which make them convenient, comfortable, and ideal for independent living. Some also have security services and maintenance services, which create a safe and livable environment.

Of course, not everyone retiring will have the benefit of good health so communities offering various levels of assisted care are also available. These include continuing care retirement communities (CCRCs), assisted living facilities, and nursing homes.

Some CCRCs more closely resemble college campuses than nursing facilities. They have a wide range of services available and allow for independent living for as long as residents can manage on their own. However, if a time arises when a resident can't manage fully on his or her own, they provide access to intermediate care services, skilled nursing services, and multiple levels of care for those suffering from physical or cognitive impairments.

3) DO understand your financial resources and implications

Once you have considered aging in-place, the second consideration is a financial one. Can you afford to stay in your present home, based on your projected retirement income? If you have a mortgage on the home, can you afford to keep paying that bill or do you have a sensible and affordable way to pay it off upon retirement?

Even without a mortgage, the costs of home ownership, especially in older homes, can be significant. Not only do you have property taxes and insurance but you also have the costs to maintain the working systems, the physical structure of the home, and the landscaping or external appearance. And if you are a do-it-yourselfer and like to mow the lawn and shovel snow, remember that there may come a day when it becomes physically impossible and you'll need to pay someone to do it for you.

If you can physically age in-place and can afford to stay financially (even with the possibility of increased costs for maintenance), you may not have to move at all—at least initially. In that case, you may want to begin the process of eliminating unwanted stuff so that if your life changes you'll have less to do at the time.

If you cannot physically age in-place or you cannot afford to stay in your present home (or both), you'll want to explore moving and ideally to do so before you are under duress to make a change.

4) DO determine desirable geographic areas

In the event of a move, the conversation about geography is about much more than just the weather. There are cost considerations, tax considerations, and family concerns.

Different geographic regions have vastly different costs of living and income tax structures. A state with no income tax could provide much needed tax relief and a better standard of living in retirement. Living where the weather requires less heating and cooling can create lower utility costs. Living in a community with proximity to shopping and dining options by golf cart can reduce transportation costs.

You'll want to make sure that you are near your hobbies and interests. If you love to golf, moving south might make more sense than north so that you can play year-round. If you love the beach or the mountains, now is the time to explore being there at least part of the year.

If you have the resources for a second home, you might want to be a snowbird, for example, spending the six cold months of the year in sunny Florida or Arizona and the six hot months of the year further north or in your hometown.

If you have grandchildren or great-grandchildren, you may want to explore living close to them, at least part of the year, or you might choose a less expensive home in your area so you can afford to travel to see your grandchildren as often as you'd like.

5) DO build a team of specialists to assist along the way

Whatever you decide to do about housing in retirement, if you keep the physical, financial, and geographic considerations in mind and if you plan ahead, you'll have lots of time to find the right option for you.

You also don't have to do this alone and, in fact, you shouldn't try. There are specialists who can work together to form your dream team of advocates for this process.

A real estate agent can assist in determining the potential value of your present home, as well as providing advice on the upgrades or repairs you might want to make to maximize the sales price. He or she can also help you find a new home, although if you are moving to a different geographic region, you'll want to have an agent in each area—one to help you sell and one to help you buy.

A mortgage advisor can assist you with determining financing options on a new home if you plan to buy. He or she can also provide options for a reverse mortgage or **reverse purchase** to determine if that strategy makes sense in your situation.

Your CPA or tax advisor can assist with the impact of a move from one state to another, which will help you measure the affordability and sensibility of a move.

If you move out of state, you'll want to consider finding an estate planning attorney in your new state so that your documents are updated based on the laws of your state of residence. Your present attorney may be able to recommend one in your new area.

And, of course, your financial advisor can assist in aggregating all of the details from these specialists and integrating them with your present financial plan to make sure you can afford the move you're contemplating—whether it is across the country or down the street.

Now that we have discussed the five DOs, let's shift our focus to the pitfalls to avoid when starting this process.

THREE DON'TS OF DOWNSIZING IN RETIREMENT

1) DON'T underestimate the impact of aging

None of us wants to envision our own frailty. When we feel young, healthy, and capable, we can't imagine being unable to care for ourselves. We may remember our grandparents getting old and may be witnessing our parents' aging but surely that process can't happen to us.

The harsh reality is that one in three adults will eventually require some type of assisted care and even more of us will lose the ability to do some of the things we once did as younger men and women. Aging isn't always fun and it isn't always easy. However, it is predictable that if we live long enough, our bodies and minds won't be as sharp as they once were.

As a result, when planning on housing decisions in retirement, maintaining flexibility is important. As life changes, medically or otherwise, be ready for your team of advisors and your loved ones to know what "Plan B" entails.

2) DON'T overestimate your financial wherewithal

For many financially successful people, decisions about spending money can feel somewhat carefree during years of full-time employment and ample income—especially for those who can earn more by working more. Once you graduate into retirement, unless you have an infusion of significant consulting income or some type of employment, your resources will become finite in a new way psychologically.

It's important to reiterate the realities about retirement:

- Life is going to be more expensive than you expect.
- You are going to live longer than you imagine.

- You will need to make sure you have resources that you cannot outlive.

It has been said that to be young and broke is an inconvenience but to be old and broke is a tragedy. One of the greatest fears that retirees have is running out of money, and the best way to prevent that from becoming a tragic reality is to plan ahead and to be realistic with your expectations.

3) DON'T keep your plans a secret

If raising a child takes a village, navigating housing decisions when graduating into retirement takes an army. You'll need to communicate openly and effectively with your team of advisors and with your family and loved ones all throughout the process.

Surprises are rarely welcome on this subject. If they are responsible adults, your grown children can be allies and resources to you during this process. Your plans do not require their permission or approval but ideally, your family members will at least have an awareness of your intentions and preferences. They may have concerns about your health and well-being; you worried about them for many years and now the shoe may be on the other foot. Try to understand their potential worries and make sure they are aware of yours. The more you communicate, the easier this process will be and the smoother any transition is likely to go.

This concludes your penultimate course and prepares you for the final capstone. Hopefully, now armed with the DOs and DON'Ts of housing and downsizing post-graduation, you'll be able to turn your attention to all of the other decisions you'll face in the months ahead of and following your graduation day.

POST-COURSE EXERCISE QUESTIONS

1. **TRUE** or **FALSE**: No decisions on housing in retirement should be made until you have formally retired.

2. **TRUE** or **FALSE**: Housing decisions in retirement are impacted by several financial factors including working assets, mortgage debt, income, and tax considerations.

3. **TRUE** or **FALSE**: To determine housing during your retirement years, you should take into consideration your present health and the likelihood that your present residence will allow you to age in-place without needing to move again in the future.

4. **TRUE** OR **FALSE**: When preparing to retire, geography will play a role in whether or not to move, especially as it relates to family members' locations and access to friends, hobbies, and medical care.

5. **TRUE** OR **FALSE**: All retirees should choose to live in continuing care retirement communities to make sure resources are available when needed.

POST-COURSE EXERCISE ANSWERS

1. **FALSE.** Planning to move is a daunting task at any stage of life but for people contemplating retirement, it is especially demanding. It is wise to start planning some three to five years in advance of retiring. For some people, the decision may be not to move or downsize right away (or at all). Even for those not planning to move, there are important steps to take around housing and to create and execute a plan properly takes time.

2. **TRUE.** You'll need to take a full inventory of assets and liabilities and to determine if a mortgage of some type will be required during retirement. Based on whether or not you have a mortgage payment in retirement, you also need to know what withdrawal rate will be required from your working assets to determine your retirement income strategy.

   This may be a good time to explore creative financing options, including reverse mortgages, to assist with cash flow, if needed. It may also be a good time to consider the impact of income taxation in different states to determine lifestyle affordability as it relates to your income and tax burden.

3. **TRUE.** If your present residence is one in which you could predictably navigate as a 10- or 20-year-older version of yourself, it may postpone or eliminate the need to move. However, if you have a home with lots of stairs, an upstairs master bedroom, and lots of space to cover, aging in-place might be more difficult than you'd think. If that is the case, try to avoid making inflexible or expensive decisions (like reverse mortgages), which could be problematic if the need to move were to arise at some point in the future.

4. **TRUE.** A successful retirement doesn't necessarily constitute a life of leisure but you'll want to be close to family, friends, and activities you enjoy for better quality of life. Also, you'll almost surely face healthcare issues in your later years and will want to know that you have access to quality care nearby.

5. **FALSE.** While some retirees will enjoy the accessibility of various resources that can be provided by a continuing care retirement com-

munity, it isn't ideal for every retiree. Each situation is unique and there are lots of living options, including independent living in a house or condominium or inclusion in an over-55 community for active adults. It is best to explore these many living options and arrangements before deciding on one, which is another reason why starting to explore this topic early can have so much impact.

EXTRA-CREDIT ASSIGNMENT

For this course, the extra-credit assignment is based on your age and how close you are to your own target retirement date.

EXTRA-CREDIT ASSIGNMENT IF YOU ARE APPROACHING FIVE YEARS TO RETIREMENT OR HAVE ALREADY RETIRED

Your extra-credit assignment is to take a hard look at your present residence. Consider access to bedrooms, bathrooms, laundry rooms, and other common spaces. While your home might be close to your present employment, consider your proximity to family, friends, hobbies, and hospitals, and determine if the geography is likely to be ideal once you aren't commuting to your present job.

If you are 65 years old, ask yourself candidly if an 85-year-old version of you could realistically manage in your present home.

If you can age in-place and have proximity to people and places likely to be important during your retirement years, check the box and make sure your financial plan takes staying put into consideration.

If you can't age in-place or expect you'll need or want to move for some other reason when you graduate into your retirement, discuss this reality with your spouse, extended family, and financial advisor, and make sure your plan incorporates the costs of a relocation.

EXTRA-CREDIT ASSIGNMENT IF YOU HAVE MORE THAN FIVE YEARS TO RETIREMENT

For younger people who aren't five years or less to your planned retirement, you can skip this assignment, unless you have parents or grandparents who are living, in which case your assignment is much tougher than the older folks completing this course.

Your assignment is to open a dialogue with your parents, grandparents, or other more senior relatives and to familiarize them with the concepts in this course. A little insight for them might make a tremendous difference—for them and for you.

Retirement Readiness 403:

THESE ARE THE DAYS... OF BIG DECISIONS

The final course of any college program is often the capstone and ends with the submission of a thesis or the presentation of a dissertation.

We will begin this course with a primer on the most major decisions facing people when they decide to retire from full-time employment, most of which need to be addressed imminently. We'll conclude with some of the smaller items worth exploring in a more leisurely way once the graduation day has passed.

THE SIX FINAL STEPS TOWARD GRADUATION

There are six primary areas where decisions are needed just before, immediately at, or just after retirement:

1. Debt restructuring or reduction
2. Long-term care insurance placement
3. Medicare and more
4. Pension election
5. Social security claim
6. Insurance review

DECISIONS <u>BEFORE</u> YOUR RETIREMENT DATE

Debt restructuring or reduction

Think back to when you were a freshman in your financial life. That might have been a few hours ago when you began reading this book and couldn't put it down or you might be holding a tattered copy that you started 40 years ago.

Way back then, we discussed the many reasons for debt reduction and now you've got another one. It is very difficult to borrow from a bank or other financial institution once you have retired. That is because one of the primary determinants of credit worthiness is income and income is easier to demonstrate with a W-2 from your employer than from a pile of investment or retirement account statements.

If you have any debts that need to be refinanced—for student loans, for your mortgage or home equity line of credit, or for any other debt obligation—complete that task before electing to retire.

Long-term care insurance placement

Likewise, applying for long-term care requires resources and is also based on attained age. If you have not yet placed long-term care insurance in force, consider doing so before you retire. In a perfect world, you'd apply some 10 years prior to retirement, but the three to five years prior to retirement is basically the last chance to get long-term care insurance affordably.

DECISIONS <u>ON</u> YOUR RETIREMENT DATE

Medicare and more

If you are retiring after attaining age 65, the medical insurance discussion is straight-forward. Medicare Part A, which is available to you with no premium cost, needs to be placed in effect at age 65 whether you have other medical insurance or not. You'll want to initiate the claim for Medicare 60–90 days before your 65th birthday to make sure the enrollment is timely.

Once you plan to leave full-time employment, if you are age 65 or older, this will be the time to enroll in Medicare Part B and Part D. These coverages will have a cost to you and will vary annually based on the plan you choose and the income you declare on your tax returns. Except in the case of some military veterans or other rare instance where retiree medical supersedes Medicare, Medicare will become your primary insurer as soon as your employer's health insurance terminates along with your employment.

The medical insurance decision isn't as simple if you plan to leave full-time employment prior to your 65th birthday. When your employment ends, if you have been a participant under your employer's medical insurance plan, the plan must offer you a continuation of benefits (under a provision called COBRA) for a period of 18 months. If you are between the ages of 63½ and 65, this can close the gap entirely between your employer's plan and Medicare. COBRA premiums are fully at your expense but you cannot lose your coverage during that time, except for failure to pay premiums.

If you are under the age of 63½ when you leave full-time employment, you will either need to join your working spouse's employer plan (if applicable) or you'll need to explore individual medical insurance through your home state's insurance exchange.

Using COBRA or getting individual medical insurance can be daunting and expensive, so explore these options and costs before retiring and make sure to make the change immediately upon retiring.

Pension election

If you are a government employee or a private-sector employee fortunate enough to have a defined benefit pension, the decision to begin income is a critical and irrevocable one. It should therefore be carefully considered before you make your election.

Under most pension plans, you have a variety of survivorship options, which will impact the amount of your monthly benefit. If you are not married (single, divorced, or widowed), you'll generally elect the single life option which provides for the maximum retiree benefit but ends immediately upon your death.

If you are married, you may have as many as five to six other choices that will impact not only your benefits but also your spouse's benefits in the event that he or she outlives you. You can provide for a joint and 100 percent survivor benefit, which means that your spouse receives the same benefit check as a widow or widower that you did as a retiree. This will usually be the lowest payment amount due to the ongoing nature of the payment at its original amount.

There may also be options for less than 100 percent of the retiree's benefit to go to a surviving spouse (often 50 percent or 75 percent) or options to continue benefits to a widow or widower for only a set maximum period of time once the retiree is deceased. Lastly, there may be an option that allows a smaller benefit initially but then increases the benefit if the retiree outlives his or her spouse.

The most important thing to understand about pension elections is that once you make them, you can never change them. You also have to make them almost immediately upon retirement so you'll want to gather the estimated benefits from your HR department and review them with your financial advisor before making the decision that is best for you.

Some of the elements that are factors in this decision include an age disparity between a retiree and a spouse, any health disparity between a retiree and a spouse, family history of longevity, financial needs during retirement years, and availability of other income streams or life insurance benefits in the event the retiree dies first.

DECISIONS <u>AFTER</u> YOUR RETIREMENT DATE

Social security claim

The rules relating to social security are adjusted by Congress with some regularity so it will be important to understand your options before making a claim, either before, at, or after retirement.

That said, there are a few general best practices involving social security:

- For anyone still working or considering working, avoid claiming social security before full retirement age. Even though you can claim at age 62, your monthly benefit will be greatly (and permanently) reduced and will be offset even further by any income you make prior to your full retirement age.

- For married couples, it is usually wise for the spouse with the higher of the two monthly benefit amounts to delay claiming until age 70. The reason is that the surviving spouse keeps the higher of the two benefits and that can create the maximum allowable survivorship benefit.

- The break-even point if you wait until age 70 to claim benefits is usually between 82–84. So if you have good health and reasonable family longevity in your genes, it may be worth waiting until age 70 to claim. On the other hand, if your mortality is compromised or your health is in question, claiming earlier may make sense.

There are certainly more considerations than these and some that may be completely unique to your personal and family situation. Avoid rules of thumb and look at your options carefully before claiming.

Insurance review

Auto insurance

As a retiree no longer commuting to work, you may be eligible for a reduced premium on your auto insurance. It's unlikely to change your financial life but any savings is worth pursuing.

Disability insurance

Once you are no longer working full time and have reached financial independence, there is generally no need to maintain disability insurance. Group coverage will expire when you terminate your employment and individual coverage can be proactively terminated to save you from making further premium payments for coverage you likely no longer need.

Life insurance

If you are covered under your employer's group life insurance coverage, typically that coverage expires when you leave your employment. In some cases, there are limited benefits for retirees of a certain age or for those who spent a certain number of years with the employer.

Not only do you need to know if any coverage will remain in force at your employer's expense during some or all of your retirement years but you may also need to know if the remaining coverage is portable. You'll need to ask if you can take it with you when you go. In most cases, group life insurance isn't portable or isn't portable favorably but depending on your health and the cost, if portability is an option, you may at least want to explore it.

This is also a good time to review your other life insurance that isn't related to your employment. Once your nest egg is large enough that you have reached financial independence and you have elected your pension benefits and filed your social security claim, you may be able to make meaningful reductions to your remaining life insurance coverage and premiums.

If you have whole life insurance, you'll absolutely want to keep it for your own future use (or your heirs'). But in the absence of any health condition that could compromise your life expectancy, any term insurance or other non-cash value permanent life insurance may not be needed anymore once you have reached this point in your life, since its primary purpose was income replacement in the event of your untimely death.

POST-COURSE EXERCISE QUESTIONS

1. **TRUE** or **FALSE**: Annual social security benefits increase from ages 62-70, but there is no benefit to delaying filing as a retiree past age 70.

2. **TRUE** or **FALSE**: Social security income is not subject to federal income tax.

3. **TRUE** or **FALSE**: Every state in the US has specific income tax rules and rates that apply to pension benefits.

4. **TRUE** or **FALSE**: It is not necessary to file for Medicare until you are fully retired so long as you have health insurance through a current or prior employer plan.

5. **TRUE** or **FALSE**: If you plan to stay in your home and need to refinance your mortgage to do so comfortably, it is best to initiate and complete the refinance before you retire.

POST-COURSE EXERCISE ANSWERS

1. **TRUE**. Social security can be claimed as early as age 62 but is subject to earning limitations and reduced benefits. After reaching full retirement age (generally age 67), there are no income limitations and benefits are not reduced but delaying the claim for benefits until age 70 allows for a larger annual benefit for life. Once you reach age 70, there is no reason to delay filing as annual benefit amounts no longer increase.

2. **FALSE**. Depending on your adjusted gross income, as much as 85 percent of your social security benefit check could be subject to income taxes.

3. **TRUE**. Most people are aware that all states have their own income tax codes that impact residents during working years. However, every state also treats income from pensions or various retirement plans differently and in some states these income sources are not taxed at all. As a result, determining where to live in retirement can be impacted by both financial wherewithal and state tax rules relating to retirement income.

4. **FALSE**. While you do not need to file for Medicare Part B or Part D until you are fully retired, it is very important to file for Medicare Part A so that it is effective on your 65th birthday, regardless of your employment situation or access to health insurance and to avoid a late enrollment penalty.

5. **TRUE**. It is much easier to qualify to borrow money while you have income that you can declare it on your loan application. Once you are retired, you may have more difficulty in demonstrating income and could be turned down for a loan or subject to higher interest rates as a result.

EXTRA-CREDIT ASSIGNMENT

The extra-credit assignment for this course may be more suited for a yoga or meditation practice than for a retirement readiness course.

Breathe.

You have major decisions to make, and some are time sensitive, so pace yourself and plan ahead. Making any of these decisions under duress will be especially hard and some of that anxiety can be relieved by proper planning.

So breathe. Give yourself the space and time to think about these decisions in advance. You've earned it.

Graduation Day

CONGRATULATIONS! NOW WHAT?

Today is the first day of the next great journey of your life. Nothing is over—one of the best times of your life is just beginning. And why not? You have more resources, time, and, of course, wisdom. This is not the time to feel tired *or* retired; it's time for adventure!

After your name is read and you walk across the stage to the roaring cheers of friends and family members, your college experience is over. In traditional retirement, this might be an office party or a family gathering, or it might just be a few handshakes and hugs and a final goodbye at the office.

Your time at Retire U wasn't really dedicated to finding the right answers, as much as identifying the *right questions* to ask. Hopefully, it has provided food for thought about what's ahead and steps you can take to build your own path. Like a philosophy class in college, the answers may be less important than the thought process.

Recent college graduates often return home to live with their parents for a period of time as they get their careers underway. Sometimes they fail to launch entirely and never really thrive professionally or financially.

When graduating into retirement, the safety valve of Mom and Dad's guest bedroom is a Medicaid-eligible nursing home. This is a last resort and not where you want to spend the last part of your life, so you'll need to make sure you have reached a level of financial independence to provide you with lots of options and opportunities.

And you have a new question to answer that perhaps you've never been asked before.

What do you want to be when you grow up?

Just because you finished college, it doesn't mean you stop learning. Likewise, just because you reach financial independence and graduate into retirement, it doesn't mean you stop living.

You now have the tools you need—the professional experience, financial resources, and a vast personal network—to be mission-driven and to contribute in any way you'd like to the success of your community, industry, and family.

As the popular saying goes, "It's never too late to be what you might have been." There is incredible wisdom in that simple statement. We ask children constantly what they want to be when they grow up. They rarely say, "I want to be a tax audit specialist." They more likely say they want to be astronauts, ballerinas, professional athletes, or lead singers in a rock band.

Why don't we ask adults what they want to be when they grow up? Is it because we somehow believe that once we're adults, we stop growing, dreaming, or evolving? Do we lose the ability to recreate ourselves, to believe in our dreams, or to chase virtual fireflies?

I don't know what I want to be when I grow up, but I have professional dreams that certainly play a role in my personal vision of my post-graduation years. Instead of merely being an authority in the financial advising profession, I yearn to be an influencer in the profession, that is, someone who can help democratize advice and make a difference on a large scale, even for individual and families I never meet personally. This book is one step in that journey but it won't be the last one. To paraphrase what Robert Frost wrote, I have miles to go before I sleep.

Whether you are age 32 or 72 right now, close your eyes and visualize what life could look like for you in five years, 10 years, even 20 years.

When you reach financial independence, will you still be working in the same profession or industry? Will you still be living in your current home or even your current state or country? Will you be teaching college classes, starting a travel blog, opening a consulting practice, volunteering at your local food bank, or spending lots of time with your grandchildren?

Maybe you'll be doing all of the above. Maybe you'll have a rhythm to your life that can only be achieved through financial independence.

Your graduation into retirement affords you the ability to choose how much you want to work, how you want to spend your time, what you want to experience, and, yes, what to be when you grow up.

Dr. Seuss wrote in his last published book during his lifetime, *Oh, the Places You'll Go,* "You can steer yourself any direction you choose." His book has been a frequent graduation present for high school and college graduates since it was published in 1990. Why don't we read it to ourselves as adults and even present it as a gift when a friend or colleague retires?

The answer lies in the way we have been wired to think about retirement. We congratulate people for retiring but then we expect them to disappear and become less relevant. We somehow see their wealth of experience and wisdom as less valuable when their business card has "expired."

American fashion icon Iris Apfel said at age 97, "For me, retirement is a fate worse than death." That is a clear sign that our adult population needs to reconsider what it means to retire and, instead, to make this a step in an exciting exodus and not a personal hibernation or extinction event. Only then will we ask adults what they want to be when they grow up and only then will we determine our own answer to the fundamentally critical question.

Leaving your legacy

The basic legal definition of legacy is "something inherited." The word conjures up visions of will readings when heirs find out which sibling got the grandfather clock in the den or the condo in Aruba. We also inherit traits from our biological ancestors, which are far more powerful than any property left behind.

In my opinion, the stuff we leave behind is not nearly as important as the stories, the values, and the wisdom we impart on others during our lifetimes. I challenge you to think of your legacy as more than your house or IRA account and to consider what you can leave for future generations—not only of your own family but of your community—that will create real value.

If you own a business, your legacy might be that the company continues after your retirement and lives on creating jobs and servicing customers or clients long beyond your lifetime.

If you have significant financial resources, perhaps some can be used to make a difference in your family and community by giving the most valuable and impactful financial gift possible to your children—the gift of *influence.*

A large gift can ensure your name is on a school building forever, but when you were on your college campus did you know anything about the donors of the funds to name the buildings, or did you just remember "Smith Hall?"

Instead of leaving a large charitable gift to put your name on a building, what if you created a family foundation or charitable fund with your resources and you named your children as directors of the fund?

Every year, your family would get together to determine how and where gifts would be made and what impact your legacy could have on the community. And your children (and someday their children) would have the wherewithal to make regular contributions, which ensures that they are able to rub elbows with the other donors.

A fund like that could eternally create influence for your family and would also mean charitable gifts to causes that are important to you during your lifetime. Maybe that donation creates a scholarship in your name, which is presented annually and changes a student's future every year.

That would be more of a legacy than a plaque on a building somewhere, and it would be perpetual and make an impact long after you're gone—to the charitable beneficiaries, the community, and your family.

How do you want to be remembered?
If your parents or even grandparents are still living, do you sometimes hear them tell stories from their childhood, which you feel you have heard 10

times before? Those stories make up a part of your parents' legacy, and your shared experiences with them are how they will be remembered—by you.

But how will your parents or grandparents be remembered by your children or grandchildren? Chances are, those stories will fade away and stop being told at the dinner table, in part because your children didn't know your grandparents, in part because you don't remember the stories well enough to tell them (despite hearing them 10 times over the years), and in part because you'll be telling your own stories to them just like your parents and grandparents told theirs to you.

It is possible to be remembered for a generation or two, and sometimes your contributions or accomplishments can be remembered longer than that by the public but your stories will generally fade away as the people who know you pass away. That means it's not easy to leave a real legacy without finding a way to capture those stories—in your own voice—during your lifetime.

I suggest that you consider leaving behind a digital video of yourself that tells some of your stories so they are captured in a much more impactful and lasting way. You can do this with your own camera on your mobile phone or you can hire a company to conduct interviews and produce a legacy video of your life. You may be thinking that your stories aren't interesting enough to record but to people you leave behind, these videos are *priceless*.

My father-in-law died entirely too young. He was so young, in fact, that my daughter doesn't remember him. I was searching for pictures to share with family and sadly there were very few. It seems that without doing it on purpose, he was always the one *taking* the pictures, instead of being in them. There are no pictures of my daughter and her grandfather and to me that is incredibly sad.

Shortly after that experience, I hired a producer of legacy videos to interview each of my parents so they could tell their stories and those they remembered from their own parents and grandparents. I introduced the concept of the videos to them as the most selfish gift of all time, by asking each of them to record these as a gift to my daughter and future generations of our family.

To say that these videos will be treasured is an understatement. Each of my parents had the opportunity to decide how they wanted to be remembered and to make it happen.

I didn't know it many years ago but today I'd give anything to have even a five-minute video of my own grandparents, to see them and to hear their voices one more time.

I am fortunate that both of my parents are still alive and well and my daughter is still in grade school, but I presume that someday on what would have been their 110th birthdays, I'll wind up watching my parents' videos with my own grandchildren and introducing them to their ancestors in the most personal way possible.

That is how to ensure that you will always be remembered and, more importantly, to ensure that you'll be remembered in the way you choose.

How can you leave behind your *values* and not just your *items of value*?

Personal stories, charitable gifts, genetic traits, and legacy videos all play a role in what you leave behind along with your property when you die. And all of those gifts are impactful in different ways. I challenge you to consider recording your personal values either in your video or in writing so that they can be preserved and passed along into the future.

It is easy to share pictures, artifacts, and collectibles in life—they are tangible and can be passed from one generation to another. But what happens to your values—the things you hold dear that aren't tangible—when you're gone? Most of the time, those are lost unless you proactively make it a point to share them in a tangible way. If you have spent your life as a champion for a cause, share the reasons why with your family. Perhaps, your efforts can be carried on in some way—financially or otherwise—by those who wish to honor your lifetime commitments.

EXTRA-CREDIT ASSIGNMENT

Your final extra-credit assignment may be the most challenging but also the most rewarding of all the work you've done since enrolling at Retire U.

Think about the messages in this chapter and how you can make a difference and leave a legacy that is far more impactful than money. Answer the following big questions and prepare to act on every one of them—and to start soon.

1. **What do you want to be when you grow up?**
2. **What legacy do you want to leave?**
3. **How do you want to be remembered?**
4. **How can you leave behind your *values* and not just your *items of value*?**

WHAT TO DO NOW: SUMMARY OF EXTRA-CREDIT ASSIGNMENTS

The content of this book is designed to be a blueprint for reaching financial independence. A brief summary of your extra-credit assignments is below. I hope you'll take the opportunity to start chipping away at the assignments that are relevant for you and to review the material in this book to help you along the way.

FRESHMAN YEAR

- Set a savings and investment target as a percentage of your income and make it happen. (Cash Management 101)
- Take a full inventory of your debt balances and interest rates. (Debt Management 101)
- If you have equity in your home, make sure you have a home equity line of credit (HELOC) in place for working capital, debt consolidation, and potential future opportunities. (Debt Management 102)
- Create a debt-reduction plan. (Debt Management 103)
- Review all of your insurance coverages. (Risk Management & Protection 101)

- Create a budget. (Cash Management 102)
- Ask your financial advisor the list of important questions or use them to find the right financial advisor for you. (Financial Planning 101)
- List your assets and liabilities to complete your initial inventory. (Financial Planning 102)

SOPHOMORE YEAR

- Start building your savings nest egg if you're planning to buy a home. (Financial Planning 201)
- Hold an open and honest conversation about your finances with your fiancé, spouse, or significant other. (Financial Planning 202)
- Understand the financial implications of having children and discuss them with your spouse. (Financial Planning 203)
- Consider a second opinion or a review of your investment portfolio. (Financial Independence 201)
- Analyze your existing portfolio holdings and make changes as needed. (Financial Independence 202)

JUNIOR YEAR

- Review and understand your employer's retirement plan and maximize your contributions and your employer's, if possible. (Financial Independence 301)
- Begin thinking about long-term care planning—for you or for your more senior family members. (Risk Management & Protection 201)
- Review your existing estate planning documents (or execute them) and update them as necessary. (Risk Management & Protection 202)
- Take a complete inventory of all your beneficiary designations and set or adjust them, as needed. (Risk Management & Protection 203)

SENIOR YEAR

- Write down your own personal bucket list. (Financial Independence 401)
- Determine the withdrawal rate you would need from your working assets if you retired today. (Retirement Readiness 401)
- Begin thinking about the appropriateness of your present home for aging in-place (or that of your more senior family members). (Retirement Readiness 402)
- Breathe. Pace yourself in making the big decisions before you retire, the moment you retire, and after you retire. (Retirement Readiness 403)

GRADUATION DAY

- Answer the four big questions about your legacy.

POST-GRADUATION

Please remember to share how this book helped you formulate your own plans to graduate into retirement. Send me an e-mail at ebrotman@bfgfa.com and tell your story about how you used this book to work your way to graduation day and financial independence. I'd love to hear your success stories!

Please also consider writing a review on Amazon or other book sites to help spread the word about your new vision for retirement–as a graduation and not a retreat.

Toss your cap in the air! You did it!

AUTHOR'S BACKGROUND

Eric D. Brotman, CFP®, AEP®, CPWA®, is chief executive officer of BFG Financial Advisors, an independent firm assisting clients with wealth creation, preservation, and distribution. Mr. Brotman began his financial planning practice in Baltimore in 1994, and founded Brotman Financial Group in 2003, which later changed its corporate identity to BFG Financial Advisors. He provides investment, retirement, estate, insurance, and comprehensive financial planning services for families, professionals, executives, and business owners, all of whom enjoy extraordinary client service from working with multiple CFP® Practitioners and a team of specialists.

Mr. Brotman is also the president of Brotman Consulting Group, LLC, an organization created to help financial advisors amplify their practices. Brotman Consulting Group creates a path for financial advisory firms to create influence and manage growth, helping advisors master the tasks that lay outside the realm of financial expertise: analyzing opportunities and threats, turning clients and employees into stakeholders, and marketing the practice.

Mr. Brotman holds a bachelor of arts degree from the University of Pennsylvania. He earned his Certified Financial PlannerTM (CFP®) certification in 1998, and completed his master's degree in Financial Services (MSFS) at the American College in 2003. He is also an Accredited Estate Planner (AEP®), a Certified Private Wealth Advisor (CPWA®), a Chartered Life Underwriter (CLU), a Chartered Financial Consultant (ChFC), a Chartered Advisor in Senior Living (CASL), and a Retirement Income Certified Professional® (RICP®). Mr. Brotman is a registered representative with Kestra Investment Services and an investment advisor representative with Kestra Advisory Services.

Mr. Brotman is serving his second four-year term on the Board of Trustees for the Maryland State Retirement & Pension System as an appointee of Governor Larry Hogan. He is a champion for financial literacy education, serving on the Business Advisory Council for the Comptroller of Maryland. He is a 2009 alumnus and former chairman of the board of Directors of Leadership Maryland. Additionally, Mr. Brotman serves on the Board of Trustees at Stevenson University, where he previously served as an adjunct faculty member, teaching financial planning and investment planning courses to CFP® students. He is a 2006 alumnus and former board member of Leadership-Baltimore County, the past-president and chairman of the board of the Financial Planning Association of Maryland, and a member of the Baltimore Estate Planning Council.

Mr. Brotman is the host of the *Don't Retire…Graduate!* podcast, available at dontretiregraduate.com, and recently published *Pay Less Taxes Now! Four Strategies to Help Reduce Your Taxes Legally*, available for free download at lowtaxbook.com. He has published two other books, *Retire Wealthy: The Tools You Need to Help Build Lasting Wealth – On Your Own or With Your Financial Advisor*, in 2014, and *Debt-Free for Life: The Tools You Need to Free Yourself from Debt*, in 2009. A sought-after speaker, he frequently gives seminars and workshops for companies, membership organizations, and fellow financial advisors.

Mr. Brotman appears regularly on television on *11 News Sunday Morning* on WBAL in Baltimore and is a frequent contributor on *Forbes.com*. He has also been interviewed by *WMAR* in Baltimore. He has appeared in print in *Wall Street Journal, The Baltimore Sun, Bal-*

timore Business Journal, The Daily Record, Investment Advisor, Fidelity Investor's Weekly, Investment News, Journal of Financial Planning, and numerous other publications. He has been featured on websites, including Yahoo! Finance, ChiefExecutive.com, Reuters.com, and Financial-Planning.com. Mr. Brotman was named as one of the "Maryland Power Players" by *The Gazette of Politics and Business* in 2010 and one of the "Very Important Professionals" by *The Daily Record* in 2011.

Securities offered through Kestra Investment Services, LLC (Kestra IS), member FINRA/SIPC. Investment advisory services offered through Kestra Advisory Services, LLC (Kestra AS), an affiliate of Kestra IS. BFG Financial Advisors and Brotman Financial Group are not affiliated with Kestra IS or Kestra AS.

Made in the USA
Las Vegas, NV
27 August 2022

54091917R00208